"*Marc Ellis is a brilliant writer, a deeply thoughtful and courageous mind, an intellectual who has broken the death-hold of mindless tradition and unreflective cliché to produce a superb account of post-Holocaust understanding, with particular reference to the Palestinian people and the moral obligation of Israelis and diaspora Jews. He is a man to be listened to with respect and admiration. . . .*"

—Edward Said, Columbia University

O, JERUSALEM!

The Contested Future of the Jewish Covenant

Marc H. Ellis

Fortress Press
Minneapolis

O, JERUSALEM!
The Contested Future of the Jewish Covenant

Book design: Debbie Brandt
Cover design: Joseph Bonyata
Cover photograph: "Israel, Jerusalem, Old City, Jewish Quarter, Jews standing on building" taken by Erica Lansner, copyright © Tony Stone Images. Used by permission.
Poetry featured on pp. 76–77: "East Jerusalem, 1987" and "'67 Remembered" reprinted from *A Few Words in the Mother Tongue: Poems Selected and New 1971–1990* by Irena Klepfisz (Portland, Oreg.: The Eighth Mountain Press, 1990); copyright © 1990 by Irena Klepfisz; reprinted by permission of the author and publisher.

Library of Congress Cataloging-in-Publication Data

Ellis, Marc H., date
    O, Jerusalem!: the contested future of the Jewish covenant / Marc H. Ellis.
        p. cm.
    Includes bibliographical references.
    ISBN 0-8006-3159-5 (alk. paper)
    1. Arab-Israeli conflict. 2. Israel—Politics and government. 3. Palestinian Arabs—Politics and government. 4. Jerusalem—International status. 5. Israel—Ethnic relations. 6. Holocaust, Jewish (1939–1945)—Influence. I. Title.
DS119.7.E443   1999
956.9405—dc21
                                                                    99-24378
                                                                        CIP

The paper used in this publication meets the minimum requirements of American National Standard for Information Sciences—Permanence of Paper for Printed Library Materials, ANSI Z329.48-1984.

Manufactured in the U.S.A.   AF 1-3159

03   02   01   00   99   1   2   3   4   5   6   7   8   9   10

To Ann
for accompanying me

To our Prophets
Aaron Moore and Isaiah Dylan
for the new beginning

To Gillian and Lynn Rose
for your witness at Auschwitz and beyond

To Gersham Nelson
who said "Covenant"

Contents

Acknowledgments

I am indebted to many over the years who have nourished me in life and thought. I think first of my parents, Herbert Moore Ellis and June Goldwin Ellis, for their encouragement and support. As they enter their eighth decade of life, I remember their early and later contributions to my sense of self and ability to persevere.

My wife, Ann, has been of tremendous importance to me especially during times of trial. Her friendship is an important part of my life. Our two prophets, Aaron Moore and Isaiah Dylan, are testimony to life and possibility. It is wonderful to be part of the beginning of their journey.

I also want to thank those outside of my family who have been with me during the time of the writing of this book. I think here especially of Ken Schubert, who committed himself well beyond what could be hoped for; Sara Roy, who made a place for me at Harvard; Rosemary Ruether, who advocated on my behalf; Souad Dajani and Connie Parvey, who befriended me in Cambridge; Tony Paris, Don Wagner, Betsy Barlow, Janet Davis, Nasser Aruri, Muhammad Hallaj, John Wilkins, and Daniel McGowan, who accompanied me. I include here Michael West, my editor, whose friendship allowed me to entrust this book to him.

The issues raised in this book are personal and communal, so the support of many is appreciated. I want to thank William Graham and Roger Owen of the Center for Middle Eastern Studies at Harvard University. The atmosphere of the Center and the facilities at Harvard have been instrumental in helping me bring this work to completion. A special thanks is due to the staff at Widener Library for their courteous assistance.

As I came to the conclusion of this book, I joined the faculty of Baylor University as University Professor of American and Jewish Studies. A Baptist university, Baylor has opened its arms to me in a bold and beautiful way. I am thankful for all those who brought me to Baylor: Roger Sanders, a lawyer committed to the question of justice, who discovered me in Bethlehem; Regent David McCall, who befriended me; Chancellor Herbert Reynolds, a man known for his leadership and integrity, who welcomed me to campus; President Robert Sloan and Provost Don Schmeltekopf, who interviewed me and shared their vision of a university guided by spiritual values and open to the world;

Dr. John Jonsson, Robert Baird, and Dianna Vitanza, whose enthusiasm was contagious; and Professors Ralph Lynn and Ann Miller, youthful and charismatic legends in the classroom and beyond, who spoke to me about the Baylor of the future. I am also grateful to Paulette Edwards, Wanda Gilbert, Janice Losak, Mark Long, Pat Cornett, Kim Davis, Dr. Michael Beatty, and Dr. Barry Hankins for listening to me and helping me in the transition from New York and Cambridge to Waco. A special thanks to Jim Bland and Pat Hambrick. They have built our new home and, in the process, engaged me in such diverse topics as shrimp boats and theology.

The welcome of Rabbi Alex Lilienthal and congregation Rodef Shalom and the local Baptist churches in Waco have been special and important. They have made me feel at home as a Jew and as a person. Finally, thanks to Derek Davis, director of the J. M. Dawson Institute of Church-State Studies, whose quiet presence and friendship have helped me become part of the Baylor family. Baylor has become a blessing to me and my family, as it has been and will be for countless others.

O, Jerusalem!

O, Jerusalem!
Once in Persia's shadow
Now here after a long wandering.
In the early light your stones are beautiful.
I hear the voices of the prophets and the children too.

Are there soldiers at Rachel's Tomb?
I see them in the distance.
Do they guard the return of the Jews?
I wonder, God, if they also guard you.

O, Jerusalem!
Shall I face you and pray?
I hear the voices of the prophets and the children too.
The early light fades away.
I dream of yesterday and the exile of long ago.

Once in Persia's shadow
Now here after a long wandering.
The voices of the prophets and the children too.
In the early light your stones are beautiful.
The soldiers everywhere.

—Marc H. Ellis

Prologue

This book emerged in the wake of the May 1996 election in Israel, which saw the defeat of Shimon Peres and the election of Benjamin Netanyahu as prime minister of Israel. It reached conclusion after the celebration of the fiftieth anniversary of the state of Israel and the signing of the Wye Memorandum in 1998.

Though there was much commentary on the election and the fiftieth anniversary, most of the analysis focused on the immediate consequences for the peace process between Israel and the Palestinian Authority. While this analysis was important in and of itself, the focus on the immediate tended to polarize positions and to trivialize the options confronting the leaders of Israel and Palestine, rendering superficial the stakes involved as the final years of the Israeli-Palestinian conflict approach. The politics of both sides are intriguing, yet still more is at stake than the negotiation strategies employed.

What is at stake is the future of Jews and Palestinians in their individual integrity and the future of both peoples together. For if their past has been shared, so, too, will their future. Moreover, the challenge of the future involves and transcends the political dimension, for the entirety of Jewish history is on the line.

The covenant that Jews accepted as a people at Sinai is tested in every generation, and, in our time, on the threshold of the twenty-first century, the impossible challenge of the Holocaust has been further complicated by the difficult history of Jews and Palestinians.

Rather than seeing the struggle of Jews and Palestinians simply as a current and contentious issue of domestic and global importance, the task of Jewish thought and theology is to recognize the stakes as significantly higher. The covenant itself, a covenant that brings together ethics and justice, repentance and forgiveness, is at stake, and the issue of justice in the Middle East affects all Jews in the deepest corners of Jewish faith and affirmation.

The demographics and geography of the Middle East reinforce the shared future of Jews and Palestinians. There are approximately four million Jews in Israel. The Palestinian population is almost a million within Israel, with over two million Palestinians in Gaza, Jerusalem, and the West Bank, and several million in the surrounding countries of

Jordan, Lebanon, and Syria. The geographic distance is small, and the proximity of these populations makes them dependent on the same scarce resources.

The Palestinian connection to the land is strong; it draws Palestinians within Israel, in the West Bank and Gaza, and those refugees on the periphery of Israel and Palestine toward the center of the disputed territories, potently symbolized by Jerusalem. When the Jewish political and religious determination to maintain and even expand its presence in Israel and Palestine is added to these considerations, it seems illusory to project a separate future for both peoples.

Yet the pressure for Jews and Palestinians to share the land they both call home transcends these considerations. Clearly the Palestinians have a right to return to Palestine and to govern themselves. They also have the need and the right to more than the small area now promised to them in the various agreements of the 1990s. The percentage of Palestine under Palestinian governance is minuscule in comparison to historic Palestine and, after decades of Israeli occupation and exploitation, underdeveloped and dependent.

The question of historic and contemporary injustice is paramount here, as is whether a structure to remedy these disparities will emerge. The choice to end the cycle of victory and defeat and begin the process of adjustment and reconciliation, or to solidify the victory of one side over the other, raises central issues in the history of both peoples.

While the Palestinian community is diverse and opinions on the Oslo accords—accords negotiated by the leadership of Israel and the Palestine Liberation Organization beginning in 1993—are divided as to their effect on contemporary life and the historic struggle of the Palestinian people, I approach these issues as a Jew involved in the history and the future of the Jewish people.

From the Jewish perspective, these accords can be seen as deciding the future of the state of Israel in many substantial ways, most importantly as a referendum on the course of Jewish history. The twentieth century has bequeathed a series of formative events to the Jewish world with horrific and startling consequences: the Holocaust, which threatened the annihilation of the Jewish people; and the emergence of Israel, which promised rebirth but also threatens to alter, perhaps irrevocably, the ethical character of the Jewish people. In the shadow of the Holocaust is now an empowered and at times militantly hostile Jewish state supported by Jews around the world. At the same time, that support has been placed within a narrative of innocence and redemption that refutes the culpability inherent in the exercise of state power and renders invisible those who have been displaced by that power.

What has been missed in the commentaries on contemporary Jewish history are the stakes involved in these formative events and their inter-connectedness. Though the Holocaust and the state of Israel are discontinuous in time and geography, they form a pattern of response and remembrance that is shaping the future of the Jewish people. In so doing, the history of the Jewish people is also being reinterpreted and transformed.

How does this history guide Jews, and what will be passed on to the next generation? How will Jews see themselves as the decades pass? Will Jews be able to identify their past as one of suffering, struggle, and healing, or will that history be defined as one that left suffering behind by displacing and conquering another people? In the conquest and displacement of another people, will Jews end the trauma of the Holocaust or find that the trauma of their own suffering intensifies?

Behind the political drama is the journey of an ancient people, which began with the embrace of a covenant. The covenant has always been difficult; its alternating rhythms of promise and disappointment have raised hopes and questions throughout the journey of the Jewish people. For many, the Holocaust represents the end of the covenant, the shattering, as it were, of the tablets that bonded God and the Jewish people. To others, Israel represents a renewal of that bond and therefore the rebirth of the covenant.

Yet for those Jews who see justice at the heart of the covenant, Israel may represent its final shattering. For can the covenant be renewed, can the decalogue be read, when refugees are created by a Jewish state and Jerusalem is emptied of Palestinians?

If the answers to these questions are unclear, it is clear that the direction is toward the intensification of trauma rather than healing. The use of the covenant to elicit support for the policies of the state, already suspect, can no longer be justified.

In these pages I try to address issues that have confronted Jews for decades and continue to confront us on the threshold of the twenty-first century. There is no need to demonize or sanctify present or past leaders of Israel or, for that matter, those who will come after this generation of leaders. The problem is more complex, the reality of empowerment more ambivalent.

The task before us is to surface tendencies in Jewish history and contemporary life that move us away from or toward a reconciliation with Palestinians and therefore with our own destiny. Are there religious ideals—intellectual concepts and political movements, hidden in the past and neglected in the present, that will help Jews confront the history we are creating—calling us toward justice? Can there be a new confrontation within the context of Jewish empowerment which calls the community to search out a path where Jews will cease to be victims and, at the same time, will refuse to be oppressors?

The path is diverse and complex. Chapters 1 and 2 trace visions of the diaspora and homeland theorized and practiced by such historic luminaries as Judah Magnes, Martin Buber, and Hannah Arendt at the time the state of Israel was being formed. The massacre of Palestinian Arab villagers at Deir Yassin in 1948, the same year as the founding of Israel, represented a challenge to these thinkers, as it does to Jews today.

The ethical and religious rhetoric that accompanied the birth of the state and the contradiction of that rhetoric in the massacre at Deir Yassin—a massacre that embodies the violent birth of Israel and the beginning of the Palestinian catastrophe—provide a perspective in analyzing the ambivalent legacy of Israel's founders, among them Yitzhak Rabin and Shimon Peres. It also provides the basis for analyzing the bifurcation and trivialization of Jewish life surfaced by scholars like Yosef Yerushalmi, David Roskies, and David Vital. In dealing with these themes I ask whether the choice of a state over a homeland has contributed to this crisis in Jewish life and why this most obvious choice is overlooked by such eminent scholars.

Chapter 3 recalls the dual anniversary of Deir Yassin and Israel as a mandate to share Jerusalem. Though many look to Jerusalem as a symbol of triumph and power, the histories of Jews and Palestinians are broken. Could the sharing of Jerusalem, as a way of restoring the ordinary life of both peoples, come about in the humility of brokenness and the desire for healing instead of the desire to fulfill a mythic and sometimes vengeful religious and ideological program? If brokenness and healing are emphasized, then Jerusalem can be reunited in justice and peace in which ethics, cultural sensitivity, and an ecumenical religiosity are emphasized.

At the same time, it must be recognized that the leaders of Israel, with the support of much of the Jewish community around the world, are actively seeking to foreclose the possibility of that sharing. Can the Jewish covenant, affirmed in religious and secular ways and born in the struggle for liberation, be used to oppress another people and increase the reality and trauma of dislocation? Can injustice, represented by Jewish domination of Jerusalem, be at the heart of the covenant?

It is important to recall those Jews who have been marginalized by the Jewish community precisely over this issue. Often secular in their expression, one wonders if the Jewish exilic community of our time—a community formed after the Holocaust and in protest over the policies of the state of Israel—is in exile searching for a covenant that is also in exile from the very community that invokes and claims it.

Chapter 4 addresses the Jewish covenant and its importance in Jewish life in more detail. At the heart of the covenant is the question of justice and the boundaries that define covenantal practice. The Holocaust brought the covenant and God into question. For many Jews, Israel represents the renewal of that covenant and the possibility of God after the Holocaust. Yet in the oppression of the Palestinian people a thick wall of scandal has entered the covenant, one that portends a surprising shift in sensibility. Could it be that at the center of the contemporary embrace of the Jewish covenant stand the Palestinian people?

This shift of boundaries necessitates the embrace of the Palestinian people as the way of embracing the covenant in our time. In this way the entirety of Jewish life is placed into question. Contemporary Jewish culture, which revolves around a national-Israeli axis, is a culture that has embraced a state that perpetuates injustice.

But the embrace of the state reaches beyond Israel: in support of Israel, Jews around the world have entered into alliances with states that militarily and economically support Israel. Thus Jewish culture and practice, once suspicious of state alliance because of its power to oppress, has aligned itself with that power over against others. I ask whether the evolution of Jewish-state culture, especially in the United Sates and Israel, portends a viable and ethical covenantal future for the Jewish people.

Chapters 5 and 6 carry this discussion forward. The alliance with the state and the attempted destruction of Palestinian life have brought Jewish history, *as we have known and inherited it,* to an end. Strategies of dealing with the state have, for the most part, failed; those who see the injustice must continue on the path of fidelity. If the covenant is in exile, so are many Jews. And in that exile are Palestinians as well, those forced into exile by the Jewish state and those now in exile from their own leadership.

The meeting of Jews and Palestinians in exile portends the creation of an inclusive Palestinian culture that seeks to share the land and institute a way of justice and peace for all those inside and outside the land often called holy. Hence the binational aspirations of the early homeland Zionists are recovered in new circumstances, after the Holocaust and the experience of exercising state power.

The creation of such a culture is part of the healing that can set both peoples free to continue on their journey. That journey will combine aspects of Jewish and Palestinian particularity while also providing the bridge toward a new identity. Important as part of that bridge is the movement toward revolutionary forgiveness, a forgiveness that can only come within the context of justice.

In revolutionary forgiveness, the past is carried with and among Jews and Palestinians as a clarion call that never again shall this injustice happen against or between either people. The march toward forgiveness begins at Yad Vashem *and* Deir Yassin and moves toward Jerusalem in a spirit of unity. From these places that commemorate suffering and catastrophe issues a dream of restoring the ordinary lives of Jews and Palestinians together.

On the joint fiftieth anniversary of the Palestinian catastrophe and the creation of Israel, revolutionary forgiveness seemed distant; both events demand this commitment and practice if their centenary is to be one of triumph over tragedy.

For many people, Jews and non-Jews alike, a positive solution to the conflict arrived in the Oslo accords. Still others feel that the situation has deteriorated to such a degree that the struggle is pointless. Both views see the end as near. Perhaps it is better, however, to see this time as a new stage of struggle, for Palestinians and for Jews, that has reached a decisive moment. Lines are drawn and commitments are called to account; the strange turn of history may be fashioning a new solidarity, even, paradoxically, a new covenant that includes Jews and Palestinians.

Such are the demands of the hour, unforeseen and for many a violation of loyalty and tradition. What are loyalty and tradition when both are guided by a power that is relentless in its claim to innocence yet also oppresses others? When do loyalty and tradition become a cover for injustice, and when does that cover deplete the center of Jewish life of its substance? At certain times in history—and today we are at such a time—loyalty and tradition demand an engagement, a battle for the survival of both.

After Auschwitz, such a struggle for the heart and soul of the Jewish people could hardly have been anticipated. Still, the birth of Israel and its expansion over the years have made this struggle a reality.

It is time to bring the era of Auschwitz to a close, and this can occur only when the era of the birth of Israel finds an end in the reconciliation of Jews and Palestinians. The sharing of Israel/Palestine will be a rendezvous with the destinies of both peoples, and, for Jews, a renewal of the covenant will be at hand. That covenant will be broad and inclusive, promising an end to the brokenness that still reverberates in the hearts of the Jewish people.

On the threshold of the twenty-first century, the covenant awaits our decision.

C H A P T E R   O N E

Visions of the Diaspora and Homeland

The ongoing struggle in Israel/Palestine has passed a series of benchmarks, sometimes forgotten in ensuing years. One such benchmark was the assassination of Yitzhak Rabin followed by the electoral defeat of Shimon Peres in June 1996. After the initial euphoria accompanying the signing of the Oslo peace accords in 1993, Rabin's assassination forced the crisis in Israel and Palestine to reemerge in the consciousness of the world community.

In fact, the situation has had a paradoxical quality over these last years, for as the climate for peace improved dramatically, the economic and political situation of the Palestinians progressively deteriorated. The peace process, so heralded in the world press and welcomed by political and religious leaders, has been one of Palestinian surrender to a victorious Israel.

Certainly the Palestinians recognized the Oslo agreements as a surrender but with the hope that over time the agreements would be expanded. The hope was for a peace dividend, which would come as the two peoples came to know and appreciate one another. Feeling more secure and benefiting economically and politically from the improved situation, the Israelis would understand that new compromises are essential to a shared future between Jews and Palestinians. These new understandings, many Palestinians hoped, included sharing Jerusalem, dismantling many of the Jewish settlements, and recognition and empowerment of a Palestinian state.[1]

The Palestinian surrender is a "negotiated surrender," one that sees the negotiations as a process necessary within the context of the Israeli-Palestinian conflict of the past century. A negotiated surrender is a political decision and tool; it is a way of working within a situation of unequal power.

Sometimes a negotiated surrender is the only viable way of preserving the possibility of a renewed struggle for equality and justice. If the

1

very presence of a people on the land is threatened, if the economic and political situation deteriorates to the point at which it is impossible to continue to preserve, reproduce, and recreate the culture of a people, then the refusal to surrender may represent a principle that will have no redress. In this situation, a negotiated surrender is itself a form of resistance, a strategy that places survival before pride, possibility before the difficulty of compromise.

At the same time, a negotiated surrender places faith in the power that has brought a people to the brink of disaster. It is a strange combination and a precarious one at that: Palestinians can only surrender on a negotiated basis, and the basis for their ability to surrender is a political decision that a moral appeal can be made to the political leadership of Israel to acknowledge their victory and begin a process of reconciliation.

With the power configuration so unequal, the negotiated surrender should only be made with the understanding that there is something in Jewish history and culture that will recognize the Palestinians as a people with their own dignity and aspirations. Jewish recognition of the dignity of the Palestinians will affect the political calculations of the Israeli state *vis-à-vis* the aspirations of the Palestinian people. Hence a new relationship will evolve over time.

The bitter arguments within the Palestinian community over this negotiated surrender illustrate the risk that Yassir Arafat and his advisors took in signing the Oslo agreements. For what could justify confidence in a state that forced the Palestinian people into exile, refused their return, humiliated them in their various uprisings, and even denied their essential claim to peoplehood and nationality?

Indeed, some Palestinian intellectuals like Edward Said see ignorance, stupidity, and corruption—even betrayal—in a leadership that signed such a surrender. How could a leadership, which has witnessed a disciplined and relentless Israeli power, believe that such a surrender will be seen as anything but weakness to be exploited to its fullest? Will this surrender provide cover for the completion of the plan to permanently displace and conquer the Palestinian people?

To add insult to injury, the agreement was signed with Yitzhak Rabin, one of the architects of Israel who, in various decades since the founding of the state, was instrumental in the displacement and humiliation of the Palestinian people. Had the Palestinian leadership living outside the land lost touch with reality by believing somehow that this very same state and political leadership would change their minds and hearts and translate that change into political realities? Would Israel, after decades of creating facts on the ground, change those facts, that is, move from a position of exclusion to inclusion, exclusivity to mutuality, singular ownership of the land to sharing the land between two peoples?[2]

Perspectives on the Jewish Return

Clearly, Yitzhak Rabin's policy of strength and peace, negotiated and carried on by Shimon Peres in the years 1993–1996, did not change the facts on the ground, which both men helped establish earlier in their careers. The redeployment and withdrawal of troops in parts of Gaza and the West Bank simply affirmed a long-standing Labor party policy of seeking maximum land for Jews while leaving Palestinian population centers outside of Jewish control, or, to put it more accurately, outside Jewish life. Rabin and Peres, like their Labor party in general, have always favored a strict separation of Jew and Palestinian, and the Oslo accords ratified that understanding.

For Rabin and Peres, the possibility of more land for Israel came up against the hard reality of Palestinian demographics; to incorporate Palestinian-population centers alters the fundamental Zionist enterprise of which they were two of the primary architects. Incorporating millions of Palestinians into Israel effectively makes the state of Israel into the state of Israel/Palestine.

In this scenario, the dream of a Jewish state crumbles in Israel's victory and Zionism becomes a phase in Jewish history to be studied rather than a mature cause solidified as the major direction of the Jewish future. In fact the future of Jews in Israel/Palestine takes on a different trajectory. Israel becomes a Jewish community among other Jewish communities, one seeking to work out its special connection with the land and with Jerusalem in a larger polity, perhaps a secular democratic state such as the Palestinians proposed and, in light of Jewish intransigence, abandoned in frustration decades ago.[3]

To agree to a broader polity of Jews and Arabs would affirm a position held traditionally by Orthodox Jews, one which has largely been abandoned by the Orthodox themselves. This position can be characterized in the broadest sense as invoking a "diaspora sensibility," believing that the scattering of the Jews is a decision by God calling Jews to greater fidelity to the *halacha*, that is, to Jewish teachings and commandments. Within this framework, Jewish presence in the land of Israel, with a special devotion to Jerusalem, is an act of piety, awaiting the response of God to the renewed fidelity of God's people.

In the main, Zionism is a reaction to this piety and the political and military weakness it encouraged. The Holocaust is the most important and last reminder of the absurdity of this position, at least from the European Jewish perspective. For what could a small Orthodox community in the Holy Land mean if the center of Jewish life, located in Europe, was annihilated? The early Zionists recognized the future of European

Jewry long before the Holocaust, and even their dire warnings were over-shadowed by the reality of the Nazi extermination program.

The founders of Israel were, in this sense, inheritors of the failed diaspora and the religiosity that made sense of the dispersion. This tradition, which spawned a secular-diaspora intelligentsia, encouraged a questioning of those with permanent homes and a state, giving rise to the great tradition of radical Jewish thought.

The secular diaspora is important and almost immediately recognizable. Franz Kafka, Walter Benjamin, Sigmund Freud, and Albert Einstein come to mind as representative of the European ethos that found Jews in between Jewish religious culture and European citizenship. Fleeing from one and on the fringes of the other, these Jews developed a tradition of insightful and radical thought. Hannah Arendt, herself a product of this diaspora, refers to this as comprising a hidden tradition, where insights from Jewish and European culture were juxtaposed and reconfigured. This placement between cultures also produced a tradition of political radicalism with such luminaries as Karl Marx, Leon Trotsky, and Rosa Luxemburg.[4]

There were those within the Jewish community who affirmed Zionism and the diaspora and, among them, some who affirmed an empowered Jewish community in Palestine alongside an empowered Arab community. In general terms, these Jewish intellectuals, rabbis, and activists supported a "home" for Jews, that is an enhanced and structured Jewish community in Palestine rather than an exclusive, religiously defined state.

Even to relate the terms of these understandings is somewhat difficult today, though some of the major figures espousing these positions lived into the 1960s and beyond. The difficulty lies in the overwhelming shift in Jewish sensibilities as the center of Jewish life as it has moved from a tradition of piety and secular-intellectual endeavors to remembrance of the Holocaust and Jewish empowerment in Israel.

This change of perspective took place within and after the 1967 Arab-Israeli war, mobilizing and ultimately militarizing Jewish life to the point that the religious-secular energies of the previous centuries, including their long-standing disputes, faded and were transformed by a tidal wave of grief over the Holocaust and support for an embattled state. Because of the force of this change, the language and thought that provided the foundation for discussion of a Jewish homeland in Palestine are simply unavailable to most contemporary Jews.

So, too, is the realization that dissent about a Jewish state—or even debate about the direction that such a state might take—did not come only from Palestinian Arabs or the surrounding Arab countries. The fact that reasoned dissent came within the Jewish community is now almost completely lost to the Jewish world. When voiced, it is often seen as a political construction that seeks to undermine Israel and even to promote the disempowerment of the Jewish people. Those who speak out or write about these views are seen as heretics with a special historical burden: encouraging the possibility of another holocaust.[5]

The "homeland sensibility" was initially embraced by such important Jewish thinkers as Judah Magnes, a Reform rabbi and first president of Hebrew University; Martin Buber, perhaps the most prominent Jewish religious thinker of our time; and Hannah Arendt, the great Jewish philosopher. Though diverse in their political, religious, and cultural sensibilities, they embraced a similar view of Jewish life in Palestine and, after the state was founded, in Israel. They saw the Jewish population increase in Palestine, and later in Israel, as a challenge and as a danger. The possibilities include contact with the ancient geographic Jewish homeland, the renewal of Jewish culture and language in a setting that gave birth to both, and the development of Jewish institutions and creative educational enterprises that further Jewish history and make a distinctive contribution to the larger non-Jewish world.

Even the political framework for such a homeland could take on significance for Jews and others. Here the Jewish spirit and intellect, aware of its historic suffering and complaints about unjust political structures, might pioneer a new way of governance that exemplifies the prophetic tradition of justice and thus serve as a light unto the nations. In short, the Jewish homeland could consolidate Jewish energy into a force for Jewish and world history.[6]

The danger is the duality of the hopes and aspirations of these religious and intellectual figures. The homeland could turn into a disaster if the models of language, culture, and empowerment assumed the quality and propensity of those lands and peoples from which Jews had fled and, within the context of the Holocaust, by which they had almost been annihilated. For those who sought a Jewish homeland, the gathering of the Jews in Palestine and Israel was justified and sustained by the pursuit of the goals they outlined, and these goals could only be pursued in ethical and strategic terms if the Arabs of Palestine were accorded the rights and the equality traditionally denied to Jews.

The possibility that Jews might deny justice to others when they had power disturbed Magnes, Buber, and Arendt in a way that startles the contemporary reader. In their view, to deny the rights of Palestinian Arabs violated the entire enterprise and compromised not only contemporary Jewish history but Jewish history in its entirety. The gamble was huge, one that put the formation of the state of Israel in a larger and secondary framework.[7]

The state itself was seen as militating against the possibility of achieving the goals that these homeland visionaries outlined. They feared that the state would create a structure of domination over Palestinian Arabs, a domination which would enter into Jewish life itself. Consumed with a perpetual war with the Arab peoples, the state might restructure Jewish life to a perpetual-war footing.

On a perpetual-war footing, Jews would be unable to pursue these utopian visions, and, if after generations of war the state emerged victorious, they would be buried so deep as to be forgotten. When brought to the surface, they would be regarded as archaic or even dangerous. For the victors must not only protect their victory, they must also guard the structures which brought that victory in the first place. A return to the homeland vision would be looked upon cynically, almost as a sign of weakness, proposing a past that placed the community in a physical danger that no spiritual or cultural ideal could protect.

If the diaspora and homeland sensibilities are rarely discussed today or are even understandable within the present climate of Jewish political and intellectual discourse, it is because the transformation that Magnes, Buber, and Arendt predicted has come to fruition. The formation, consolidation, and expansion of the state of Israel have mobilized energies around its own identity and continuation, as do all states, but with a peculiar intensity.

Newly won national identities are often complicated. Insofar as they displace and replace old political and identity structures, they consume tremendous quantities of material and intellectual energy. The emerging Jewish state added the dimension of an ancient people with a religious and messianic identity that could be used to mobilize political activity in forming state institutions. This added impetus—along with the dispersed, suffering quality of contemporary Jewry and the place of Jewish history and symbolism in the Christian West—sparked a movement of religious and secular fervor that fueled the building of the state and, as we see in the divisions within Israel today, threatens to overwhelm the foundation of the state itself.

The state of Israel is defined as a secular state in service to the Jewish people, therefore, at the calling of a history ultimately grounded in a transcendent reality, or at least a reality that cannot be simply limited to the cultural, sociological, or political realms. Of course, the founders of the state, including Rabin and Peres, did not claim that God was the author of the state they were building and indeed would deny that as a reason for the Jewish state. Like the true giant of the founding fathers of Israel, David Ben-Gurion, Rabin and Peres were often more antireligious than nonreligious, and the thought of their being grouped with the Jewish religious community would be offensive to them. Nonetheless, it is true that their own rhetoric of war and peace is full of religiously charged language, and the history they relate and feel a part of is a history that moves beyond the mundane.

When Rabin spoke on the White House lawn in September 1993, he invoked the ethical ideals of Jewish history as communicated by the prophets, the Jewish liturgy of destruction as it comes down through the ages (with special reference to the Holocaust), the ancient Jewish messianic yearnings found in the Hebrew Bible, and the liturgical prayers developed in an exile of over 2,000 years. What else merits the attention paid to Israel, and why do Jewish leaders think themselves so important as to merit such attention, if this broader vision of significance beyond politics and time does not?

From the perspective of Rabin and Peres, at least, the attention to Jews is obvious; it is an attention merited by the role played by Jews throughout history. Even the desire for normality is couched in the messianic language of Judaism—of Deuteronomy and Ecclesiastes—as when Rabin asserted the desire of Jews and Palestinians to build homes, to bequeath those homes to their children, and to affirm the seasons when it is proper to make war and to make peace, a time to kill and a time to love.[8]

Ambivalent Legacy, Uncertain Future

To recall these sensibilities—the diaspora vision of the traditional Orthodox; the homeland vision of Magnes, Buber, and Arendt; and what might be termed the secular-religious sensibility of the founders of the state, including Prime Ministers Rabin and Peres—is to help understand the present configuration of Jewish discourse regarding the future of Israel. For if Rabin and Peres are seen as battling and losing to the right-wing vision of the religiously devout, they should also be seen as involved in their own enterprise of religious history and the struggle to embrace, balance, deflect, and even bury aspects of their own inheritance.

Rabin and Peres battled the transformed diaspora-Orthodox position, which often appears today as a militant-settler Judaism, but they also struggled against a homeland and secularized-diaspora mentality that has resurfaced, albeit in different forms and on the periphery of contemporary Jewish thought. In this sense, Rabin and Peres are not only the last of the founders to hold the highest office in the land, they are the last to have lived within the internal struggle of Jewish culture and intellect over the formation of the state and its relation to Jewish history.

The legacy they leave is ambivalent. From the perspective of Jewish history, Rabin and Peres will be remembered by some as having laid the foundation of independence, strength, and an energetic secular social democracy. Other Jews will remember both as secular Jews who fought for the state but erred in their vision of Jewish faith and history. Lacking this ultimate commitment, they faltered at the end, attempting to cede areas of the land of Israel to the enemy. In their denial of the religious nature of Jewish life, Rabin and Peres were willing to settle for a political empowerment that violated God's will and law. In doing this, they became traitors to the Jewish people. Still other Jews will see them as upholding aspects of the Jewish tradition of justice and peace in their rhetoric while violating that tradition in their use of power.

Rabin spoke of the biblical notions of justice *and* also ordered the breaking of Palestinian bones during the Palestinian uprising; Peres spoke even more eloquently of a new Middle East *and* did not hesitate to bomb villages and civilians in a pre-election show of strength in 1996 seeking to ensure his election as prime minister. From the Palestinian perspective, both men were as flawed as the enterprise of state-building itself. Palestinians experienced both men and their policies and rhetoric, spoken from the heights of Jewish history and in eloquent language, as a reign of destruction and death. In fact, the rhetoric of Rabin and Peres is part of the Palestinian predicament; it covers over the policies of expropriation and death that defines the Palestinian experience of Jewish ethics in the past century.[9]

Yet, at the same time, both Rabin and Peres crossed boundaries that have changed the relationship between Jew and Palestinian forever. Much of this change is in the realm of the symbolic, as, at first, the reluctant handshake of Rabin and Arafat and then, in their subsequent meetings, the evolution of a more cordial, even respectful relationship. It was also realistic, as Rabin came to understand Arafat's role within the context of the Palestinian struggle. When negotiations were brought to a standstill with the assassination of Rabin, Arafat, with the permission of Peres, journeyed to Tel Aviv to console Leah Rabin. Arafat's presence in Israel and in the home of the slain prime minister—with photographs of the visit published around the world—was even more powerful a symbolic gesture than their initial handshake.

It was as if the cycle of dislocation and destruction, so identified with these two men, had come to an end, or at least the potential was there for an ending. The assassination of Rabin and the perilous quality of Arafat's own survival brought a profoundly human touch to a conflict rife with ideological posturing. In the end, both Rabin and Arafat recognized each other as adversaries *and* as representatives of their peoples, for decades involved in war and now seeking to resolve the dispute that many on both sides saw as intractable. The opening of Leah Rabin's home to Arafat and Arafat's offer of praise and sympathy for the slain prime minister raised the possibility of a mutual recognition well beyond the details of the accords themselves.[10]

In this evolving relationship and recognition, nurtured and carried on by Shimon Peres, a hope was born that the negotiated surrender would bear fruit in the future, even as the immediate situation of the Palestinians deteriorated. The symbolism of the evolving relationship among Rabin, Peres, and Arafat touched off heated debates in both communities about motives, substance, and hope for a future beyond the present.

In the Jewish world, anxieties and hope commingled. The militaristic strain of Jewish life, which seeks the complete defeat of the Palestinians and the expansion of Israel, intensified, as did the liberal strain, which hopes for a resolution of the conflict by way of Israeli security and some sense of justice for the Palestinians.

The militaristic and liberal camps have diversity within them and a center as well; the Likud and Labor parties carry these views into a politics fraught with an intensive, almost obsessive concern. Both camps recognized that a decision was being made that could set the course for Israel over the next decades, if not forever. One path sees Israel as perpetually embattled, on the defense, expanding, and with a historic and religious mandate. The other path sees Israel as a limited state, secure within the framework of peace, a Jewish state fulfilling its destiny by providing a place for Jews to live in harmony with their neighbors.

Yet there are other strains of thought and commitment that haunt both camps, even without their verbal articulation or recognized and structured following. The question of the mission of Israel with regard to the Jewish people and Jewish history and the question of the meaning of Palestinians to that history in their displacement and empowerment infused the debate with a passion that ultimately led to the assassination of Rabin and the defeat of Peres. The militaristic and the liberal strains recognized this foundational debate even as the party platforms, policies, and actions of Labor and Likud denied these differences. The initial dislocation of Palestinians was carried out by Labor, not Likud, as were the settlement policies that provided the foundation of Israel. Rabin fought in the 1948 war, commanded the Israeli military in its sweeping victory in the 1967 war, and sought to crush the Palestinian uprising in 1987. Could the difference between Labor and Likud be so great as to justify this emotion and anger?

On election day in 1996, when Peres' lead shifted to Benjamin Netanyahu, Leah Rabin threatened to pack her bags and leave Israel for good. An Israel led by Netanyahu was unrecognizable to her as the Israel her husband lived and died for. Was there such a profound difference in thought and policy between Peres and Netanyahu or, for that matter, between her slain husband and the new prime minister? How could the welcome of Arafat into her home be seen in light of her refusal to accept any form of condolence from Netanyahu? Was all of this simply a personal animus toward the man she blamed for helping create the climate for her husband's assassination?

Leah Rabin's meeting with Arafat takes on a double significance. Perhaps she came to understand Arafat's insistence on Palestinian rights *and* accepted Palestinians as a people intimately involved in a Jewish future of peace and prosperity. Netanyahu represents the politics of a past that no longer has an emergency situation—the birth and defense of the state—to justify it. For Leah Rabin, Netanyahu's politics of might and hate continued a cycle her husband hoped to end.[11]

What Rabin and Peres ultimately represent, and what is perhaps their ultimate contribution to Jewish history, is the realization that mobilization and militarization of Jewish consciousness cannot be pursued forever and, while perhaps necessary at certain points in history, can cripple and distort Jewish culture and ethics if carried beyond the need for self-defense. Clearly they were guilty of this offense themselves, but ultimately, when faced with the "other" in a personal and secure setting, they recognized the limitations of these policies. In short, a current in Jewish history and tradition precluded the normalization of unlimited power against a defeated foe.

Both Rabin and Peres helped create a catastrophe for the Palestinian people, but something in Jewish culture and life prevented that victory from being celebrated without remorse and ultimately without some kind of reconciliation. At least with their leadership, the Palestinian surrender seemed to bode an outcome that generations later might celebrate as the decisive moment for sharing the land of Israel/Palestine.

The Present Challenge

In the past century, the discussion of Jewish destiny has been informed by a variety of currents but dominated by one: the power of the state. The Holocaust is the classic example of the need to emphasize the unity of the Jewish world simply to survive the destructive power of the Nazi state. The emergence of the state of Israel has forced Jewish thought into the service of a small and fragile entity that carries the special burden of surviving the Holocaust and the admonition that its failure would lead to another holocaust.

In this climate, diaspora and homeland sensibilities have been submerged and disciplined. Yet it is their very revival that may point the way to the future, as they have been the repositories of ethical challenge to limit non-Jewish and Jewish state power. As the century-old emergency situation of the Jews comes to an end, it is crucial that these visions reemerge from the background and join the imperatives of the state on an equal footing.

Though the diaspora and homeland visions of Jewish history were formed before the founding of Israel, in a condition of relative powerlessness, their dream is not a return to a world that is dangerous for Jews. It is clear, however, that the era of state power, without diverse value centers challenging that power, has liberated Jews from powerlessness but not from the corruption and injustice that accompany power.

If Jewish powerlessness reached a dead end in the middle of the twentieth century, Jewish power has also reached a dead end as the twenty-first century is upon us. The first generation experienced the Holocaust, the second perpetrated the oppression of the Palestinian people. Caught up in both events, Rabin and Peres struggled for a way out but failed in vocabulary and ideas. And if the vocabulary and ideas were still lodged within them—and why else would they, at least at the end of their lives, recognize the face of the other as an opportunity for reconciliation, indeed a necessity—could they dare articulate these views without fear of being derided, dismissed from power, or even assassinated?

The era that featured Auschwitz and the birth of Israel is coming to an end, as both Rabin and Peres seemed to understand. Yet, there are those who have a vested interest in continuing this era. The realm of Jewish politics, religion, and institutional fund-raising, crystallized in this era, seeks to persevere. In this sense, the possibility of a normal life for Jews in the Middle East is a threat to the Jewish status quo since it contradicts the state of emergency that fueled the rise of these ideas and institutions.

Will Jews continue to support a politics and religiosity that see the Jewish world as endangered if Jews no longer perceive their world in these terms? In fact, the situation has already changed over the decades as Israel has become a secure, even dominant power, and Jews in the West have become integrated and affluent constituents of Europe and America. Jewish politics and religion exist on borrowed time by promoting scenarios of future destruction that have less and less resonance with present reality.[12]

Beneath the surface, Rabin's handshake with Arafat had as much effect on the Jewish perception of the contemporary world as it did on the relations of Jews and Palestinians. Underlying this shift of Jewish perception is an anxiety that runs deep in Jewish history. If the era of

Auschwitz and the birth of Israel are over, what will continue to motivate Jewish commitment?

The Holocaust and Israel provided the impetus to renew a commitment of millions of Jews to the Jewish people when the post-World War II world beckoned them to integrate into the secular-democratic nations of the West. The post-war integration continued the process that was interrupted in the Nazi period. and, even with this interruption—predicted by Zionist thinkers and reinforcing, at least in their mind, the need for a Jewish state—integration was chosen again by the majority of Jewish people after the Holocaust. Paradoxically, the renewal of Jewish commitment with regard to the Holocaust and Israel served as a way of integration into the West with a pride and status rarely experienced in the annals of Jewish history.

The mobilization of the Jewish community in the West had a further anxiety in this process of renewal: it was as much about their contemporary life as it was about the victims of the Holocaust and support for Israel. Integration with pride and status as Jews allows an assimilation into Western culture while seeming to retain the separate and distinctive quality of Jewish life. Over time, this distinctiveness is less and less discernible to the outsider and more difficult to define within the Jewish community itself.

Support for Israel and Holocaust memorials define this change— even trumpet it—as the pattern of daily life for Jews becomes almost indistinguishable from non-Jews. Paradoxically, the normative identification of contemporary Jews is dependent on the exceptional crisis situation of a past event, the Holocaust, and on Israel, which is no longer in danger and where most Jews choose not to live. From this vantage point, Rabin and Arafat together in Washington, and perhaps one day in Jerusalem, threatened the entire structure of Jewish life, casting the Jewish future into jeopardy.

Perhaps contemporary Jews desire assimilation *with* distinctiveness, as it provides security, status, and a sense of fidelity to Jewish heritage. Surely it is a less taxing form of affiliation than previous ways of being Jewish, as it requires only a minimal institutional structure and will countenance little interference from internal structures and authorities. Perhaps this, too, is part of the continuity of Jewish life interrupted by the Holocaust and the birth of Israel: the struggle to be free of the ghettos and rabbinic control in the eighteenth and nineteenth century is complemented by the desire to be free of the Holocaust and Israel as we enter the twenty-first century.

Jewish leadership fears that such an attitude will lead to an assimilation without distinctiveness, a final assimilation, as it were, from which there is no possibility of revival and renewal. The desire of many Jews to live and be defined only as citizens of the country within which they live is seen as unacceptable for, carried to its ultimate realization over generations, this would mean the end of the Jewish people. Here is where the diverse understandings of Jewish history and visions within that history are crucial to the future of the Jewish people. The assimilationist sensibility, for example, is found outside and within Israel and is utilized to normalize the Jewish situation in the larger world. Those who argue for a citizenship based on a democratic Israel rather than Jewish heritage seek the transformation of the Jewish definition of the state. They argue that almost 20 percent of the population of Israel is non-Jewish and deserving of equality within the state and that the Jewish definition of the state gives power to a militant Orthodox community, which seeks to define the ordinary life of Jewish and non-Jewish citizens. As in Western democratic states, citizenship, rather than religious or ethnic affiliation, should define the responsibilities and the freedom of the person. Religion can be practiced, indeed may even become more important to many, when it is free of the state and religious authorities linked to state power.[13]

Paradoxically, with such a definition of citizenship, the traditional Orthodox diaspora position might take on a renewed significance. A sizable and empowered Jewish community in Israel could provide the nourishment and hospitality for religious Jews who seek to live within the Holy Land and draw near to Jerusalem. Because of this presence, the ability to attract others to this way of life and to form communities around this sensibility could be strengthened.

A mutual desire to be free to live in the Holy Land and enjoy the possibilities of that life without state interference or coercion may form a common agenda for the secular and religious-diaspora sensibilities. If the secular community is free to be secular and the religious free to be religious—along with the freedom to move from one community to the other—both are also able to be connected to other Jewish communities around the world. The secular-diaspora communities in the West can be linked to Israel, as can the religious communities. Because of these connections, the experience, substance, and vision of diverse Jewish communities may be expanded.

The Jewish homeland vision is crucial here as well. The struggle for empowerment without oppressing another people has remained an important element of Jewish consciousness from the beginning of the state. Once the choice had been made for a state, the homeland forces struggled within the state framework to keep alive the values that, they argued, could best flourish without a state structure.

Over time, these voices were made mute through death—Magnes in 1948, Buber in 1965—and through attrition, for by the late 1960s Arendt became silent on the issue of Israel because of the vehement attacks on her loyalty to the Jewish people. Other, less well-known voices worked quietly on the issues important to them or were disciplined by the loss of jobs or grants. In short, an entire segment of committed Jews were relegated to the sideline or "excommunicated" from Jewish life, by default finding their way to other venues.[14]

As with the diaspora sensibility, those who proposed a homeland for Jews in Palestine were swept away by the tide of Holocaust remembrance and mobilization for Israel. The values they proposed, however, remain and may even be more important today then when they were initially proposed. For what purpose have Jews gathered in the land of Israel? If survival is a major aspect of that gathering and if survival has been secured, what direction should the life of the Jewish community take now? Should a cultural, educational, and linguistic revival prevail, deepening the particular gifts of the Jewish people and offering them to the wider world? Can that be done without reconciling the claims of the Palestinians who have been injured in the creation of the Jewish state?

A homeland vision within the state could surface values of justice and compassion as well as the original intentions of cultural and communal revival. It could warn against political and cultural boundaries that impose separation among Jews and between Jews and Palestinians, both of which promote isolation and injustice. The strength of Jewish life is demonstrated by its ability to interact across internal and external boundaries to the point where crossing boundaries and absorbing values and insights from different perspectives enhances each sensibility and community rather than threatens it. Like the diaspora sensibility, the homeland vision can encompass religious and secular points of view, promoting both even as they may transform each other. For often the religious understanding is broadened by its interaction with secular culture, just as secular culture is deepened by its interaction with religious culture.

With regard to Palestinians, the diaspora sensibility and homeland vision demand an understanding that is confessional and inclusive. The appetite of the state is for more territory and power without remorse or pause; the historic-diaspora experience of Jews identifies with the diaspora of the Palestinians and their continuing suffering. It recognizes Jewish culpability in the creation of the Palestinian diaspora and the responsibility to remedy the situation insofar as it is possible.

Because of the historic exile of the Jewish people, the Jewish-homeland vision recognizes the need to reestablish a homeland for Palestinians as a way of recreating a center for Palestinian life, one that can absorb part of the diaspora and provide a home community for those Palestinians who choose to remain outside their homeland. Moreover, the diaspora and homeland experiences of both peoples provide a connection in experience and a common hope, a normalization of a previously untenable situation that also affords a creative possibility, perhaps even a model, for surviving adversity and flourishing in a new configuration.

Perhaps this commingling of the Jewish and Palestinian diaspora and homeland in Israel and Palestine can begin in Jerusalem, the ancient and contemporary site of the longings of both peoples. As the religious center of Jews, Muslims, and Christians, Jerusalem is well-suited to confront Jewish and Islamic fundamentalist groups who, armed with state power or the desire to gain it, threaten to destroy the possibility of mutual interchange and reconciliation. As commentary on the central role of Jerusalem, Jewish and Palestinian political and intellectual ideologies have also found their strength emanating from this ancient city.

A different view of Jerusalem from the diaspora and homeland sensibilities might refocus debates about these secular and national ideologies that provide the matrix for the exercise of state power. As the understanding of Jerusalem changes, the entire constellation of the struggle between Jews and Palestinians might take on a different coloration. If Jews and Palestinians can live together in Jerusalem, if their religious, secular, and national views can be intense *and* compassionate, and if this city, so exceptional in the history of both peoples and the world, can yield an ordinary life of prayer, commerce, and politics, how can this be denied to other parts of Israel and Palestine, or to those Jews and Palestinians who live outside the land?[15]

The ordinary quality of life in this new configuration of Jerusalem would, in light of the present circumstances, be extraordinary. This "extraordinary ordinary," so to speak, could provide a renewed vision for both peoples. For Jews, Jerusalem will represent a true homecoming and an end of the era of Auschwitz and the birth of Israel, which includes release from the burden of oppressing another people.

The end of the forced exile from the Holy Land is joined by a natural interchange of the diverse elements of Jewish life that were created over the last 2,000 years. Instead of a forced march of narrowing Jewish life, the entire tapestry of Jewish history can unfold. Each part of the tapestry takes its place, reinforcing, critiquing, and even, at times, judging aspects of Jewish life that threaten to become dominant.

A checks-and-balances reality is established that focuses on the possibilities of Jewish history and life, while disciplining the excesses that are also part of Jewish history. If it is true that a diaspora and homeland without power is in danger from those outside the Jewish community, it is also true that Jewish power without restraints is in danger of undermining the values that make it worthwhile being Jewish.

Surely the engine of the state, with its ability to organize society and to enforce its authority through military and police force—and even its ability to manufacture crisis and encourage intellectuals and theologians to do its bidding—can easily override the hopes of what is left of the diaspora and homeland vision. In this sense, the surrender of the Palestinians *vis-à-vis* Israel is similar to the surrender that the diaspora and homeland sensibilities have made within Israel and the Jewish world. The surrender is out of necessity and has, in fact, already occurred. A public, negotiated surrender, however, as with the Palestinians, places the issue back into the public realm where another, perhaps final, discussion can take place.

If the diaspora and homeland sensibilities surrender publicly, there are no treaties to be signed, as with the Palestinian surrender. Rather, the negotiations are on moral and intellectual grounds. Issue is joined if a public declaration is made on the need to change directions and if the consequences of continuing on the same path are made clear. By surrendering in public, a form of intellectual and ethical negotiations might begin in which the resources for change are placed before the Jewish community and the constant refrain of having no other choice is confronted with alternatives.

As with the Palestinians, the strategy of the diaspora and homeland surrender includes the hope that there are enough values left within the Jewish community to recognize the claim against it and to begin the process of change to include the victim and hence embrace an alternative vision. A surprising strength can be found when the voice of the vanquished appears in the public discussion, especially when that voice is recognized as part of the internal qualities of a people.

Who could have predicted that Yitzhak Rabin would come to understand aspects of the Palestinian question from a Palestinian perspective or that the leader of the Palestinian resistance would journey into Israel to mourn the loss of her husband with Leah Rabin? It could be that decades from now the understanding of Israel as a Jewish homeland—and Palestine as a homeland for Palestinians—and Jerusalem as a place where Jews and Palestinians in their home and diaspora communities will welcome each other, might be achieved as if it were the most natural and normal way of life for both peoples.

There have been Jews, from the beginning of the renewed Jewish settlement in Palestine, who have recognized this connection of Jewish and Palestinian lives and who have paid the price for that understanding. Their interest was in justice, to be sure, but also as much in the harm that injustice would do to Jewish ethics and life.

One hears the voice of Martin Buber in 1949, just one year after the birth of the state of Israel, publicly lecturing Prime Minister David

Ben-Gurion on the plight of the Palestinian Arab refugees, or one reads Buber's letter to Ben-Gurion on the Jewish massacre of Palestinian Arabs at Deir Yassin. In both cases, Buber's words were strong and, for the most part, unanswered. Ben-Gurion's silence has endured until Buber's words have become virtually unknown to contemporary Jews.[16]

Still, these words resonate throughout Jewish history, awaiting rediscovery and, even more, awaiting contemporary voices to speak as clearly, in a time of security, as Buber did in a time of uncertainty and danger. At the end of their journey—and as representatives of a state that did not listen to Magnes, Buber, or Arendt—Rabin and Peres struggled toward a vision that could, at a great distance to be sure, respond to their vision.

Who will speak now and venture the next step to reconfigure the Jewish journey, a journey that remains vibrant even as it becomes more ancient? Who will help rescue a millennial dream threatened with nightmare? In short, who will lecture the current prime minister, now on the threshold of the twenty-first century, as others did in the middle of the twentieth century?

Even more important is the question of how Jews will seek security *and* justice, embrace values of strength *and* compassion, and mobilize so that their voices will change the course of Jewish life rather than remain voices unheeded. For the distance between the voice of the diaspora and the homeland and ours is great in time and depth.

If not heard today, one wonders how these voices of dissent will be heard or recovered decades from now. By then the situation within the Jewish world and between Jew and Palestinian will have been decided. The vocabulary and vision of the diaspora and the homeland might be unavailable, perhaps even indecipherable.

That the Holocaust and the state of Israel loom large in Jewish memory and concern is understandable. That both have begun to recede in Jewish consciousness and, in the decades and centuries ahead, that they will recede even further is inevitable. A Jewish world formed around a memory centuries old or mobilized around a state that has assumed a normal pattern of life is difficult to imagine. It would mean that the struggle for rebirth after the Holocaust, symbolized by the birth of Israel, had failed, become ossified, and the Jewish people would be a fossil people. It would mean a further narrowing of Jewish perspectives until only that of power is allowed.

Those who speak now align themselves with the hope of creating a meaningful future. They also help rescue the voices of Jewish history from an oblivion that they do not deserve. As is so often the case in Jewish history, the time is late, the circumstances are complex, and the wager is great. As is often true in Jewish history as well, the time is now. For what other time do we have than now?

CHAPTER TWO

On Memory and Justice

Few concepts are so intimately linked in Jewish life as memory and justice. Contemporary Jewish scholars have spent much of their energy in thinking through this connection in the post-Holocaust era.

Memory is of the past, but remembrance is always in the present. Both point toward a future where justice, once denied, will be embraced. This pattern began in the Exodus, where God, remembering injustice and the promise of the covenant, forged a future of justice anchored in remembrance. The link between memory and justice has always been central in Jewish life, though the Holocaust has made it less clear or even has created an unbridgeable chasm.

Still Jewish thinkers persist. One such person is Yosef Hayim Yerushalmi.[1] Yerushalmi finds the core of Jewish survival and identity in the Bible, where a type of historical and mythical remembrance is called for by God. Exhortations to remember are numerous and are seen as a religious imperative for the entire people. These exhortations reach a crescendo in Deuteronomy and the prophets; these books recall the wonders that God has done for the people Israel and call Israel to remember what their enemies have done against them. The defining moment of remembrance in Jewish history is found in the Bible as well: "Remember that you were a slave in Egypt . . . ."[2]

Memory, of course, is problematic; memory can be a force for justice, but it can also be deceptive, even treacherous. The obligation of Israel to remember is selective, tied to God's acts of intervention in history and Israel's positive and negative responses to them. Remembrance is found within ritual and recital, and thus the narrative of Israel is both liturgical and historical. Though the mission of Israel is tied to God, it is traced through history; the covenant is a bridge between God and history, embodied in Israel itself. Remembrance is central to the covenant and the security of the relationship between God and Israel.

If memory is central, the failure to remember is disastrous. More than a momentary lapse of attention or an excusable human failing, the lack of memory is fraught with tremendous anxiety, as it threatens to sever the relationship that is so important to Israel and the world. Yerushalmi points out a peculiar and revolutionary aspect of this remembrance in that God is also enjoined to remember.

Like Israel, God is bound in the covenant. The remembrance found in ritual and recital is also a way of reminding God of the commitment jointly shared, to be found and demonstrated in history. Memory can thus be a hymn of praise but can become a query, even an accusation, when the promises of God are found to be wanting.[3]

Memory has rooted the Jewish people throughout history, especially in the years of exile and suffering, but the role of memory in contemporary Jewish life is deeply problematic. The dangers of memory, with their focus on exclusivity and chosenness, have traditionally coexisted with its possibilities, a sense of relationship with God and the protection of God within suffering. Contemporary Jewish life, however—especially after emancipation in Europe, the Holocaust, and the birth of Israel—has taken on a bifurcated character.

As a result of emancipation in Europe and America and national sovereignty in Israel, Jews have fully re-entered the mainstream of history. Yet, as Yerushalmi notes, "their perception of how they got there and where they are is most often more mythical than real." Though myth and memory provide the foundation for action, some myths are worthy of preservation and reinterpretation while others "lead us astray" and must be redefined. Still others are dangerous; they must be exposed and jettisoned.[4]

Yershulami ends his lectures without specifying which myths are worthy of preserving and which are dangerous. Nor does he specify the danger that Jewish life is in beyond tracing the rise of secular culture, a modern scientific understanding of history, and consequent decay of Jewish memory. The dangerous juncture reached in Jewish history, after the Holocaust and the rebirth of a national identity in Israel, seems to be defined as the vulgarization of Jewish life or its oversimplification, that is, a trend toward a superficial discussion and embodiment of Jewish life. "Nothing has replaced the coherence and meaning with which a powerful messianic faith once imbued both Jewish past and future," Yerushalmi writes. "Perhaps nothing else can. Indeed, there is a growing skepticism as to whether Jewish history can yield itself to any organizing principle that will command general assent." The danger here is movement beyond vulgarization and superficiality toward assimilation. Perhaps all three trends will come together sometime in the future.

Yerushalmi is honest when he states that there are no obvious solutions to the issues he has raised.[5]

As complicated as his argument is, and as tentative as his proposals for the future are, one cannot help but think that he has left out an important aspect of contemporary Jewish life and, with it, a major element of the memory that needs to be acknowledged. Though his first lecture was delivered in Jerusalem, and though he identifies nationalism as an important part of the contemporary Jewish experience, Yerushalmi nowhere mentions the complicated history of Jews and Palestinians as part of the collective memory of the Jewish people.

If Jewish memory has become abstract, unable to bridge myth and reality or to fashion a coherent center for contemporary Jewry, is it possible that this lack of remembering contributes to the problems that Yerushalmi surfaces? There is a history between Jews and Palestinians to record, to recite, perhaps even to ritualize in the city where these lectures were delivered. Yet if this history does not record that memory or even allude to it, then perhaps Jewish life is further bifurcated.

While lecturing in Jerusalem, Yershulami seems blind to the history around him, including those people struggling under Israeli domination. Or perhaps he was unable to articulate this change in Jewish history within the framework in which he was trained and sought to articulate. Either through ignorance or inability, was he actually contributing to the vulgarization, superficiality, even assimilation of Jewish life? Did including Palestinians in Jewish remembrance threaten to historicize the Jewish experience to such an extent that the traditional framework of Jewish life would be overturned? And if the Palestinians are not included, how can Jews decide which myths are worthy of preservation and which are dangerous and need to be jettisoned?

One wonders if a third category of Jewish memory has been created, even as it remains unarticulated by most Jewish scholars. The injunction to remember God's acts in history and the peoples who have threatened Jewish existence is joined with the need to remember acts Jews have undertaken against others, in this case the Palestinian people. As with the first two injunctions, forgetting or pretending that the deeds have not taken place creates a further rupture within Jewish history, one that allows myths such as Jewish innocence and exclusive redemption to triumph. The balancing factor of history, which grounds the work of God in the life of the people—in many ways the essence of the covenant—fades.

As the covenant becomes more and more mythicized, God becomes abstract or even peripheral to the people. The center of Jewish life, which is also the place of affirmation and resistance, begins to lose its force, and the people drift from cause to cause until there is only power or apathy to attract them. Religious and secular orthodoxies predominate as both refuse the tension of God and history.

In contemporary Jewish life, the Holocaust and Israel have assumed their rightful and complicated place within this void as emotional attachments to a mythologized history in which most Jews are not participants. Viewed from afar and uncritically, the Holocaust and Israel may lose their place in history and assume a mythic status as protectors of the void.

The Jewish Liturgy of Destruction

This need for revision is true for the Jewish liturgy of destruction as well. In his work, David Roskies, Professor of Jewish Literature at Jewish Theological Seminary, explores remembrance in the context of Jewish writers and artists during the Holocaust. Roskies finds that in the midst of the Holocaust catastrophe, religious and secular writers and artists alike used the Jewish tradition of remembrance to articulate the difficulties, sorrow, and anger of their predicament. By using ancient Jewish archetypes of divine promise, election, and the mission of Israel and its place among the nations, counterposing them to the present circumstances, Jewish writers and artists were simultaneously able to locate themselves in a history of suffering and promise over against the Nazi vision of the Third Reich *and* carry on a transcendental dispute with the God of the Jewish covenant. Here the interaction of myth and history is placed in full mobilization.

A narrative emerges that is fully engaged with the present yet rooted deeply in the past. The history articulated reads almost like a liturgy, a liturgy of destruction, to be sure, but also a liturgy of resistance. An example is Yitzhak Katzenelson, a secular poet, who organized a public reading of the Bible on the day the Warsaw ghetto was sealed. This was to demonstrate a continuity of history as a people rather than belief in God. At the same time Hillel Zeitlin, a modern religious existentialist, began translating the Psalms into Yiddish. When his ghetto tenement was blockaded, Zeitlin arrived at the roundup point for deportation dressed in a prayer shawl and tefillin.[6]

If the liturgy of destruction fulfills the Jewish understanding of myth and history in its deepest interaction—providing an identity, a strength, a framework for resistance, and a search for meaning during the Holocaust—it also exhorts the interaction of ritual and recital. Memory here is the recovery of an entire history, which includes myth, history, ritual, and recital in a dynamic way.

The sense of collectivity is invoked within the context of individuality, transforming, in Roskies words, "collective disasters into individual rites of mourning and individual deeds into a model of collective sacrifice." What greater testimony to the strength of Jewish life can there be than recognition of a common history, one filled with diversity and argumentation, suffering and resistance, where the collective and the individual find their place and thus plant the seeds for the continuation of the people, even in their darkest night? The liturgy of destruction is created by martyrs for themselves in continuity with the past and as a link to a future that the martyrs themselves will not be alive to witness. Their martyrdom is a sign of fidelity to history and the moment, to the covenant even in its shattering, and to a future that will rise from that martyrdom.[7]

The liturgy of destruction spans Jewish history, and the writers and artists of the Holocaust are heirs and innovators within that tradition. For the most part, contemporary Jewish thinkers serve as narrators of that liturgy, recovering and naming the disparate voices of the European diaspora. These thinkers enable the present generation of Jews to see the continuity of the tradition even as it seems to be shattering. Paradoxically, the loss of tradition is the call for its survival, indeed the proof of its importance and vibrancy, if only the post-Holocaust generation will embrace it. Post-Holocaust writers and artists deal with these themes extensively, placing the traditional Jewish archetypes, such as the *Akedah*, the Exodus, the covenant at Sinai, the destruction of the Temple, and the pogrom, in a radical and subversive context.

It is here that the problem surfaces. What is to be done with this liturgy of destruction and the archetypes as they are handed to the next generation? If, as Roskies states, the catastrophe itself endows the Jewish writer and artist with "unprecedented authority," and, if, at the time when the "traditional doctrines of redemption and retribution had lost their power to console, visual icons of Jewish suffering came to symbolize the staying power of the people," what will endow the symbols and structure of a secure and established Jewish life with purpose and meaning? Can the broken tablets pictured in Samuel Bak's "Proposal for a Monument," or his "City of Jews," which features a devastated urban landscape with the tablets themselves a part of the tableaux, speak to Jews today? In the "City of Jews," the only sign of life is a smoking chimney; the city itself is sinking under the weight of God's commandments, "dying under the sign of its chosenness." For Roskies, Bak's midrash on Jewish history is as follows: "To live as Jews means to uphold the covenant even as it is desecrated, to exist both in the shadow of eternity and on the brink of destruction. There is no return to the Decalogue except via Vilna and Ponar. The tablets have been broken—in order that they may be pieced together again. One cannot build them other than on ruins. The sacred symbols, though defiled, are the only ones left."[8]

The Holocaust itself has become a Jewish archetype, and this, too, is a reference point for the future. The Holocaust archetype, however, is as ambiguous as it is powerful. "City of Jews" represents a destruction that challenges the future to a depth of recollection and reconstruction which the present may be unable to bear. One cannot ignore the symbolism of dying under one's own chosenness, for it represents a deep rendering of the Holocaust experience.

Nor can one look askance at someone seeking to "forget" that experience. For how can one "remember" this city—which represents the collective experience of the Jewish people—without desiring to forget it at the same time? Surely there are ways of simultaneously remembering and forgetting, thus trivializing the Holocaust even as one employs the rhetoric derived from it.

Roskies sees the danger primarily in the universalization of the Holocaust, which arises from the designation itself. Though the word *holocaust* refers to burnt sacrifices in the Bible, the word itself, derived from Latin, is extrinsic to Jewish history. This being so, the term *holocaust* lacks the resonance of Jewish history and discourse and makes it available to the broader non-Jewish community, which is then free to define and redefine the parameters of the event or even compare their own experiences within that framework.

The danger Roskies sees is the diminution of the horror of the Holocaust and the loss of its particularity. This gives rise to a confusion by which the catastrophe, "once the most private of Jewish concerns, becomes part of the public domain," with the resulting problem that "external perceptions replace inner realities, and borrowed words and archetypes are enlisted to explain the meaning of destruction" to Gentiles but also to Jews.[9]

Here the fear of superficiality, trivialization, and assimilation is raised again. The fear of assimilation is paramount as Roskies notes that the inner cadences of Jewish life are challenged by the invasion of foreign symbols, especially the Christian symbols of Christ's crucifixion found in the paintings of Marc Chagall and the work, at least in its interpretation by Christians, of Elie Wiesel. Roskies is caustic when he denotes the crossing of the boundary of Christian symbolism into Jewish life as a "real breakthrough." Picturing the travails of the Jews as a crucifixion in a sense hands Christians a victory to their own claim of universality and, at the same time, overrides the internal dialogue and history of the Jewish community *vis-à-vis* the liturgy of destruction and the animosity between the two communities. The use of Jesus can also be a form of resistance, however, as in Uri Zvi Greenberg's statement against Jesus and the Christians who claim him, graphically laid out in the form of a cross.[10] It can even be an attempt to speak to the Christians in a language they can understand, forcing them to ponder their transgressions.

Still, the acceptance of Jewish evocations of the Holocaust in the non-Jewish world requires a self-censorship, an editing of particular Jewish symbols and inner dialogue. The understanding of writing and art becomes dependent on interpretations wholly foreign to the Jewish experience. With Wiesel, this happens in the introduction of his work by the famous Catholic writer, François Mauriac, with his invocation of Wiesel and the Holocaust victims as a symbol of Christ's crucifixion. It ends by Wiesel's highlighting the themes of existential doubt and the post-war isolation of the individual over the appeal to fight the anti-Semites who would consign the Holocaust to oblivion. As Roskies sees it, since "no one in the literary establishment of the 1950s was ready to be preached to by a Holocaust survivor, existentialist doubt became the better part of valor."[11]

The cost of this "valor" is high, at least from Roskies's point of view. The theme of catastrophe particular to Jewish sensibility is a way of consoling fellow sufferers and provides a message of hope and continuity; the theme of existential despair leaves the survivors in a generalized exile and breaks the dialogue between Eastern European writers and their Jewish audience. The replacement of the particular with a nonparochial message reduces the message of the Holocaust, as difficult and ambiguous as it is, to one of "complete despair." When Wiesel and others edit out the shared expressions of faith to concentrate on the terrifying plight of the individual, Roskies believes they embrace a cultural rapprochement and sever themselves from the Jewish liturgy of destruction.

The implication is that individual advancement and larger cultural acceptance of their work takes precedence over fidelity to the family and communities that perished in the Holocaust. Whether intentional or not, the universalization of the Holocaust carried out by Jews themselves is a form of alienation and a further exile from the Jewish ethos that was threatened with destruction in the Holocaust. Implied but not specifically addressed is the most paradoxical of conclusions: that the near universal attention that the Holocaust has received, in large part due to the ability of Chagall, Wiesel, and others to communicate the horror of the event to those outside the Jewish world, may facilitate the loss of Jewish identification and understanding, except in the most vulgar and superficial modalities.[12]

What Roskies does not see is the possibility that Chagall, Wiesel, and others might be attempting to bridge the gap between Jew and Christian for reasons other than acceptance and self-advancement. Perhaps they recognize that the shattering of the tablets represents the shattering of traditional Jewish discourse, and that the archetypes of Jewish culture and liturgy will be lost if not interpreted within a broader framework. Perhaps the danger of the Holocaust is so deeply felt by them that security takes precedence over anger; reconciliation is necessary so that the next generation will remember the Holocaust rather than be faced with a similar event in their lives. Continuation of the Holocaust, even as an event of catastrophe much smaller than the destruction in Europe, might mean the end of the Jewish people.

The attempt to bridge the communities could also mean that these writers and artists retain faith in the possibility of the humanity of those defined as "other," a faith in the "conversion" of Christianity to the plight and hope of the Jewish people through recognition of Christian culpability in Jewish suffering. That this latter hope could come from victims of the Holocaust who had no reason to harbor such hope seems incredible. Could the shattering of the tablets and the weight of God's chosenness mandate a final appeal for a breakthrough beyond the violence and destruction of human history?

Another possibility locates the theme of survival within the West and the birth of Israel. It could be that these writers and artists recognize that an appeal to remembrance in an expanding dialogue on the Holocaust is crucial to the post-war integration of the Jews into the West *and* the mobilization of support for Israel. The end of the Holocaust and the birth of the state are separated by only three years, so the emergence of post-Holocaust literature parallels the origins of the state.

It is hardly coincidence that the interest in the Holocaust, in fact its very naming as such, occurs within the context of Israel's victory in the 1967 war. Further, most historians see the memory of the Holocaust either within the larger context of the suffering of World War II or as beginning to fade by the late 1950s. By that time, Western Jews were busy with life in Europe and America, and Jews in Israel were distancing themselves from suffering as a long, shameful chapter in Jewish history that they were determined to end.

Paradoxically, then, the Holocaust assumes its significance and its narrative power for Jews and non-Jews just as Jews are integrated in the West and assume power in Israel. The way of the future for American and Israeli Jews is seen as the wedding of both communities via the Holocaust in Europe. And the future of Israel is found in the narrative of Jewish suffering and rebirth, which can be embraced by those in Europe and America who had traditionally been the enemies of the Jews, that is, Christians. Perhaps the paradox of all paradoxes is that Jewish intellectuals, theologians, and activists recognized immediately that the future of the Jewish people was in the hands of those traditions and peoples responsible for the conditions leading to the Holocaust itself.

This embrace by Jewish leadership is complex in the extreme, as are the motivations behind that embrace. Self-advancement and security are important, but so, too, is a sense of responsibility for the collective safety and flourishing of the Jewish people after the Holocaust. Critical to this project is the assertion and preservation of Jewish innocence, certainly in the Holocaust, but also with much more difficulty in relation to Israel. In some ways this can be seen most clearly in the works and life of Elie Wiesel after the publication of *Night*, as he creates a narrative in which remembrance of the Holocaust story is dependent on the Jewish and Western sense of innocence in the building of Israel.

By the 1970s, most Holocaust writing functions as a way of asserting the mission of Israel in light of the Holocaust and the presumed innocence of all Jewish behavior, including in Israel, because of Jewish suffering in the Holocaust. An archetype is added to Jewish history, that of the perpetual innocence of Jews regardless of circumstances, in suffering *and* in power. Henceforth, internal and external criticism of Israeli policies is filtered through the Holocaust, just as Palestinian voices will be. When the Holocaust narrative is at its peak, as in the 1970s, the Palestinians are invisible; their emergence in the 1980s is as a peripheral player in the larger Jewish drama.[13]

Holocaust theology emerges in the 1960s in the matrix of remembrance of the Holocaust and the empowerment of Israel. The emphasis by Roskies and Yerushalmi on the themes of remembrance and the predicament of post-Holocaust Jewry are possible and make sense to a Jewish and non-Jewish public because of the religious reflections pioneered and popularized by Wiesel and other serious Holocaust thinkers such as Richard Rubenstein, Emil Fackenheim, and Irving Greenberg.

The dynamics of Holocaust theology emphasize the suffering of the Jewish people in the Holocaust and the necessity of their empowerment in Israel. A subset of themes, which dovetails with the general framework, emphasizes the innocence of the Jewish people and the possible redemptive aspects of Jewish empowerment in Israel. The survival of the Jews is seen in a familiar light: a combination of memory, myth, and history cast in the realm of the liturgical. For when one listens to Wiesel speak on the Holocaust—whether in a local synagogue or accepting the Nobel Prize—the refrain and cadence is liturgical. In Wiesel's speech, Bak's midrash on history comes to life reconfigured, as the tablets are broken *and* made whole, the Jews are suffering *and* are empowered, the whole world is arrayed against the Jews as the same world is commanded to enter the mystery of Jewish death and rebirth.[14]

As Yershulami and Roskies implicitly criticize this reconfigured midrash, they are also dependent on it. Yet, even leaving aside this unannounced dependence, the criticism of the superficiality, vulgarization, even assimilationist aspects of Holocaust theology, remains abstract. The criticism falters when the missing connection to a life of depth is sought. There is no way back to the worlds that these authors explore.

But where is the road ahead? Or at least what paths need to be explored to create a Jewish framework worthy of the past and able to be passed on to the future? Can the myths of Jewish history be brought into the dynamics of history so that Jewish purpose in the world will be grounded in reality? Can the liturgy of destruction be transformed into a liturgy of healing and creation?

Perhaps the answers to these questions can be found in confronting historical events that have been neglected or suppressed by the Jewish world. As Jews know all too well, on the other side of innocence and redemption lie those who are cast off and displaced, those made invisible and forgotten. It may be that recovery of this history is key to confronting the dangers that Yerushalmi and Roskies surface.

If memory is problematic, sometimes deceptive, even treacherous, does it also retain an explosive power that can transform a people's search for survival and identity? Can the memory of suffering inflicted on Jews one day come to terms with the suffering that Jews have inflicted on Palestinians? And could that dawning realization of the difficult struggle for survival and the loss of innocence propel the Jewish people into a search for life beyond being a victim or an oppressor? Perhaps such a recovery of memory can limit the bifurcation that is so much a part of Jewish life. It may also lead to a reconciliation with the "enemy," which often as not portends a reconciliation with oneself.

For has the trauma of the Holocaust, which is remembered, recited, and ritualized today more than at any time, led to a healing of the Jewish people? A corollary question is whether Jewish empowerment in the West and in Israel has healed Jews of fear, anger, and the brokenness that post-Holocaust writers and artists portrayed so vividly.

Through memorialization and power it is difficult to argue that Jews have finally put the era of Auschwitz behind them. One wonders if the theme of Auschwitz remains part of the landscape awaiting, at least in the Jewish psyche, a rebirth in a future scenario of destruction.

Remembering Deir Yassin

Jews around the world celebrate the birth of the state of Israel as a formative event in Jewish history. The memory of that birth follows the lines that Yerushalmi probes, existing in the tension of myth and history and creating a narrative that is recited and ritualized. In this memory, the birth of Israel is linked with the Holocaust.

Although the birth of any state is dramatic, the drama of Israel is magnified by the overwhelming suffering in the Holocaust and by the fact that many Holocaust survivors fought in Israel's war of independence. The drama is intensified even further because of the millennia-old travails of this ancient people. Ancient archetypes of exile and liberation, featured in a radically subversive way against the Nazis and even against God in the Holocaust, are employed here in a way that reinforces the return of the Jews to the land of Israel and raises the possibility that God might be returning to the people.

The power of Holocaust and Israeli imagery overrides the actual history of this return and the creation of the state; those on the other side of this Jewish drama are either made invisible or dramatized as a mythic enemy whose opposition to their own displacement takes on cosmic significance. For who can oppose the fulfillment of Jewish destiny, the recreation of Jewish life, and the mending of the broken tablets, except those whose agenda is ungodly and demonic?

Yet beneath the mythic structure of the creation of Israel are people, Palestinian *and* Jewish, who saw the struggle quite differently. Their experience of the struggle, while retaining aspects of myth and history, was transformed in the actualities of everyday life. Some experienced the birth of Israel as a collision of different worlds and histories. In this collision their vision of the future was tested. Diverse opinions and actions were held and taken, risks were great, time was short, lives were at stake.

Looking back on these events today, one is moved by the difficulty, complexity, and honesty of the participants in the founding of the state. The tragedy was that in this birth lay a future of divisiveness and brokenness. Nowhere can this complexity, this tragedy, and the future be seen more vividly than in the events at Deir Yassin, a Palestinian Arab village, where over 100 Arabs were massacred by the Jewish paramilitary group known as the Irgun in April 1948, whose leader, Menachem Begin, would later become prime minister of Israel.

My involvement in the issue of Deir Yassin helps frame the historical issue in contemporary terms. As I was working through the question of memory and Jewish history, rereading Yerushalmi and Roskies in the summer of 1995, the Israeli-Palestinian negotiations reached another milestone with further Israeli withdrawal from occupied Palestinian territory and the expanded assumption of governance by the Palestinian Authority. It was at this time that I received an invitation to join the Board of Advisers of a project titled "Deir Yassin Remembered." The project has as its purpose the creation of a memorial site to commemorate the massacre. Though I was aware of the massacre, and even met survivors of it, the details of the atrocity were vague to me.[15]

Through my meetings with Palestinians over the years, I realized that Deir Yassin was important to them on both historic and symbolic levels. In historic terms it signaled escalation of the violence of the war, so that the very presence of Arabs in Palestine was threatened. Symbolically it represents the forced displacement of Palestinians and the beginning of their catastrophe.

For Palestinians, Deir Yassin contradicts in the most profound way any claim to Jewish innocence and raises the question of the cost of Jewish empowerment. Over the years, the "forgetting" of Deir Yassin has stood, at least for Palestinians, in direct contradiction to remembrance of the Holocaust. In Roskies's terms, Deir Yassin has remained part of the inner landscape of Palestinian life, as the Palestinians, to a large extent, have been unable to articulate their tragedy in the West.

The cultural integration achieved by Jews after the Holocaust has been the driving force behind this inability of Palestinians to make their case before the larger public. Roskies's complaint about the transformation in Jewish consciousness because of public discourse about the Holocaust is a luxury that Palestinians might look forward to dealing with. For the loss of remembrance of Deir Yassin in Jewish and Western consciousness is part of the historic and symbolic defeat of the Palestinians, just as public acknowledgment of the Holocaust is part of Jewish and Israeli empowerment.[16]

How was I to relate to this project of memorialization? At this same time, the situation in the Middle East seemed promising, at least in comparison to previous years. The deal between the government of Israel and the Palestine Liberation Organization deliberately side-stepped the historic grievances of both parties, and the intellectual atmosphere surrounding the agreements concentrated on the present rather than rehashing the past.

Though the celebratory atmosphere of the initial signing in 1993 had faded considerably by the time I received the invitation, the emphasis remained optimistic. Was this the time to join a committee that had as its aim the remembrance of a massacre symbolizing the destruction of Palestine? Equally fascinating was the committee's intent to lobby the Israeli Knesset for permission for such a memorial. What would it be like at this juncture of history, and as a Jew, to travel to Jerusalem and lobby the government of Israel for a memorial that would contradict—even indict—the sense of Jewish innocence?

Though by the spring of 1948 both sides of the Jewish-Arab conflict in Palestine were growing accustomed to the human cost of war, the massacre at Deir Yassin provoked an outrage that to this day remains a sensitive part of the history of both peoples. Located strategically on high ground in the corridor between Tel Aviv and Jerusalem, Deir Yassin had a peaceful reputation among its neighboring Jewish settlements and had entered into a mutual non-aggression pact with the Givat-Shaul and Montefiore settlements. When Arab forces asked permission to use Deir Yassin as a military base, the village leaders refused, pleading that its strategic location would expose the village, especially its women and children, to great danger.

Deir Yassin's leaders foresaw the possibility that arrived despite their delicate and seemingly successful negotiations with the Jewish villages and Arab combatants, for Deir Yassin was captured after an unsuccessful defense against the Irgun and the Haganah, the mainstream Jewish army. After the Haganah withdrew its men, the Irgun remained.

Looting and murder followed the surrender of the village. The message that the Irgun successfully conveyed to the Palestinian Arabs was that they must flee the advancing Jewish armies or face dire consequences. Within weeks of the massacre over 300,000 Arabs fled their homes. As Menachem Begin noted in his memoirs, the "legend" of Deir Yassin was "worth half a dozen battalions to the forces of Israel." After the massacre, Begin sent a message of congratulations to the conquerors of Deir Yassin: "Accept congratulations on this splendid act of conquest. Tell the soldiers you have made history in Israel."[17]

After initially claiming that a group of Arab rebels was responsible for the massacre, the Jewish Agency acknowledged that Jewish soldiers belonging to dissident organizations were responsible for the "savage and barbaric" acts at Deir Yassin, and they cabled an apology to King Abdullah, the leader of Transjordan. A year later, as plans for resettlement of the abandoned village by Jewish Israelis were being formulated, Martin Buber and three other Jewish scholars—Ernst Simon, Werner Senator, and Cecil Roth—wrote to Prime Minister David Ben-Gurion asking that Deir Yassin be left uninhabited, or at least that its resettlement be postponed.

Noting the tremendous pressures of resettlement resulting from the displacement of Jewish populations during World War II, the authors still pleaded for a higher consideration. For Deir Yassin had become "infamous throughout the Jewish world, the Arab world and the whole world. In Deir Yassin hundreds of innocent men, women and children were massacred. The Deir Yassin affair is a black stain on the honor of the Jewish nation." The letter continued by stating that it would be better to let the "lands of Deir Yassin lie fallow and the houses of Deir Yassin stand uninhabited, than to carry out an act whose negative symbolic impact is infinitely greater than the practical resolution it can offer." For Buber, resettling Deir Yassin within a year of the crime would amount to an endorsement of, or at least an acquiescence with, the massacre: "Let the village of Deir Yassin remain uninhabited for the time being, and let its desolation be a terrible and tragic symbol of war, and a warning to our people that no practical or military needs may ever justify such acts of murder and that the nation does not wish to profit from them."[18]

Ben-Gurion did not respond to the letter, despite the fact that Buber and his compatriots sent him copy after copy, anticipating a response. Eventually the prime minister's secretary responded that Ben-Gurion was simply too busy to read their letter. Meanwhile plans for resettlement continued unabated. Indeed the press reported the resettlement of the village, with the new name of Givat Shaul Bet, as if it were like any other. Israeli historian Tom Segev writes that "several hundred guests came to the opening ceremony, including Cabinet Ministers Kaplan and Shapira, as well as the Chief Rabbis and the Mayor of Jerusalem. President Haim Weizmann sent written congratulations. The band of the school for the blind played and refreshments were served."[19]

When I received my invitation to join the commemoration committee, I thought of this history of atrocity, the letter of conscience, and the silence of Ben-Gurion. Surely Ben-Gurion was a busy man, as the creation of a state takes an extraordinary amount of energy, ingenuity, political maneuvering and vision. The deed done, a thousand issues confronting him at the time, who would not excuse him this oversight, or even refusal, to reply? The celebration is also understandable, for the creation of a new community is typically a cause for festivities rather than confessions of misdeeds and atrocity.

From another perspective, Ben-Gurion's silence signaled a question that to this day has yet to be answered. According to Israeli historian Benny Morris, it was during the time of the massacre at Deir Yassin that Ben-Gurion "explicitly sanctioned the expulsion of Arabs from a whole area of Palestine." Ben-Gurion's silence may have been an attempt to dismiss or even bury the reality that the founding of Israel was marked by atrocity and violence, rather than innocence, and that many survivors of the Holocaust achieved security and prosperity through the spoils of war and the displacement of another people. The Israeli newspaper *Davar* reported this haunting possibility without ambivalence: "At the sound of the Israeli soldiers marching, the Arabs were seized with a great terror and left their homes, with their heavily-loaded camels and donkeys, *en route* for the border. . . . And now in Jamsin—renamed Givat Amal—live new residents, recently arrived via Cyprus, survivors of the camps of Europe. They sit around a long table, with one remnant of the abandoned furniture, and tell their tales." At the time of the resettlement of Deir Yassin, and hundreds of other formerly Arab villages, a Knesset member, Yosef Lamm, stated, "None of us behaved during the war in a way we might have expected the Jewish people to behave, either with regard to property or human life, and we should all be ashamed."[20]

If the building of state and the emergency circumstances of the Holocaust can account for the silence of Ben-Gurion—indeed the silence of much of the Jewish establishment inside and outside of Israel since Deir Yassin—one wonders what accounts for the silence today. Should letters like Buber's, updated and expanded over the years for still other displacements and atrocities, remain unanswered? Should festivities that surrounded the signing of the Declaration of Principles in Washington, D.C., in 1993 or the fiftieth anniversary of Israel in 1998 be the order of the day, rather than remembrance of the cries accompanying the end of Palestinian life and the beginning of new life for Jews in Israel? In short, should Deir Yassin, buried in Jewish consciousness, be raised again at this new and more promising moment in history? Or do remembrances of past transgressions freeze Jews and Palestinians in a past from which there is no escape?

It is interesting that this last argument is often promoted by parts of the Jewish establishment, even as they mobilize funds to create memorials such as the United States Holocaust Memorial Museum. Jews will not allow the world to forget Jewish suffering at the hands of the Nazis and choose, within the context of unparalleled security and affluence in America, to emphasize the Holocaust as an essential element of Jewish identity. Few Jews see the emphasis on Jewish suffering in Europe as stifling a promising future in America and in Jewish communities around the world.

Elie Wiesel's words at the fiftieth anniversary commemoration of the liberation of Auschwitz speak eloquently to this point: "Close your eyes and listen to the silent screams that terrify mothers. Listen to the prayers of anguished old men and women. Listen to the tears of the children. Remember the nocturnal procession of children, of more and more children, so frightened, so quiet, so beautiful. If we could simply look at one, our heart would break. But it did not break the hearts of the murderers. Do not forgive the murderers and their accomplices. God, merciful God, do not have mercy on those who had no mercy on Jewish children." Wiesel spoke these words as a survivor of Auschwitz but also as an author, respected university professor, and Nobel Prize recipient.[21]

One wonders if this remembrance, so detailed and yet at the same time so liturgically rendered, is the very key to remembering the suffering of those at Deir Yassin. The context and the magnitude of suffering were vastly different. There is no need to compare the tragedies to recognize that the tears of the children, the silent screams that terrify mothers, the prayers of anguished old men, resound in the history of the Palestinian people—in their catastrophe—just as they are heard in contemporary Jewish life. For if the Holocaust represents a tragic end to Jewish exile and powerlessness, the creation of Israel represents the beginning of Palestinian exile and powerlessness. While the tragedies of the Holocaust and the Palestinian exile are separate in geography and magnitude, what connects them is a cycle of displacement that compounds and deepens the tragedy.

Many Jews do not recognize that this cycle carries the wounds of both peoples into the present and, in a sense, makes them more difficult to heal. For can Jews be healed of the trauma of Holocaust by displacing another people? Could it be that atrocities committed against the Palestinian people in Deir Yassin and beyond, and the inability to admit and confess this atrocity, have further wounded the Jewish people and made it more difficult for Jews, even with the power of Israel, to be healed? Wiesel's words, while so moving and powerful, mean less when he, like Ben-Gurion, responds to an invitation to remember Deir Yassin—to be part of the Board of Advisers—with silence, and a brief mention that "things are improving." Jews hardly minimize the Holocaust because "things are improving." On the contrary, the naming of the historical injury deepens precisely at this moment.[22]

Perhaps Wiesel is so immersed in commemorating the Jewish dead and celebrating Israel that he is unable to remember the cries of others whose lives are remembered by their own families with as much affection and horror as Wiesel has for his own family. Perhaps, at a deeper level, Wiesel is traumatized by the Holocaust and unable to think through the ambivalent feelings he might have toward both Israel and the Palestinians. Clearly it would be difficult for Wiesel to listen to a Palestinian man of his own age, whose parents and siblings were murdered at Deir Yassin, recite at the fiftieth anniversary of the massacre, "Do not forgive the murderers and their accomplices. God, merciful God, do not have mercy on those who had no mercy on Palestinian children."

As Buber's letter to Ben-Gurion illustrates, not all Jews were too busy or were silent in the face of Deir Yassin. In fact there were Jews who attempted to stop the massacre. Meir Pa'il, a young Haganah officer who helped coordinate the initial attack on Deir Yassin, pleaded with the terrorist leaders to stop their men and women from slaughtering the Arab civilians after their surrender. According to Pa'il, when members of the neighboring Jewish village of Givat Shaul heard about the massacre, they came to Deir Yassin to stop the killing. As Pa'il relates: "They were just Jews, citizens who were ashamed. They began to shout and cry and the massacre was stopped."

Unfortunately, despite the intervention of the Jewish villagers, the terror continued a few days longer. Some of the Arab survivors of Deir Yassin were loaded into freight trucks and "led in a victory parade like a Roman triumph" through the Mahaneh Yehuda and Zichron Yosef quarters of Jerusalem. After the parade, they were executed. Jacques de Reynier, a Swiss doctor working for the International Red Cross, arrived at the village as "mopping up" operations were being conducted. De Reynier witnessed, among other acts, a young Jewish woman stab an elderly man and woman "cowering on the doorsteps of their hut" and "a beautiful young girl with criminal eyes, showed me her knife still dripping with blood, she displayed it like a trophy."[23]

The horror of Deir Yassin continued to haunt Martin Buber. In an address to the American Friends of Ichud in New York in 1958, Buber recalled the breakdown of moral fiber witnessed a decade earlier: "It happened one day, however, that outside of all regular conduct of the war, a band of armed Jews fell on an Arab village and destroyed it. Often in earlier times Arab hordes had committed outrages of this kind and my soul bled with the sacrifice; but here it was a matter of our own, or my own crime, of the crime of Jews against the spirit. Even today I cannot think about this without feeling myself guilty."

In this speech Buber accepted the verdict of history—that a Jewish state had come into being—and that contemporary Jewish life would be worked out within that structure. Still Buber felt that those Jews "who will truly serve the spirit must seek to make good all that was once missed: he must seek to free once again the blocked path to an understanding with the Arab peoples. . . . There can be no peace between Jews and Arabs that is only a cessation of war; there can only be a peace of genuine cooperation." These comments harkened back to his letter to Ben-Gurion in which he wrote: "The time will come when it will be possible to conceive of some act in Deir Yassin, an act which will symbolize our people's desire for justice and brotherhood with the Arab people."[24]

The Path Chosen

The distance between Martin Buber and Elie Wiesel on this issue is worth noting, for it illustrates how far the Jewish community has moved over the years. The distance cannot be explained simply by the origins or experience of either man, for both were formed in the crucible of the Nazi onslaught, and in their survival both were celebrated within and outside of the Jewish community.

To understand their differences does not require us to romanticize Buber, as he was a man of his time, European in outlook, colonial in mentality, Zionist in his vision. But he was also able to deal with the issues of the Holocaust, Israel, and the Palestinian Arabs in a critical and humane manner. In 1953, for example, Buber traveled from Jerusalem to accept the Peace Prize of the German Book Trade at Frankfurt and, in a controversial speech, differentiated between those Germans who committed genocide against the Jewish people, those Germans who remained silent during the Nazi era, and those who actively resisted fascism.

Buber shared, in only a strictly formal sense, a "common humanity" with the perpetrators; knowing the "weakness of men," he could not condemn those who were unwilling to oppose the Nazis at risk of their own or their families' lives. For those who became martyrs, however, Buber felt a "reverence and a love, a special intimacy which binds us at times to the dead and to them alone." On the question of Palestine, Buber was a confirmed and outspoken proponent of a binational state, a land of two peoples jointly governed with a shared civic, defense, police, and economic system. After the establishment of the state of Israel, Buber argued for a federation within the Middle East and a healing of wounds within historic Palestine.[25]

Two examples beyond the letter to Ben-Gurion regarding Deir Yassin illustrate Buber's direct confrontation of Israeli state power with regard to Palestinian Arabs: a March 1949 debate on the moral character of Israel with Ben-Gurion, just after the latter was installed as the first elected prime minister of the new state, in which Buber spoke of the Arab refugees as a moral question for Israel; and a March 1953 letter to the speaker of the Knesset protesting the draft legislation entitled "Expropriation of the Land," which legalized mass expropriation of Arab land within Israel. In the debate with Ben-Gurion, Buber challenged the new prime minister to convene an international, interfaith congress with the cooperation of Jews and the "neighboring peoples" to consider the refugee problem, adding the poignant question, "Were we not refugees in the diaspora?" In his protest against expropriation of Arab lands, Buber wrote, "We fail to understand why, according to press reports, hardly a single Jewish member of the Knesset has raised his voice against a law intended to give the stamp of legality to acts and deeds which he would consider a grave injustice if they were directed against himself or against Jewish property."[26]

We do not need or want to demonize Wiesel in this comparison. Buber was expelled from Nazi Germany; Wiesel survived Auschwitz as an orphan, having lost his immediate family there. After his expulsion, Buber lived in Palestine and then Israel and so was more closely attuned to the realities and the possibilities of the conflict between Jew and Arab. After several years in Palestine and Israel, Wiesel made his home in France and America and thus observed Israel from a distance. Perhaps because of the immediacy of the situation, the Holocaust became for Buber the backdrop for the establishment of a Jewish home in Palestine in cooperation with the Palestinian Arabs.

In a February 1939 letter to Mohandas Gandhi, Buber condemned Gandhi's insistence on nonviolence for German Jews and disputed

Gandhi's characterization of Jewish settlement in Palestine as a purely colonial endeavor, while still arguing for Jews and Arabs to share Palestine. For Buber, Gandhi misunderstood both the absolute and unstoppable evil of the Nazi menace and the Jewish sense of peoplehood. Even within the dynamic of fascism and conflicting interests in Palestine, though, reconciliation and cooperation were possible. Hence Buber's travel and public lectures in Germany in the 1950s, at a time when Wiesel was observing his ten-year vow of silence on the Holocaust.

When finally, in the 1960s and 1970s, Wiesel spoke and wrote on the question of Jews and Palestinians, he did so within the context of the Holocaust, projecting the past into the present. That is why Wiesel flew to Israel on the second day of the 1967 war, expecting Israel's defeat and a second holocaust. Because of this expectation, the victory of Israel became a miracle, assured not by military strategy and tactics, but by the "millions of martyrs of the Holocaust [who] were enlisted in the ranks." For Wiesel, these martyrs were like the biblical pillars of fire, shielding their spiritual heirs. With this assistance, Israel could not be defeated, and the Israeli victory became a watershed experience for Wiesel and the Jewish people.[27]

For Wiesel, Israel represents a moral victory as illustrated by the fact that during the war Israeli soldiers, rather than becoming cruel, became "sad." In his view they fought without hate and, instead of becoming proud, were humble and humane in their victories. Clearly, though Buber thought Jews superior to Arabs, he did not accord his own people this posture of innocence and, as with Deir Yassin, was direct and uncompromising concerning Jewish transgressions.

Buber saw Jewish ethics sorely tried in Palestine, then Israel, and the justification for Jewish renewal in the land was not innocence but a responsibility to a future for both Jews and Arabs. Both Buber and Wiesel correctly believed in Jewish innocence regarding the Holocaust. But Buber understood that the creation of a Jewish home, though absolutely essential, was not innocent in its reality, while Wiesel projects into the messy business of state-building the innocence of the suffering.

This sense of Jewish innocence allows Wiesel to project a culpability on Palestinians that, from the Palestinian perspective, especially in light of Deir Yassin, should rightfully be applied to Jews. In a letter "To a Young Palestinian Arab," published in 1975, Wiesel relates how Jews after the Holocaust "opted for Man" instead of vengeance. The pursuit of Nazi war criminals, for example, was to "remind man of his need to be human—not of his right to punish. On behalf of the dead we sought consolation not retribution."

In terms of Palestinians, Wiesel affirms in a general way responsibility for what happened to them. Still he cannot abide by what Palestinians have done with their anger: "From Munich to Maalot, from Lod to

Entebbe, from hijacking to hijacking, from ambush to ambush, you have spread terror among unarmed civilians and thrown into mourning families already too often visited by death. You will tell me that all these acts have been the work of your extremist comrades, not yours; but they acted on your behalf, with your approval, since you did not raise your voice to reason with them. You will tell me that it is your tragedy which incited them to murder. By murdering, they debased that tragedy, they betrayed it. Suffering is often unjust, but it never justifies murder."[28]

It is this sense of innocence, rather than a commitment to Israel, which allows Wiesel to write these words without understanding that, to an outside observer, they are immediately relevant to contemporary Jewish history. For, in light of Deir Yassin and the Palestinian catastrophe, it is untrue to say that Jews opted only for humankind or that Jews did not seek vengeance.

Can we see in this massacre that the Jews who maimed and killed—remembering that the leader of the Irgun, Menachem Begin, later became prime minister—in Wiesel's words, "debased that tragedy, they betrayed it?" As Wiesel writes, "Suffering is often unjust, but it never justifies murder." Perhaps this is the subtext of Arthur Hertzberg's open letter to Elie Wiesel in August 1988, at the height of the Palestinian uprising, criticizing Wiesel's virtual silence on the Israeli occupation and his refusal to criticize Israeli policies publicly. Hertzberg ends his letter with words reminiscent of Martin Buber: "We show the truest love of Israel and the Jewish people when we remind ourselves that, in strength or in weakness, we survive not by prudence and not by power, but through justice."[29]

Perhaps it is more accurate to say that peoples survive through prudence, power, and justice and that, in order to achieve these goals, critical analysis of the history of one's own people is as important as analysis of other peoples' history. In a history of any duration, this examination will at times be weak or nonexistent, for aspects of prudence, power, and justice vary in intensity of themselves and in relation to one another. A balancing of these elements and a reassertion of critical analysis will periodically come into view, only to be diminished and resurface still later. One can see this dynamic in relation to Deir Yassin: a suffering people committing atrocity; a suffering people trying to end atrocity; those who speak forcefully and those who are silent; one who sees commemoration as movement toward a future of reconciliation and cooperation; another whose immense suffering raises questions to the oppressor that also, though not consciously recognized, raises questions to one's own people.

Surely we can say that after the Holocaust and the birth of Israel the liturgy of destruction so hauntingly rendered by Elie Wiesel now includes the suffering of the Palestinian people. To be silent, deflect, or minimize Jewish responsibility for that suffering is no longer possible. Nor can the consequences of such suffering be buried in peace agreements, troop withdrawals, or gala affairs. In the arena of history, one can speculate whether Buber's plea to take Deir Yassin seriously would have chastened a newborn state, so that Wiesel's celebrated Israeli victory in 1967 would not have given birth to decades of military occupation that included violations of human and national rights, massacres, and deportations. Could the memory of Deir Yassin, attended to forthrightly, have significantly altered a future of victory and blood?

Today that memory of atrocity includes a deep rendering of Jewish history as a path already taken rather than a hypothetical future. In the past Deir Yassin, at least in Buber's understanding, could act as a moment of choice in the direction of the state. Over time it is clear that Begin's, rather than Buber's, sensibility carried the day.

In contemporary Jewish life, the memory of Deir Yassin is distant and foreclosed, almost buried under Wiesel's articulation of Jewish innocence. Yet it remains a subversive memory waiting to explode in Jewish consciousness, a permanent reminder that in the Jewish assumption of power another people has suffered. Jews have committed and therefore are always capable of committing acts that we lament and rage against when directed against us.

At the same time, Jews are reminded that more than the peace of the powerful and surrender of the vanquished is necessary to come to grips with this history. Acts of reconciliation and justice are possible and necessary at this late moment. Decades after the liberation of the death camps, memorials, museums, restitution, apologies, and confessions are still being made for and to the Jewish people. Could it be that on the fiftieth anniversary of Deir Yassin and the Palestinian catastrophe, similar memorials, museums, restitution, apologies, and confessions should have been made at Deir Yassin and in Jerusalem by Jews, including leaders of Israel, to a Palestinian people *en route* to their belated and necessary empowerment?

Memorialization without justice is an empty symbol that may compound the injury. Justice gives a hearing and meaning to the victims and the possibility of a future that remembers the pain of the past as a difficult road to a place from which a shared life may emerge out of a shared tragedy.

CHAPTER THREE

Jerusalem and the Broken Middle

Unearthing the atrocity at Deir Yassin resurrects deep ambivalences of Jewish historical memory. Does emphasizing atrocity necessitate recitation of other atrocities, including those committed by Palestinian Arabs in their fight against the Jewish state and later within the context of their forced exile from the land? Can the emergency years of the Holocaust override consideration of morality and ethics?

Establishment of the Jewish state, made possible in part by Deir Yassin, could only be accepted and celebrated with the silence of David Ben-Gurion and the later narration of Elie Wiesel, a symbiosis that finds Jewish history to be of primary importance and Palestinian history to be peripheral and secondary. Surely I, as an empowered Jew in America, benefit from Menachem Begin's audacity and terror—indeed benefit from the existence and power of the state of Israel.

Do I refuse to bloody my own hands, and therefore accede to that extreme violation of human and national rights, while maintaining my sense of innocence? Perhaps I am a weak diaspora Jew who lacks the will to fight physically and intellectually for my own people. Does remembering Deir Yassin consign all of Israeli history to error and atrocity? This could lead to the condemnation of the history of all peoples, for the price of all empowerment at some stage includes subjugation and atrocity.

In the end, a memorial at Deir Yassin is important less as a resolution of all questions or even to minimize ambivalence. Rather, the voices of the dead, forgotten by Jews and now heard again, remind us of the cost of Jewish empowerment and compel us toward a confession and justice. And, as importantly, they serve to rescue the voices of the defeated from history, at least to record their testimony for the future.

In Martin Buber's letter to Mohandas Gandhi, he wrote: "Testimony without acknowledgment ineffective, unobserved martyrdom, a martyrdom cast to the winds—that is the fate of innumerable Jews in Germany. God alone accepts their testimony. God 'seals' it, as is said in our prayers. Such martyrdom is a deed, but who would venture to demand it?" By remembering Deir Yassin, do we as Jews finally acknowledge, make more effective, and observe a martyrdom now no longer cast to the wind? Buber continues: "Dispersion is bearable; it can even be purposeful if somewhere there is ingathering, a growing home center, a piece of earth wherein one is in the midst of an ingathering and not in dispersion and from whence the spirit of ingathering may work its way out to all the places of the dispersion. When there is this life, there is also a striving, common life, the life of a community which dares to live today, because it hopes to live tomorrow. But when this growing center, this increasing process of ingathering is lacking, dispersion becomes dismemberment." Perhaps it is now incumbent on Jews to apply these words to an ingathering of Palestinians, in terms of refugees, political empowerment, and the sharing of Jerusalem.[1]

Paths of Resistance and Affirmation

The distance traveled between Buber and Elie Wiesel is vast, the language and conceptual framework that Buber inherited and was innovative within has virtually disappeared. It returns as a haunting memory, one spoken into a void to a vanishing audience. The lesson of powerlessness has been taken to heart.

Yet it remains the case that when Jewish intellectuals and theologians celebrate the empowerment of the Jewish people, they rarely speak of power. Instead they speak of destiny, return, purity, and innocence. This linguistic cover confuses those who support the creation and expansion of the state at any cost and those who resist the state or aspects of its policies. For if Israel is built on destiny and innocence, the very discussion of power is suspect.

If the conceptual framework of Buber is lost to contemporary Jews, so, too, is the language of politics. In the theological realm, the discussion of Israel is depoliticized to the extent that criticism is often seen as a sin, one for which "excommunication" from Jewish discourse is the preferred remedy. After all, how can one resist innocence without having a sinister motive? Such a resistance could only come from an internal self-hatred or even a desire to create the context for another holocaust.

The hidden quality of Jewish dissent in relation to Israel is a secret waiting to explode. For many within Jewish leadership positions, this is part of the paradoxical quality of the various peace processes and anniversaries. On the one hand, they threaten to destabilize the institutional and identity structure of the Jewish community built up over the years; on the other hand, they might bury forever this undercurrent of dissent so the community could proceed as if nothing of significance had occurred in building the state. Jews are empowered and innocent, and the questions of displacement and murder that Deir Yassin raises remain buried. Israel, as a response to the Holocaust, is the watchword while Deir Yassin and the Palestinian catastrophe fade into oblivion.

Yet the massacre of Palestinian worshipers in Hebron by Baruch Goldstein in 1994 and the assassination of Yitzhak Rabin in 1995, *after the Oslo agreements,* by a devotee of Goldstein, Yigal Amir, as well as the continuing expropriation of Palestinian property and the de-Palestinization of Jerusalem, *during and after the celebration of the fiftieth anniversary of the state of Israel,* raise the stakes of internal Jewish dissent and what, indeed, has happened to us as a people since the Holocaust. For if Deir Yassin can be dismissed as a regrettable incident in a war for survival, how can the Hebron massacre and Rabin's assassination be explained?

The typical response of those with liberal leanings is to disown the perpetrators as Rabin, in a Knesset address, did so forcefully of Goldstein. Those with conservative leanings also disown the perpetrators, as many Orthodox rabbis did with regard to Amir's use of *halacha* to justify the murder of the "traitorous" Rabin. It is as if Goldstein and Amir were formed within another people. But then, who are the thousands of Jews who come to pay homage to a memorial to Baruch Goldstein and who, after Rabin's assassination, placed the banner at the West Bank settlement Maale Amos—a settlement named for the prophet Amos—which read, "We are all Yigal Amir"?[2]

The tendency toward a militarism disguised in the rhetoric of innocence is the legacy of a community that refuses to acknowledge the complex journey from suffering to empowerment. One thinks of the warning signs along the way: the Jewish villagers neighboring Deir Yassin who hear the cries of the wounded and run to the beleaguered village to stop the killing; Meir Pa'il, who witnesses this action and reports "they were just Jews, citizens who were ashamed. They began to shout and cry and the massacre was stopped"; or the young Rabin, who, during the 1948 war, orders his men to empty Lod and Ramle of Palestinian Arabs and encounters resistance among some of his men.

Rabin's autobiography relates the problems he had quite directly: "Great suffering was inflicted upon the men taking part in the eviction action. Soldiers of the Yiftach Brigade included youth movement graduates, who had been inculcated with values such as international fraternity and humaneness. The eviction went beyond the concepts they were used to. There were some fellows who refused to take part in the expulsion action. Prolonged propaganda activities were required after the action to remove the bitterness of those youth groups and explain why we were obliged to undertake such a harsh and cruel action." The villagers who pleaded for the massacre to end and the soldiers who refused to participate in the expulsion were warning signs that those who have suffered were now causing others to suffer and that the humanity forged in that suffering was being violated in the violation of others. Some Jews intuitively saw in these "harsh and cruel" actions the beginning of the end of the Jewish ethical tradition and, therefore, at great risk to themselves, refused that end.[3]

The dissent continues through the years. Israel's initial incursions into Lebanon in the late 1970s and early 1980s, for example, occasioned an outburst in the Jewish community that was heard around the world. For the first time, some Israeli soldiers refused to serve when called up for duty or, once in Lebanon, left to return to Israel. Those who refused called themselves *Yesh Gvul* (There is a Limit) and wrote to the prime minister of their stand. In response to the massacre at Sabra and Shatilla in 1982, hundreds of thousands of Jews marched in Tel Aviv and Jerusalem.

Henry Schwarzschild, who fled Berlin with his family in 1939, went even further as he wrote a letter of resignation from the editorial advisory board of *Sh'ma,* citing his inability to support a Jewish state any longer. Having been troubled for a decade by the "chauvinistic and repressive effects" of Israeli nationalism, Schwarzschild experienced the war in Lebanon as a "turning point in Jewish history and consciousness" similar to the end of the Second Commonwealth and the Holocaust. For Schwarzschild, the resumption of political power after 2,000 years of diaspora is a "tragedy of historical dimensions." To allow the state of Israel to lay claim to be the modern incarnation of the Jewish people is to "betray the Jewish tradition." Because of this, Schwarzschild renounces the state of Israel, disavows any political or emotional connection to it, and declares himself its enemy.[4]

Schwarzschild's opposition to Israel raises the question of the homeland option, though with a new problematic. By the 1980s the path had already been chosen, and the prime minister who orders the invasion of Lebanon and the bombing of Beirut is Menachem Begin, the same man who congratulated his forces on their victory at Deir Yassin. Israel is not only independent, it possesses one of the most sophisticated military forces in the world. The state as warrior is accepted without being named as such, and the military people who refuse to serve are remnants of a consciousness that is narrowing and almost inaccessible to most Jews.

Palestinian Arabs, who were in the forefront of homeland consciousness as partners in Palestine, are maligned or dismissed even by some of those who refuse service in Lebanon. Progressive intellectuals who oppose the war in Lebanon, like Amos Oz, argue that Jews should maintain a dignity higher than the neighboring peoples, and the issue is one of self-defense and divorce, that is, Jews and Arabs come from different cultures and should be permanently separated.

The partition which the homeland Zionists fought is now accepted and argued for by the dissenters themselves. In a strange coincidence, as Schwarzschild lay dying of cancer in April 1996, the Israeli bombing of Lebanon began again, this time under the leadership of Shimon Peres. In this much smaller operation, 170 Lebanese were killed and thousands of refugees were created. The code name changed as well: in the 1980s Israel's war in Lebanon was called *Peace for Galilee,* in the 1990s *The Grapes of Wrath.*[5]

Between the wars in Lebanon is the dissent surrounding attempts by Israel to crush the Palestinian uprising. This dissent featured a desire to retain a morality that many Jews felt was slipping away. A major fear expressed was that the violence against Palestinians was coming home and that the occupation of another people could lead to a brutalization of Jewish consciousness and life. For these dissenters, Palestinians deserve a state, though often unmentioned is the fact that the state proposed is so small, divided by Jewish settlements, and without Jerusalem, that its ability to support or even govern itself cannot be assured. The state is also to be demilitarized and the Israeli military will have outposts in Palestine. In a strange twist of fate, Israel will even be responsible for the military security of Palestine.

Yet beneath the strategies of the commentators who assume Israeli dominance and Palestinian subservience is a horror similar to the one Schwarzschild expressed over Lebanon. The stories of Israeli brutality reported in the Israeli and Western press shocked many Jews who remain within the Holocaust narrative of suffering and innocence. The beating of Palestinian youth to teach them the lesson of Israeli superiority, the mass imprisonment of Palestinian resistors in sprawling concentration camp-like prisons, and the policy of deliberately humiliating mothers and fathers in front of their children, brought back memories of Jewish suffering.

Had the experience of the Holocaust brought Jews to this kind of behavior? Are Jews really capable of doing to others what had been done to us?

Clearly for most Jews the lessons of Deir Yassin had already been lost; even the war in Lebanon and the continuing Israeli occupation of parts of Lebanon had become commonplace. And Rabin, who as Minister of Defense ordered the beatings, is the same man who ordered the expulsion of thousands of Palestinian Arabs from Lod and Ramle.

The difficulty Rabin's men had expelling villagers in 1948 is the same difficulty he had with his forces in 1988. Some Israeli soldiers refused to participate in the beatings; others publicly protested the occupation policies. A similar reeducation policy was implemented for those who refused, but, again, the distance between 1948 and 1988 is significant. For those who protested during the Palestinian uprising, the Palestinian Arabs have a diminished place in Palestine that ought to be respected; the Israeli soldiers see themselves as occupiers in a strange and dangerous country. That many of these Palestinians arrived in the West Bank and Gaza as refugees from the Israel these soldiers call home is rarely mentioned.

It is as if the dissenters are trying to stop Jews from creating a new history of conflict rather than seeing themselves as the logical extension of the formation of the state, that is, in continuity with a history within which these soldiers were born and which they are now extending. That is why progressive Jews in Israel see no contradiction in organizing peace marches that originate from Rabin's tomb, as if this is a sign to Palestinians of their good intentions. For Palestinians, of course, Rabin's life and death carry a profound ambivalence that Jewish progressives seem unable to understand.[6]

A Covenant in Exile

The question of resistance to injustice perpetrated by Jews is raised within the evolving tradition of Jewish dissent. This tradition is long and, as with remembrance and the liturgy of destruction, is found in the origins of the Jewish people.

The command to remember is located in the covenant between God and Israel. Dissent is found within this covenant as well, as Moses and Aaron struggle with the people and sometimes with God. The early narratives of the experiences of the wandering tribes are filled with affirmation, questions, *and* dissent. Job is one who struggles with suffering; Abraham, Isaac, and Jacob are hardly docile followers of God or are even content with their calling. Later, the prophets are critical of the behavior of Israel, at times foreseeing its destruction. This history of dissent continues through the destruction of the temples, the wanderings through Europe, and even within the Holocaust.

The birth of Israel was also a dissent from the traditional diaspora position and from the homeland visionaries. With the establishment of the state, dissent increases, even as it loses a language and matrix from which to argue effectively. For who could argue that the tradition of dissent as it manifests itself today has achieved its goals?

Does it matter to the Lebanese civilians that Schwarzschild declared himself the enemy of Israel? Did *Yesh Gvul*, in announcing its limits, actually forestall the destruction of Lebanon? As important, it is difficult to argue that the cumulative effect of this tradition—for example, Buber's voice, unheeded in the 1940s, when added to the voices of Schwarzschild and *Yesh Gvul* in the 1980s and the protesters against the brutal crushing of the Palestinian *intifada* in the 1980s and 1990s—will one day end or significantly reverse the Palestinian catastrophe.

It is a forbidding prospect that the tradition of dissent has failed and may, because of its attempt to announce and reclaim the innocence of the Jewish people, actually be complicit in the displacement of the Palestinian people. Tracing this dissent within the context of Israel is possible only within the parameters of the state's expansion; it is like a holding action that fails to hold, as if the victory of power is inevitable and the protest a fulfillment of the need to articulate opposition. The protest is full of emotion, and rightfully so. It is a desperate attempt to lay claim to the part of Jewish identity that remembers the wandering and suffering of exile, that makes the equally desperate attempt to believe that somehow the Jewish people are different, that Jews will not oppress when given the chance, and that the tradition of dissent against unjust power is not simply self-serving.

Though most contemporary dissent is couched in secular language, it is, like the vision of Rabin and Peres, religious in its own way. One wonders if this dissent is an attempt to hold onto the covenant even as the language that surrounds it becomes unfamiliar. A significant reason for this unavailability of religious language is the use of covenantal language to project or protect the very power the dissenters oppose. Religious language has become so debased over the years that there seems no way back, and for many a complicity appears in the language itself.

For is the covenant present when a Palestinian is displaced or humiliated at Deir Yassin, in Lebanon, during the *intifada*, or with the Israeli death squads that have operated in parts of the West Bank and Gaza over the decades? Is the covenant present when rabbis in Israel justify these actions as ways of furthering the destiny of the Jewish people? Or when, through the language of suffering and innocence, rabbis in the United States and Europe refuse to acknowledge that these actions are taking place? Has the covenant been so abused that it is no longer possible to speak its language, to rest secure within it, or to find one's destiny within its commandments?[7]

Surely the religious allusions of Judah Magnes's challenge to the development of Jewish nationalism are distant today, yet the force of his challenge may be even more relevant. In a journal entry in May 1923, Magnes wrote: "Will the Jews here in their efforts to create a political organism become devotees of brute force and militarism as were some of the later Hasmoneans, and will they, like the Edomite Herod, become the

obedient servants of economic and militaristic imperialism? Is it among
the possibilities that some day it may become political treason for someone sincerely to repeat in the streets of Jerusalem Isaiah's teaching that
swords are to beaten into plowshares and men are to learn war no more?
Or will the Jews of Eretz Israel be true to the teaching of the Prophets of
Israel and attempt to work out their ideal society so that Jerusalem may
be restored and Zion redeemed through righteousness and peace?" Contrast this with the writing of Ari Shavit, the Jewish Israeli essayist, and his
comments on the Israeli bombing of Qana, Lebanon, in April 1996—a
disputed military target where hundreds of Lebanese civilians took
refuge: "So now Qana is part of our biography. Precisely because we have
tried to deny and ignore this outrage, it remains affixed to us. And just as
the Baruch Goldstein massacre of praying Muslims in Hebron and the
murder of Yitzhak Rabin were extreme manifestations of some rotten
seed planted in the religious-nationalist culture, it now seems that the
massacre at Qana was an extreme manifestation of seeds dormant in our
secular Israeli culture: Cynicism. Arrogance. Egocentrism of the strong.
A penchant to blur the distinction between good and bad, the allowed
and the forbidden. A tendency not to demand justice, not to be adamant
about the truth."[8]

Though the language of Magnes and Shavit is distinctly different,
with biblical allusions replaced by historical detail, the appeal to remembrance and the testing of history is similar. For Magnes, the prophets of
Israel are part of the biography that calls Jews away from militarism and
empire. For Shavit, the contemporary memory of atrocity and assassination functions as a critique of domination and arrogance. Where Magnes
cites ancient Scripture as a reference for the conduct of Jews, Shavit uses
events in the life of contemporary Israel as a form of judgment.

A new Scripture is being forged in the creation of Israel, as Scripture
was originally forged in the creation of the Jewish people. Whereas for
Magnes the venture of Zionism is dependent on the fulfillment of the
covenant, a covenant already formed and laid out, for Shavit the experience of Israel is in process. The prophetic voice is in the historical event
that is still unfolding. The path is being chosen and the judgment on the
religious-nationalist and secular culture in Israel is found in the atrocities committed against the other.

In 1923, Magnes wrote, at the beginning of the journey, with hope
and trepidation. Unlike today, there was little concrete biography to the
Zionist movement. At the turn of the century, the biography itself is the
source for reflection, and the history is more complex. In 1923, the question was what relation the diaspora had to Zionism and what goals the
movement should have in relation to European Jewish history. At the
turn of the century, cries of the defeated are the center, and the Jewish

narrative focuses on a covenant unraveling within the context of Jewish power.

In Shavit's view, the Jews of Israel are failing to create a culture and society that respects others and therefore itself. From a different vantage point and in different language he seems to be reaching the same conclusion that Magnes held at the very creation of the state in 1948: the biography of Jews in Palestine and Israel is so stark as to raise the question of whether an error of immense magnitude has been made in the creation of the state.

As both Magnes and Shavit witness and participate in this unfolding enterprise, neither asserts innocence. They have seen too much. Shavit ends his essay with his own experience in Qana in 1978: "It was no big deal—only a limited military action. First we shot at the village with machine guns, then we entered in one column of armored vehicles and two columns of infantry. Finally, we found three terrorist youth and stormed them in the most idiotic way possible, losing two of our own. I have not stopped thinking about Qana. Its place in our lives. Our lives are in it. I recall how we appeared on its horizon in 1978, leaving some casualties behind and vanishing. And then we came back."[9]

Shavit's words are haunting, almost liturgical in their cadence. They are like the words of Elie Wiesel, though the destruction is now carried out against another people. A new midrash is forming, harkening back to Samuel Bak's "City of the Jews," again with a transformation difficult to imagine for those who survived the Holocaust. An artist who survived Qana might title her drawing "Power of the Jews" and use the symbolic imagery of the star of David or even the tablets as crushing the people of Qana. Perhaps Shavit, looking at Bak's drawing today, would see his own image transfigured because of what he and his people have done.

Shavit's words—"and then we came back"—provide an image of destruction like a fate visited upon a defenseless people. But whose fate is on the line here? The dead, to be sure, but also the living, the soldiers, including Shavit himself, who are suffering from a loss of direction and an inability to distinguish right from wrong.

One feels that Shavit's fate and the fate of Israel are being decided in Qana. The accusation that Shavit levels on behalf of the dead of Qana is clear; like Uri Zvi Greenberg's statement against Jesus and the Christians who claim him, graphically laid out in the form of a cross, the complaint of the people of Qana might be similarly laid out in the form of the star of David. And among the signatures is Shavit's.

Such an internal indictment places Magnes's warning in perspective. To the question of whether it is possible that one day the repetition of Isaiah's teaching of peace in Jerusalem might be considered political treason, the answer is yes. As important, however, is the response that

Magnes could not foresee: that some involved in the violation of Isaiah's teaching would question themselves and the state that sponsors that violation without reference to the prophet.

The call for critique comes less from God or the mission of Israel than it does from the experience of militarism and empire. This involves a further transformation from the biblical call to remember those who caused suffering to the people Israel and adds a third element of Jews causing suffering to others. Without God and Bible, Shavit takes on the responsibility of causing others to suffer as intimate to the Jewish experience. "So now Qana is part of our biography," Shavit reports in a tone as intimate as Magnes assumed Isaiah to be.

Perhaps it can be said that both Isaiah and Qana are now part of the Jewish biography, along with Sinai, the Second Commonwealth, the Holocaust, the birth of Israel, Deir Yassin, the massacre in Hebron, and many other events in Jewish history. Some of these events are spoken of in overtly religious terms, others in decidedly secular, even antireligious terminology. Despite the differences in time and geography, a commonality emerges in the sense of peoplehood and the structure of the narrative.

Herein lies remembrance, ritual, and recital, the mixing of myth and history, and, as David Roskies writes, the transformation of "collective disasters into individual rites and of individual deeds into a model of collective sacrifice." This then is joined by speech, about the sacrifice of others for reasons of the state of Israel, spoken by individuals on behalf of the Jewish people and Jewish history: individual speech portrays a collective culpability.[10]

Isaiah's calling, though specific to his time, is seen by Magnes as reverberating through Jewish history. No matter how the community responds to this challenge, it is accepted as part of the canon. Paradoxically, to betray Isaiah's call is to affirm its challenge. Magnes wonders whether Jews in this phase of history will respond in the affirmative or betray this vision that nonetheless lies at the heart of Jewish life. As part of the canon, Isaiah remains and becomes even more insistent if the community opts for power rather than justice.

Shavit's challenge can be seen in light of Isaiah. Can his own experience of pursuing war instead of peace, with the culpability that this entails for the Jewish people and state, be judged by Isaiah's vision? Or can it stand alone, these actions judging themselves? Can the prophetic challenge come from injustice toward a Palestinian Arab or a Lebanese national as it once came from a Jew? Can the other become the center of Jewish history as Isaiah once was? Or does the other become central because Isaiah remains central, even if his words are not quoted, or, when quoted, his vision is ridiculed? Is Shavit's inclusion of Qana a log-ical extension of Isaiah's vision?

For Shavit there seems to be little choice. The violence done in Lebanon and the violence done in Palestine are part of the history that challenges the religious and secular communities to think again about the path they have chosen. The people Israel have reached a dead end with the state of Israel. Neither the religious nor secular foundations of contemporary Jewry provide the ability to judge critically the history being created and stop it before the "biography" includes so many vic-tims as to overwhelm any possibility of dignity and peace for the Jewish people.

In an earlier essay written during the Palestinian uprising, Shavit explores a still more devastating arena. His actions as a guard in an Israeli prison camp filled with Palestinian resisters reminds him of the Nazi camps that held so many Jewish prisoners. Shavit is reluctant to acknowledge this parallel. Still the reminders are there: "Like a believer whose faith is cracking, I go over and over again in my heart the long list of arguments, the list of the differences. There are no crematoria here, I remind myself, and there was no conflict between people there. . . . But then I realized that the problem is not in the similarity—for no one can seriously think that there is a real similarity—but that there isn't enough lack of similarity. The problem is that the lack of similarity isn't strong enough to silence once and for all the evil echoes, the accusing images." Having heard the cries of Palestinians being tortured in the camp, Shavit concludes: "And now, as the screams grow weaker, as they change to a kind of sobbing, wailing, you know that from that moment on nothing will ever again be as it was. Because a person who has heard the screams of another person being tortured is already a different per-son. . . . A person who has heard the screams of another person being tortured incurs an obligation."[11]

What is this obligation? Is it to fulfill the covenant through remem-brance of this suffering Shavit has witnessed? He is calling the attention of the community to the dwindling difference between what has been done to it and what it is now doing to others. Perhaps the obligation is to lament a journey that has taken the community from victim to oppressor.

Shavit is acting in a contemporary way, as Hillel Zeitlin acted in the Warsaw ghetto, facing history in the depths and publicly affirming his Jewishness regardless of the cost. Zeitlin arrived at deportation in prayer shawl and tefillin, affirming the dignity of the Jewish people; Shavit, as a soldier in a Jewish state, writes of the martyrdom of others and, in this, affirms the dignity of those who Jews have been taught to despise.

The blurring of the difference between the Nazis and the Jews, which Shavit hesitates to and yet is forced to affirm, confers the obligation of

Shavit's dissent even as it highlights Zeitlin's symbolic protest. Shavit attempts to rescue Zeitlin's haunting act before it, like the vision of Isaiah, can no longer be understood.

For in the destruction of others, Jewish archetypes of the prophetic and suffering are rendered ineffectual, receding from memory and vocabulary, just as the diaspora and homeland vision disappear. The systematic denigration of a people renders the entire history of the Jews problematic, threatening to silence the articulation of myth and history so foundational to the Jewish enterprise. Shavit is cautioning Jews that the ultimate triumph of the Jewish spirit, represented by Zeitlin, is threatened with extinction.

With Deir Yassin and Qana as part of the biography of the Jewish people, Jewish history carries within it a new and disturbing archetype, one of destruction unleashed against others, which, itself, has a history and a danger of repetition. Shavit is in Lebanon in 1978, at the Gaza Beach Detention Camp in 1991, and writes about Qana in 1996. He recalls the massacre at Hebron in 1993 and the assassination of Rabin in 1995. The war in Lebanon is the work of Menachem Begin, who is also the commander of the Irgun who carried out the massacres in Deir Yassin in 1948. The assassination of Rabin recalls his own role in the attempt to end the Palestinian uprising, as it brings to mind his orders to expel Palestinians for Lod and Ramle in 1948. "And then we came back" is a cycle Shavit surfaces in relation to Lebanon, but it is actually a metaphor for Jewish empowerment in Israel.

The relative youth of Israel allows us to see this cycle in specific individuals and events, for example, in the lives of Begin, Rabin, and Shavit. The broader issue, however, is that many Jews have been part of this history in an intimate way, as soldiers, politicians, bureaucrats, businessmen, intellectuals, rabbis, and theologians. Israel, like any state, has its own imperatives and its own momentum, so to lay the blame solely on the state is to evade responsibility. The founding, building, defending, and expanding of Israel have been a collective effort of the Jewish people. Most Jews take a collective pride in Israel; there is also a collective culpability. The return of Jews to power has mostly been seen as a miracle in light of the Holocaust. Today it may also be recognized as a disaster.

What do Jews do when they recognize that a project of ultimate importance, one widely supported and celebrated among Jews and non-Jews in the West, is at the same time a disaster for Palestinians and for Jews as well? What happens to the unity of a people when more and more Jews see the displacement of the Palestinians as a stain on Jewish history?

Henry Schwarzschild resigned from the enterprise of state-building in a public letter, and many Jews simply leave Jewish life because of an inability to be heard on this issue. Schwarzschild's resignation is, in one respect, a strong commitment to the dialogue on the future of the Jewish people, for he takes his Jewishness so seriously as to risk public scandal. In his anger, we hear the testimony of the Jewish prophets and the vision of Isaiah. Wrestling with the covenant is the framework within which Schwarzschild's opposition to the state makes sense. Schwarzschild speaks for those Jews who "resign" from their Jewishness without public notice or who, while remaining within the Jewish community, become silent.

Part of the "disaster" of Israel, then, is an increasing number of Jews who are in exile within the framework of Jewish empowerment, an unexpected internal exile within a time period and a collective effort that promised the end of exile. Shavit should be seen in this context as well: as a committed participant in the Jewish return whose faith is "cracking." Where once Jews were forced into exile by the powers of the world, Jews, by creating an exile for another people, have created one for themselves.

Jews have carried the covenant with them in exile for thousands of years. Today the question has shifted: *How do Jews carry the exile within the promised land, and what is the covenantal obligation in this new wandering?* This exile, so often thought of in negative terms of assimilation, abandonment, and aid to the enemy, may be a last desperate attempt to refuse assimilation to power and to rescue the community abandoning its central values. In this light the "enemy" is seen as a bridge to a recovery of the covenant and the direction of Jewish history.

To the criticism of leaving Jewish life, those in exile may see no other alternative if that life is to be preserved. The question of assimilation, of the superficiality and vulgarity of contemporary Jewish life—usually thought of in terms of Jewish knowledge, observance, and Hebrew language skills—are exactly those elements of Jewish life seen as complicit in injustice by those in exile. Those in exile are arguing for a reckoning with the covenant that participation in the community helps to obscure.

What Schwarzschild and Shavit point to is a solidarity with the victims of Jewish power as a way of confronting a community that is complicit. In the Jewish world, solidarity on the question of Israel is maintained within the framework of innocence and redemption. By breaking with this framework, the presumption is that one is breaking with Israel. Still, the community accepts a silence on Israel as a way of maintaining solidarity.

Jews like Schwarzschild and Shavit confront silence as a force in the continuation of injustice, so that the ordinary functioning of the community is seen as allowing Israel to continue on its path. The exceptional acts in military force in Lebanon, for example, which sometime cause an outcry, are made possible within the ordinary functioning of the state and the community that sanctions the state. The exception, then, is part of the ordinary, and thus the ordinary is called into question. That is the conclusion reached by Schwarzschild and Shavit in the 1980s and 1990s and, earlier, by Magnes in the 1940s.

Their conclusion suggests a series of difficult questions: How do Jews with these understandings fulfill their sense of the covenant, especially as these "normal" workings of the community continue to add to the biography of the Jewish people? *Could it be that in this era of empowerment, the only way to fulfill the covenant is to remember the victims of Jewish power, that is, to include the Palestinian people as part of Jewish history and destiny? Since they are already part of our biography, is it incumbent on Jews to embrace the Palestinian people as intimate to the covenant itself?* Perhaps it is time to expand the covenant to include the Palestinian people, or perhaps it has already been expanded without Jewish acknowledgment. One wonders if this expansion is the missing connection that Jewish scholars discuss but cannot find.

It is a complicated picture, to be sure, and the midrash found in Bak and Wiesel is now complemented by Magnes, Schwarzschild, and Shavit. Such are the complications of history and the evolution of the covenant. Those in exile may see this call to solidarity as the next step in the long unfolding of Jewish history. They acknowledge that the liturgy of destruction has now become inclusive and, therefore, that the covenant is found in that inclusivity.

If the Jewish covenant now includes the Palestinian people as an obligation born of injustice and suffering, then separation of the two peoples is impossible. A strict separation of Jews and Palestinians formalizes an injustice done to Palestinians, as they are relegated to a tiny percentage of what was once their home.

In formalizing this injustice, a strict separation also formalizes the victory of Israel, thus placing at the heart of the covenant, in a permanent way, a structure of injustice from which Jews benefit. *The covenant becomes the guardian of oppression rather than its questioner; either overtly or covertly, and the commandments become the fence around relations of oppression.* Of course, those relations will remain unspoken even as they solidify as a way of life. Remembrance embraces myth without history, as the ancient archetypes recall an innocence betrayed in the life of the community.

Over time, the archetypes lose their force because it is precisely when myth is divorced from history, or in this case contradicted by it, that the transcendent is seen as a farce. The exilic community of Jews will continue to grow until later generations forget those myths that were once found wanting. The assimilation that occurs at that time will be bereft even of rebellion, and a silent, almost pathetic, end of Jewish history will be at hand.

The other side of this silent assimilation is an orthodoxy embraced as a form of militancy against history, whose *raison d'être* is an acceptance and promotion of power to shield against the subversive message of the covenant itself. This is a religious assimilation that claims to be the authentic inheritor of Jewish history. One pictures here the reversal of the image of Hillel Zeitlin arriving at the deportation site wearing prayer shawl and tefillin. Instead, we are left with the image of Orthodox Jews praying at the Western Wall in a Jerusalem cleared of Palestinian dwelling places and inhabitants. Jerusalem is reconstructed as a Jewish city without the haunting images of those dispossessed of their homes.

In the eyes of Palestinians, the Jewish shawls and tefillin worn in prayer become symbols of deportation and expulsion. The transformation of the archetype of suffering becomes complete and perhaps irretrievable in its original context. The archetype shifts away from the Jewish people who claim the covenant and resides in exile among the Palestinians, a people who have a claim on the Jewish community.

Jerusalem and the Broken Middle

The diaspora and homeland vision seek to fight assimilation to injustice, and the exilic community seeks a way to reclaim and express its sense of Jewishness. Both are engaged in a fight for justice for Palestinians that is also a fight for Jewish history. This fight is a public one within the context of a negotiated surrender of the Oslo years. The question remains: How do these visions and this community place before the Jewish world the obligation of the expanded covenant and the path to realize its demands?

On the one hand, the demands of the expanded covenant might be seen as extraordinary, calling Jews to a heroic level of vision and sacrifice. Looked at another way, this covenant might begin with seemingly the opposite, that is, a search for the ordinary within an extraordinary situation. Perhaps the expanded covenant is a call to redefine the heroic in terms of the ordinary, the search for a renewed life of routine and interconnectedness. In fact, the search is to recover the ordinary, a status taken from Jews in Europe and Palestinians in Palestine.

Within the cycle of dislocation, settlement, wars, uprisings, torture, and poisonous demonization of the adversary, it seems an impossible task to envision a return to the ordinary. For what can the ordinary mean in such a situation? A context that has not existed in decades, for example, the Palestinian Arab way of life in the 1930s, cannot be recovered. If there is an understandable longing for this return on the Palestinian side, one can likewise understand the fear of Jewish refugees from the Nazi state, for the ordinary life of German Jews was already unavailable to them and there is no dream of return to Hitler's Germany.

Clearly both the dream of the Palestinians and the nightmare of the Jews are unattainable. The actual reality has long since become incapable of return and such sensibility is a fantasy with dangerous implications for both peoples.

Restoring the ordinary in terms of the past is impossible when it invokes contexts that have long since disappeared. But the pursuit of the ordinary—the restoration of a normal way of life, the fight to reestablish the ordinary recognizable in the histories of both peoples, one that can continue to evolve in the future—is more than mere fantasy. This restoration is rooted in the complex reality of the past, is capable of understanding the possibilities and limitations of the present, and is committed to a future encompassing both past and present, even as it refuses to be bound to either. Restoring the ordinary establishes a connection among past, present, and future to root the ordinary in something other than domination or submission.

At one level, we desire to rid the discussion of myths, for example, the Jewish myth of innocence and redemption, so that we can proceed to the root of the problem. The hope is that once the root is exposed, a solution will become obvious. But myths are part of the discourse itself. Myths, repeated often enough, blur the distinction between truth and fiction. After so many years, myths themselves are part of the fabric of life, and the fear of these myths unraveling may encourage a rage more destructive than the myth itself.

The challenge seems to be somewhere else, to uncover the myth but in the broader pursuit of finding a middle ground between opposing sides. Over time the middle ground will take on a life of its own, thus establishing a basis from which the next steps can be taken. New questions arise from this middle that will ultimately displace aspects of the original myths or transform them into new configurations. The deliberate and unconscious myths are still in need of exposure, but when new ground is reached their importance and the need to defend them are diminished.

In this sense, Rabin's rhetoric, though contradicted by his actions, may be used as a bridge to that middle to which he pointed but did not himself reach. Though his intentions are important to investigate, they are less important than the hope he outlined. Hope can be seen as the next arena of the struggle to move beyond the present. The next arena will likely also hold its own myths and become a place from which further struggle is needed.

"The" solution in its finality always eludes us as we move toward an ever-evolving middle ground. As the late Jewish philosopher Gillian Rose remarked, the middle is always broken and with reason. Life itself is broken, and the images, philosophies, ideologies, and theologies we create are flawed. From Rose's perspective, the attempt at closure through the elimination or purification of the myths, half-truths, and lies, covers over what one sought to eliminate. Something less than the purification should be attempted, that is, the need to build upon a "broken middle" which recognizes myths *and* history, flaws *and* movement, injustice *and* the pursuit of justice, the fears within each community *and* the possibility that fears can be overcome in the process of forging a new relationship.[12]

To approach the broken middle in Israel/Palestine is to face the difficult subject of Jerusalem. Jerusalem stands for a diverse array of symbols and realities to Jews and Palestinians. For some Jews, Jerusalem represents the hope of return nurtured for almost 2,000 years of exile. In this sense, Jerusalem is a religious and national symbol whose power cannot be overestimated. Other Jews, while embracing both the religious and national symbolism, see Jerusalem as the geographic center of an empowered and expanding Israel. Jerusalem is to them as much present as future. With the prayers of return having been realized, the challenge now is to Judaize the city and expand its boundaries.

Though rarely spoken or written about, there are Jews in Israel and elsewhere who are wary of Jerusalem, with its history of religious fanaticism, its Middle Eastern flavor, and the present-day-religious and settler movements that have flourished since the Israeli annexation of Jerusalem following the 1967 war. The cities of Jerusalem and Tel Aviv still define a fundamental fracture in Israeli society. Jerusalem denotes a religious and continually expanding Israel; Tel Aviv denotes a more European, secular, and limited state.

Palestinians are also intimately involved in the question of Jerusalem. Jerusalem is central to their history as a religious site of prayer and pilgrimage for Muslims and Christians. It is also a sign of their defeat and displacement, as the annexation of Jerusalem has had the effect of denying Palestinian governance and, at the same time, through demolition of Palestinian housing and land confiscation, steadily decreasing the number of Palestinians living in Jerusalem.

Jerusalem has been, and remains today, the intellectual, cultural, and economic center of Palestinian life. The end of Jerusalem as a Palestinian place of prayer and activity divides the Palestinian population, north and south, east and west; hence the segmentation and ghettoization that have increased in the past decades. For Palestinians who look to Jerusalem as a religious symbol, as well as those who see the city in secular, economic, and cultural terms, the loss of Jerusalem is devastating.

Without seeking to universalize or romanticize the experience of Jews and Palestinians, it is important to realize the commonality of how Jerusalem functions in the imagination of both peoples. Both Jews and Palestinians see Jerusalem in symbolic and practical terms. Religious Jews and Palestinians are drawn to Jerusalem for religious reasons, while secular segments of both peoples have more mixed feelings about the city. Secular Jews and Palestinians may be drawn to Jerusalem for historic, economic, or political reasons; yet they tend to be ambivalent, sometimes stridently so, about the religious militancy that is part of Jerusalem's past and present.

For both peoples, Jerusalem represents destruction, exile, and hope for restoration. Though the messianic message continues to emanate from this ancient city, the cycle of domination and destruction is evident in the very architecture of the city. For can Jews and Palestinians be unaware that the one who controls Jerusalem today is the same one who is exiled tomorrow?

The broken middle is found here, in the myths, historical experiences, common aspirations, the attraction to and ambivalent feelings about the city which is called holy and eternal. The fact is that Jews and Palestinians are now living side by side in a proximity that has engendered suspicion and bloodshed, but one that could also provide a visible, bodily encounter with those who are primarily known as the other.

The broken middle recognizes the other as a challenge and possibility to fulfill aspects of the internal longing and needs of each people while respecting and seeking to understand and facilitate the longing and needs of the other. Both peoples have claims, have suffered, and seek dignity and justice. Both histories have been broken in the twentieth century, and both have struggled for a rebirth that is whole and complete.

Clearly the Palestinians have failed in this effort of rebirth, with loss of land, swelling refugee populations, and loss of a meaningful sovereignty. In a physical sense, the Jewish people has succeeded in reversing its loss, and some even hail the foundation of Israel, with its capital in Jerusalem, as the beginning of redemption. Yet it is difficult to accept the redemption of one people at the expense of another. It is difficult to celebrate the Jewish return to Jerusalem when Palestinians are relegated to segregated precincts, ghettos if you will, like those that too often have formed the landscape of Jewish history.

Perhaps, then, the broken middle begins with the hope of return, and the failure of both peoples to achieve the result they aspired to historically and in the present. It can encompass, as well, the terrible result of achieving an end that includes the conquest and displacement of the other. This furthers the cycle of displacement and death, calling into question the moral worth of victory.

It is difficult to envision how Jews and Palestinians can be healed of their trauma by inflicting wounds on each other. Rather, the opposite is the case: the wound inflicted on the other deepens the trauma of the initial injury. Thus, the broken middle includes hope, failure, a desire to end the cycle of destruction, and the realization that a true healing of a people can only come by including the other as significant in one's own hopes and aspirations.

It may be that opting for the broken middle begins the dissipation of the other as other and that the commonality initially recognized becomes the life of a community in the making. The other becomes the neighbor with whom one begins to share a common life. In so doing, both embark on a new history with its own symbols, aspirations, ambivalence, and failures.

To many Jews, the thought of a new community brings fear of a final assimilation, as if a life without barriers might make Jewish identity unattractive. The fear is that there is little compelling left to Jewish life and that another people might replace that attraction. In Israel/Palestine the fear is also cultural, as if a European Jew is somehow lost to the Jewish community because of involvement with Palestinian and Arab cultures. Since a majority of Jews in Israel are of Arab and North African descent, this possibility invokes fear only insofar as Jewish life is defined by European background and culture.

If Jewish and Palestinian cultures come into close contact and intermingle freely and on an equal basis, do European and American Jews fear that the Western orientation of Israel will disappear in favor of a new configuration of an Arab and North African Israel/Palestine? Since the Holocaust is so central to the European experience but peripheral to Jews of Arab and North African descent, this shift in consciousness might mean that the narrative of European Jewish suffering will be displaced as the guiding principle of Israel.

The broken middle, while attentive to history, does not freeze that history or seek to develop an orthodox theology beholden to it. Rather the broken middle seeks to recognize the openness of history by addressing the next questions that face a people; it refuses to allow past suffering to be used as a shield against accountability in the present. Though the broken middle refuses utopia, it also refuses paralysis and the pretense of innocence.

The broken and the middle become a path where history is worked out with reference to the past, present, and future. The connection among the three may be obvious, for it is difficult to see how a people can arrive at a destination, and how that arrival can be understood with any depth, unless the connection of past and present is understood.

Yet the connection is neither linear nor preordained. Rather, the future always involves new elements and configurations, and—though preservation and continuity may remain a goal of some, even to the point of inventing a mythic continuity where little or none exist—a new reality has already come into being.

It is important to note that when there is freedom to choose, Jews choose, even after the Holocaust, to live in a democratic and secular framework in contact with other cultures and religions. That is, Jews continue to hope for a society and a way of life beyond what they have known, and they continue to pioneer new realities in their own lives and in the cultures in which they live.

Holocaust survivors who remained in or returned to Europe after the war and American Jews who continue to live in America despite the availability of Israel attest to this determination to live in the broken middle. To live among Christians with their symbolism, theology, and culture after the Holocaust event, so intertwined with Christian complicity, is an example of the choice of the broken middle. It is difficult to propose honestly that a wager on the broken middle in the Middle East is higher than a wager on a civilization that burned Jewish bodies day and night for years.

The passions that have been raised in the more than fifty years of struggle between Jews and Palestinians are important to identify and affirm. Clearly both sides feel in need of protection, and this includes the need for physical safety. The particularity of each culture has been under assault in this century, and the necessity of ensuring a sense of cultural continuity is as important as the political structures that ensure the physical integrity of each community.

In the broken middle, healing and the future of the Jewish and Palestinian communities must have a structural base from which to evolve. With regard to Jerusalem, this might mean a dual governing entity that allows autonomy for each community, and a larger entity that provides joint governance of the city. Jerusalem becomes the capital of Israel and Palestine and, over time, the capital of Israel/Palestine. The city remains undivided, and the possibility of the resurgence of Palestinian life comes into being.

It is here where difficulty is found. Despite the ebb and flow of agreements and rhetoric, a structural division is in place that separates Jews and Palestinians. The broken middle cannot be one that accepts this division or the future that this structure envisions for both communities. With reference to Jerusalem, the present political, military, cultural, and population configurations must be equalized or at least allowed a process that will in a relatively short time provide a rough parity between the two communities. This means, among other measures, increasing the Palestinian population of Jerusalem, as well as housing main political institutions of the Palestinian government there.

From Jerusalem, further expansion of the agreement can occur that will include, in a structured and orderly way, Palestinians within Israel and Palestinian refugees around the world. For to achieve a broken middle, their inclusion and return must be recognized as part of the brokenness of the past and present, so as to become part of the future. Ignoring these realities mistakes the rhetoric of peace for a future beyond the past. The difficult realities will remain only to paralyze Jews and Palestinians in a cycle from which there is little chance of escape.

Azmi Bishara, a Palestinian who is also an Israeli citizen, understands the limits of the present agreements as catalysts for the revival of the binational idea once current in Jewish and Palestinian circles. To achieve this binationalism in the future, Bishara envisions the need to mobilize Palestinian and Israeli democratic forces who champion binational values over narrowly nationalist values: "We will have to point out to the Israeli Left that its current slogan of separation . . . is actually a racist slogan: it legitimizes Israel's ongoing domination of another people; it legitimizes the idea that Palestinians are a demographic threat. In its stead, we must propagate political programs that emphasize the genuinely binational values of equality, reciprocity and coexistence."

Bishara echoes the words of Judah Magnes that he wrote to a friend in 1929: "It must be our endeavor first to convince ourselves and then to convince others that Jews and Arabs, Moslems, Christians and Jews have each as much right there, no more and no less, than the other: equal rights and equal privileges and equal duties." For Magnes, this was the sole ethical claim for Jewish life in Palestine, for without this equality the quest for a Jewish homeland would turn into a nightmare. The visions of Magnes and Bishara could prompt a search for the broken middle to be found in the ancient city of Jerusalem.[13]

CHAPTER FOUR

The Covenant on the Threshold of the Twenty-First Century

In 1948, Hannah Arendt predicted that the creation of Israel would polarize the Jewish and Palestinian Arab communities into rival, bitterly hostile camps. Unfortunately, her prediction has come to fruition. Those on both sides who seek compromise are often forced to choose extreme positions that they do not actually, in principle, hold.

With the declaration of Israeli statehood in 1948 the middle ground gave way; those who declined to enlist with either extreme were deemed disloyal. In fact, Arendt foresaw a strange reversal in the making, a reversal that still haunts the public discussion of Jerusalem and Israel/Palestine. The middle—those who see the possibility of a solidarity between Jew and Arab that limits the demands of each community so as to accommodate the possibility of achieving the greater good of harmony and peace—are labeled as extremists. The extremists—those who desire to maximize the success of one community at the expense of the other community—are labeled as moderates, often engaging in battle with ideologies and policies that are even more extreme than their original views.[1]

The transformation of extremism into moderation is defined as the debate itself narrows. For many, Menachem Begin and Yitzhak Rabin are seen in confrontation, as ideological opposites, even bitter enemies, but it is difficult to distinguish many of their policy decisions and actions. Both were challenged by those on the left; they were also harassed by those on the right. Their attitudes and policies toward Palestinians were, in their early and later years, surprisingly consistent and part of the mainstream of Israeli and Jewish life. Atrocity and expulsion, deportation and settlements, even agreements with Arab countries and Palestinians, characterized their attitudes and politics. By contrast, Judah Magnes and Azmi Bishara, whose positions were once considered moderate, are today seen as radical beyond possible thought.

In the present configuration, the transformation that Arendt foretold and tried to avert has almost become complete. Tikva Honig-Parnass, an Israeli journalist and editor of *News from Within*, refers to this transformation of the definition of extreme and moderate as a statist-tribal consensus that began with the state and is actually solidified on the threshold of the twenty-first century. "The apparent 'historic compromise,'" she says, "has not included any substantive recognition of the national rights of the Palestinian people or of the PLO as a national liberation movement. It is still viewed as a gang of terrorists, which by force of circumstance—an unfavorable balance of power—was compelled to come to terms with Israel. The public discourse, whose parameters are set by the political establishment, has no space for genuine soul-searching regarding the historical nature of the Zionist movement, the dispossession of the Palestinian people from their land since 1948, and Israel's state terrorism in the territories occupied in 1967 and in Lebanon."[2]

For Honig-Parnass, the opposite seems to be occurring as the government continues to hold up the "joint credo" of Zionism, referring to the Jewish "historic right to the land of Israel" and the readiness to "give up" territories in it. Despite the rhetoric and even the apparent political divisions in Israel, the consensus is firm. Honing-Parnass confirms what Arendt wrote years earlier: that a consensus of division and power would emerge that would ultimately seem centrist and commonplace.

Honig-Parnass wrote of this consensus in the wake of the assassination of Rabin and before the election that brought Benjamin Netanyahu to power in 1996. In his first visit to the United States after his election as prime minister, Netanyahu affirmed the continuity of the consensus in Israel by referring to the Rabin assassination as tragic, complimenting the defeated Peres for his contributions to the state, and affirming the status of Jerusalem as the eternal and undivided capital of Israel.

In an address to a joint session of the Congress of the United States, Netanyahu affirmed that there will "never be a re-division of Jerusalem," a view previously endorsed by Rabin and Peres, and added, "We will not drive out anyone, nor will we be driven out of any street of our capital." According to Netanyahu, the unification of Jerusalem under Israeli sovereignty guarantees the freedom of all, and the Jewishness of the city is assumed as a historic right and contemporary good. The politically implemented Judaization of Jerusalem and the consequent decline of Palestinian population and culture there are never mentioned. In this sense, the "historic right" of Jews covers over the politics that have guided the remaking of Jerusalem since 1967. The possibility of the broken middle disappears in the rhetoric of Jewish innocence and power.[3]

After his address to Congress, Netanyahu visited the United States Holocaust Memorial Museum, laying a wreath and pausing for a moment of silence to honor the victims of the Holocaust. The visit to the museum was even more poignant, as Netanyahu's wife, Sarah, lost almost her entire family to the Holocaust.

One wonders, however, what those who perished in the Holocaust would think of two of Netanyahu's initial cabinet appointees, Raphael Eitan and Ariel Sharon. Eitan commanded a unit in which scores of captured Egyptian soldiers were executed in the 1956 Israeli-Egyptian war and predicted in the 1980s that the expansion of Israel into the West Bank would ultimately reduce Palestinians to "drugged cockroaches." Sharon presided over the massacre at Quibya in 1953 and was a prime architect of the war in Lebanon in the 1970s and 1980s. Sharon was also found culpable by the Kahan Commission, who investigated the massacre of hundreds of Palestinians in Sabra and Shatilla in 1982, forcing his resignation as defense minister.[4]

The reaction to Netanyahu's election was diverse. From the conservative side, Henry Kissinger, former secretary of state under President Richard Nixon, saw the security-conscious reputation of Netanyahu as a positive force to solidify Israelis behind a viable peace agreement. Unlike Kissinger, Norman Podhoretz, editor-at-large of *Commentary,* was pessimistic as to whether the new prime minister can halt the process of creating a Palestinian state and a consequent civil war between the Palestine Authority and Hamas. For Podhoretz, this would lead to a "Lebanonization" of Palestine and inevitably draw the other Arab states into a "last effort to wipe the Jewish state off the map." On the liberal side, David Grossman, an Israeli novelist and political commentator, felt that the election shows that most Israelis are not "mature enough" for the peace process: "They want peace, of course—everyone wants peace—but they're not willing to make the concessions it takes." Grossman finds this ironic, because this is "exactly what the right wing used to say about the Arabs, that they're not mature enough to make peace."

From the Palestinian perspective, Edward Said commented that the peace process was at an end, for he remains unconvinced that anything but a small minority of Israelis has had a change of heart about peace. His comments are almost bitter about the prospects of peace: "Having been in the territories a couple of months ago and seen what the devastation of the Israeli-American peace process has wrought on the Palestinians, I came to the painful conclusion that better a crude and brutal Netanyahu than a posturing—but also crude and brutal, judging by his actions in the territories and in Lebanon—Peres." Elie Wiesel countered Said's understanding by counseling that the worry over Netanyahu is misplaced: "There is something called the wisdom of the people, and we must have faith in it. A Jewish wise man once said, 'Trust the people, for they may not be prophets, but they are the children of prophets.' History is irreversible. Think about tomorrow. There will be negotiations. During the campaign, Netanyahu spoke like Peres; Peres spoke like Netanyahu. So don't worry. It will be O.K."[5]

The division between Said and Wiesel on Netanyahu is telling and perhaps symbolic of the entirety of the Jewish return to Palestine. What is acceptable from the Jewish side is a disaster for the Palestinians. Negotiating from strength, the process of seeking solutions is complex and requires time. The strong are rational and, in this case, heirs to the prophetic vision. Leaders are sustained by the collective wisdom of the people. Those on the other side of that power experience a form of oppression, and the heirs of the prophetic vision become their doom.

Said prefers the crude and the brutal, the straight talk and actions that advise his own people of their real situation. Netanyahu is little different than Peres or, for that matter, Rabin. Said seems to echo the response of a Palestinian in Gaza to the assassination of Rabin: "Am I sorry? Yes—I am sorry for us, not for Rabin. The one who killed him is a Jew, so why are the Palestinians locked up? Even when it is open Gaza is still behind bars. The Israelis haven't absorbed the fact that we are here as human beings and partners. To them we are marginal." Said counters to Wiesel that "it will be O.K." is simply a cover for a brutality that continues under different Israeli leaders who, despite their rhetoric, carry on essentially the same policies. That, at least, is the common wisdom of the Palestinian people.[6]

Can this common wisdom of both sides be transformed through a vision and policy that probe deeper than Wiesel and help shift Said's desire for an honest reckoning of the crude and the brutal? In the twenty-first century, is there hope of a dialogue to place the unity of Jerusalem as a path of justice and reconciliation rather than the celebration of a victory over the Palestinian people? Perhaps the hope and despair that attend assassinations and elections are themselves part of the problem. The continuity of the consensus is represented in the policies of Israel from the beginning so that the focus on personalities and political parties may be a diversion. If Wiesel asserts that Peres and Netanyahu sound alike, and Said asserts that they act alike, then the change in leadership and governing coalitions makes little difference.

The future seems bleaker when the weakness of the diaspora and homeland visions are factored in, and even the rhetoric loses touch with the ethical tradition of justice and mercy. For when the rhetoric loses its connection with that tradition, the appeal of an alternative path disappears. Perhaps Netanyahu neglected the Jewish ethical tradition in his rhetoric because it is no longer available to him. It is less a matter of personal preference, style, or even politics, than a history that has stripped this rhetoric of its power to invoke a vision. Even Wiesel, who is at home in the language of that tradition, is reduced to allaying fears without suggesting any specific outcome or ideal.

Thus the consensus that arrived unbroken in Netanyahu has lost the subversive memory of the tradition. His much-publicized attendance at an Orthodox synagogue on the Sabbath in New York is paradoxical and informative on this matter. Rabin and Peres downplayed and sometimes ridiculed the Orthodox yet maintained the tension of the tradition's dream in their public speech. Netanyahu exhibited none of this tension even as he displayed his religious credentials.

Though this disparity may seem opportunistic on Netanyahu's part, the reality is much more serious. Netanyahu represents the transformation of the religious-diaspora vision into a religiosity that blesses and lives off state power. At the same time, he symbolizes the transformation of the secular-diaspora and homeland-Zionist visions into an assertion of rights and power and disavows the right of Palestinians to their own home. Netanyahu embodies the destination Arendt predicted.

What the future holds is difficult to predict. Contemporary Jewish leadership represents the consensus that has governed Israel from the beginning: the negotiations and accords will continue with different rhetoric but minimal difference in policy. Israel will continue to fashion its victory, strengthening its hold on Jerusalem, "thickening" the settlements, dominating the resources and infrastructure of the area, and allowing a limited autonomy to Palestinians without recognizing their political and national rights. Over time the closures will be lifted and Palestinians will be welcomed back to Israel as cheap and unskilled laborers if, in fact, foreign workers have not taken their place. The denial of rights and the continuing economic problems that accompany a limited autonomy might give birth to new uprisings. Future sustained revolts could be less disciplined and more violent than the previous ones, for the conditions of the Palestinians have deteriorated and hopes for a negotiated surrender will have dissipated. For Palestinians the gamble will have been lost, and the Palestinian leadership will be discredited.

Palestinian desperation will be matched by the coarsening of the fabric of Israeli society and leadership. With the tension of ideal and reality in Jewish speech and thought depleted, one wonders what kind of military response will be applied in such a scenario. Will there be Jewish dissent as with the previous uprising? How will that dissent be articulated, and what actions will flow from it? Will the exilic community continue to grow, fleeing a tradition that supports the troops and the bullets with prayers and rabbinic rulings? Will the limits of force continue to expand as they have throughout Israeli history until there is no limit?

There is the possibility of muddling through with enough give and take to keep the lid on the explosion. The breakthrough of the Oslo accords was that a bridge beyond violence and stalemate could be glimpsed ahead. Though distant, that bridge filled the world with hope and, in so doing, galvanized Jews and Palestinians to bring closer that time when Isaiah's vision could be spoken again in Jerusalem.

That time has receded. Still it awaits rediscovery, even if the language has changed, and the words are spoken from an exile that grows larger and more alienated from the mainstream of Jewish life. Or perhaps that exile is becoming the mainstream itself, hidden, inarticulate, and searching for a home once found in the covenant. Perhaps, against all expectation and announcement, that covenant already resides among those in exile in solidarity with the other who is called enemy.

Boundaries and the Covenant

Exile is a recurring theme in Jewish history, the commentary about which is found in both ancient and contemporary sources. Exile bears traditionally religious connotations, relating to the loss of the promised land and the connection with God and the community.

Probing the meaning of exile reveals great depths of religious testimony and questioning. For the chosen people to be displaced and to suffer—to wander through strange lands among diverse peoples, often to be displaced again—penetrates to the very heart of God's promises. Does this people, singled out by God to be God's own, have as a destiny to be subjugated to other peoples who have not been chosen?

The rabbis often interpreted exile as the responsibility of the people for their hubris in attempting to supplant God with human intention and power or their laxity in observing Jewish law. Both were regarded as sins to be punished by God, with the consequent message that a return to humility and obedience would repair the relationship with God and restore the people to the land from which they had been dispersed.

Punishment was seen in the context of parental love, a wayward child being punished so that the homecoming would restore the relationship and charge it with a renewed vigor. To be sure, the punishment of exile was rarely accepted without protest, and a tradition grew up in the Jewish community of arguing with God, a tradition that has its roots in the Bible and has reached its peak in the aftermath of the Holocaust.[7]

Reflections on the exile and the larger framework of the covenant itself are ostensibly about hubris and obedience. Yet these elements are important only in the context of boundaries, boundaries about God and community originally agreed upon at Sinai and interpreted in the history that unfolds from that agreement. Once the boundaries have been drawn and agreed upon, queries about the boundaries and their apparent violation take place within a certain formula, what Anson Laytner terms the law-court pattern of prayer. The components of this prayer include an address to God the judge, the complaint and petition brought against God and to God, and a concluding petition or request by the individual or the community. Sometimes an additional component is added that identifies God's response to the petition.

In this sense, prayer is a challenge, sometimes an accusation, in a court-like structure. If the individual and the community can be accused of crossing the boundary of the covenant, both can petition God for redress or a lighter punishment; both can even expand the accusation of violation to include God. The law-court structure allows the accusation against God to be heard and, if judged appropriate, to be settled in favor of the person and the community. Within the covenant, God can accuse and punish; God can also be spoken to honestly, accused, and convicted. The exile is a trial of Israel, but it can also become a trial of God.

Laytner identifies Elie Wiesel's work as the latest and perhaps last addition to this tradition of arguing with God. In his autobiographical *Night* and his play *The Trial of God*, Wiesel pushes this argument to the limit, accusing God of betraying the people through silence and inactivity. There is also the issue of power, as the enemies of the Jewish people are making a mockery of the promise of God's protection. While God is either unwilling or unable to protect the people, the Nazis assume the power that God once displayed.

As for promises, Wiesel is objective in declaring that only Adolf Hitler kept his promises to the Jewish people. Why pray to God for protection, for God is impotent in the face of the Nazi challenge. God punished Jews for crossing the boundaries of hubris and obedience, but Adolf Hitler crosses the ultimate boundaries of life with God's chosen and does so with impunity. For this, God is guilty, and the idea of Jewish suffering as a form of punishment is rejected. The penalty may be the same one inflicted by Hitler on millions of Jews: death by starvation; disease; firing squad; gassing; or, in the famous scene from *Night,* of the slow, pitiful death of a young boy, death by hanging. The death of God is a public death witnessed by the Jewish community, just as the covenant was witnessed to at Sinai. The covenant begins and ends in public; the promise of life ends in a death that is unopposed by God.[8]

One can see this in Elie Wiesel's novels that follow *Night.* In *Dawn* and *Day*, a positive progression from a world of darkness to a world of light is portrayed but also a reverse progression in terms of God's presence to the Jewish people. At the beginning of *Night,* God is present; in *Dawn,* God is killed so that humans can live; and in *Day,* God is absent. As Wiesel's titles become brighter, the presence of God becomes dimmer, so that by the publication of *Day,* humanity lives without God and without meaning.

For Wiesel this is a journey of pain, which begins in the outward event of Holocaust and continues internally in this new consciousness of the loss of God. The loss of God is at the same time the loss of the covenant or, if you will, a shifting of the covenant from God and Israel, God and humanity, to the Jewish people and its memories of pain and death, God and meaning.

What remains of these memories of the Jewish people, their encounters with God, and a world once infused with meaning, is the overwhelming experience of death; this is what is available to Jews in the present. With this memory and void, Wiesel proposes an additional covenant, one emphasizing solidarity, witness, and sanctification of life.

Wiesel's additional covenant leads neither to the messianic event nor to redemption but leads instead to acts of solidarity designed to triumph momentarily over the void. This solidarity is universal in its reach and particular in its expression: a renewed solidarity with the Jewish people is exemplified in support for Israel. If Sinai is confronted by Auschwitz as a counter-testimony, Auschwitz demands an unremitting solidarity with the Jewish state.[9]

If this void is felt by Jews and other people who have suffered, is shared across boundaries of time and peoplehood, and if this void is now shared in a particular way by Jews and Palestinians, perhaps, then, a covenantal obligation is shared as well. Wiesel's additional covenant might extend to an inclusive covenant of Jews and Palestinians, both bound by memories of God, of a world infused with meaning, and the overwhelming experience of dislocation and death. Here the messianic and redemptive can be glimpsed in the present within memory and a future shared by Jews and Palestinians.

Can the renewal of trust and the healing of wounds occur in isolation, with reference to a past that becomes more and more distant, or in the mutual embrace of a past and future that are concretely shared? Perhaps reestablishment of the covenant and the possibility of reaffirming God can be found in this recognition of a shared memory and future that can, in the present, be touched, struggled with, wept over, and celebrated.

One wonders, then, if Wiesel's progression from *Night* to *Day* in relation to God can be reversed, as a journey toward a renewed embrace and presence where the void is acknowledged and bridged by an activity of healing that transforms memory into an active solidarity. Wiesel's sense of solidarity as counter-testimony to Auschwitz is transformed into a solidarity with a center of engagement that seeks to leave Auschwitz behind or, more succinctly stated, seeks to place Auschwitz in a broader historical perspective and as one reference—significant, to be sure, but no longer *the* guiding center—in the history of the Jewish people.

Jewish understandings of Israel shift as well. No longer is Israel seen simply as a response to the Holocaust; as an embattled, besieged state always threatened with another holocaust; or as a redemptive dream without its own tainted history. Rather, Israel is seen as a place where active solidarity with the Palestinian people and an inclusive vision of mutual empowerment are experimented with and over time brought into reality.

The messianic and redemptive are seen in the possibility of Jews and Palestinians normalizing their lives after their catastrophes and struggles. Jews and Palestinians living normal lives—in Yitzhak Rabin's vision, building homes, planting trees, loving, living side by side in empathy, as free human beings—could represent the healing of wounds, the renewal of trust and, in this sense, the end of the era of Auschwitz.

The possibility and danger of the contemporary political situation are now seen in a context that moves beyond politics into the very question of covenantal affirmation after Auschwitz. The possibility is that a tragic history is transformed and, with that, comes a healing of wounds and renewal of trust. The danger is that opportunity will be delayed or even squandered, for if time does not heal all wounds, it can most certainly increase them through distance and continued violation.

At some point, healing may become unavailable, and the wound at the heart of Jewish and Palestinian history may simply become an uncontrollable rage. On the Jewish side, if empowerment continues without reconciliation, Auschwitz will end, but in a different way. Israel will become without memory of its founding and without an anchor that may temper a militarization penetrating deeper into the fabric of Jewish life.

If this occurs, even the memory of God and a world with meaning, which presupposes the possibility of reclaiming both, will fade. The dialogue with the covenant will come to an end and the additional covenant, which takes shape only with reference to the original, will also become increasingly distant and ultimately unavailable.

The failure of a deep solidarity with the Palestinian people may then affect Jewish history and Jewish belief in a way that rivals or even surpasses the Holocaust, for the struggles within the Jewish past may be seen as an irrelevant distraction. Wiesel's greatest worry may be fulfilled; the complete trivialization of the Holocaust or even its disappearance from memory. Recognizing the Jewish liturgy of destruction as an inclusive one will cease to be an arena of struggle. There will be no liturgy to commemorate the dead or to reconcile histories infected by atrocity.

Those who carry the memory of Jewish suffering and act in solidarity with the Palestinian people may ultimately decide the future of the covenant and the Jewish people. These Jews may transcend the limitations of Wiesel and translate the rhetoric of Yitzhak Rabin and Simon Peres into an efficacious political framework of justice and peace. If the political opportunity is missed, they will remain as witnesses to the squandered opportunities for reconciliation and as a resource for a renewed struggle to be faithful in the future. Perhaps those who carry the memory and act in solidarity are key to a future beyond the era of Auschwitz, even if their witness is buried in the affluence and power of contemporary Jewry, as the diaries and pleas of Holocaust writers were buried in the rubble of ghettos across Europe.

Many Jews who embody this future are, of course, marginal to the Jewish community today, for they exist in exile. Many were originally moved by the words and images of writers like Wiesel and sought a path to carry that message into the future. Some who were heavily involved in Jewish life have, in the face of disappointment and anger, disappeared from organized Jewish public and religious institutions. Those who have been unable to resolve the contradiction of a universal and particular solidarity that minimizes or excludes Palestinians found little in the way of spiritual nourishment to sustain them in their journey. They instead have found homes in other religions, such as Christianity, Buddhism, Hinduism, and a variety of cults that have Jewish participation disproportionate to the Jewish population in the larger society.

These Jews can be encountered everywhere, attempting to live a solidarity that propels them to destinations paradoxically encouraged and warned against by people like Wiesel and members of the Jewish establishment. Most often, Jews in exile lack an ability to articulate the reasons for their deep passions of justice or that their intuitive movement toward inclusion represents a loyalty to Jewish history rather than a sinful aberration. Often they are fellow-travelers who articulate their solidarity in recently acquired ideological and theological languages.

The boundaries that Wiesel draws are similar to those Yosef Yerushalmi and David Roskies come up against but with a particular force. The liturgical aspects of Wiesel's articulation of the additional covenant draw Jews to the depths of Jewish identification. The sense of loss and consequent responsibility are felt at a deep level. Even as the past is invoked with a haunting pathos—the memory of a world infused with meaning and God—however, the present is left without that same depth. Solidarity with the Jewish people and Israel is heard, but what does one do with the cries of those who have been displaced since the loss of Wiesel's world?

The boundaries of Wiesel's world were broken and, in that, the boundaries of the Jewish world as well. Wiesel mourns that violation; Yerushalmi and Roskies analyze the aftermath and find bifurcation and assimilation. A new boundary has been violated that is difficult to reconcile with the additional covenant, for how can a people continue to invoke the violation of their boundaries when they are violating boundaries of another people?

The additional covenant, which emerges as a testimony to, and in confrontation with, the original covenant, is in its very articulation itself violated. The boundary whose crossing is correctly protested calls forth a further protest when crossed again. Yet the message is mixed and confused. As the violation of the Jewish people is held above and beyond the violation of others, anger is encouraged in the face of the violation of Jews while silence is counseled, even mandated, in response to the violation of Palestinians.

It is strange, perhaps, that part of this marginalized Jewish constituency is found in the adult children of Holocaust survivors, children for whom the Holocaust liturgy is an intimate reality. Some of these adult children of survivors have found, in the Palestinian resistance to Israeli occupation and Jewish responses to that resistance, an arena of struggle that sees the memory of suffering as a path toward a life beyond suffering. For these Jews, of course, the tension of Holocaust, Israel, and Palestine is almost unbearable, and, in their poems, stories, and essays one finds expressed the difficulty of living in this tension.

The struggle of the children of Holocaust survivors is hardly abstract; the shattering of their parents' lives and their experience of growing up in that shadow compel them to cry out against further pain in the lives of others. At the same time, they realize that the present situation does not shatter only the lives of others but is a shattering within their own lives as well. Some come to feel that their own healing can only come with the healing of the other who has been broken by Jewish and Israeli power.

Irena Klepfisz, essayist and poet, is one such person. Her father, Michal Klepfisz, was an activist in the Bund and a member of the Jewish Fighters Organization in the Warsaw ghetto. In early 1943, she and her mother were smuggled out of the ghetto by her father, and he also smuggled in weapons and materials used to produce weapons later used in the ghetto uprising. On the second morning of the uprising, three days after his thirtieth birthday, Michal Klepfisz was killed while protecting other ghetto fighters as they escaped. After the war, Irena and her mother, Rose Perczykow Klepfisz, emigrated to Sweden and then to the United States.

Klepfisz's experiences of the war, memories of her father, and life with her surviving mother were, in retrospect, hardly easy. Grappling with the issue of Palestinians and Israeli power was no less easy, but in the end it provided Klepfisz with an arena to come to a new understanding of the possibilities of personal and communal healing after the Holocaust.

After traveling to Poland and Israel, Klepfisz helped organize, in April 1988, the Jewish Women's Committee to End the Occupation of the West Bank and Gaza, which shortly thereafter began to hold weekly vigils in New York City at the offices of the Conference of Presidents of Major American Jewish Organizations.

The group's proposal to end the violent repression against the Palestinian uprising, support of an international peace conference, and proposal of a two-state solution was often greeted with hostility. Some Jews insisted that the Holocaust precluded such political action. One Jewish man told Klepfisz that he wished she were buried in Poland like his own parents. A few Jews wished another holocaust on the demonstrators. Still others felt that their actions would lead all Jews, including them, "back to the ovens."

In different ways, Klepfisz and the committee demonstrators were accused of disloyalty and of being collaborators with historical and contemporary Nazis. As Klepfisz writes, "We were told that to give the Palestinians a state was to give Hitler his final victory, that our behavior was desecrating the Holocaust of the 1940s and ensuring the Holocaust of the 1990s, perhaps even the 1980s."[10]

Understandably, Klepfisz experienced a mixture of shame, fear, and anger, emotions she had experienced her entire life as a child of a ghetto fighter and a Holocaust survivor. Still she remained resolute: "Knowing that the world was passive and indifferent while six million Jews died, I have always considered passivity and indifference the worst of evils. Those who do nothing, I believe, are good German collaborators. I do not want to be a collaborator." Klepfisz took seriously the admonition of a Palestinian woman she came to know in Jerusalem in 1987: "Write about what you see. Write what is happening to us."

In reflecting on the Palestinians' challenge, Klepfisz reflects on the disturbing analogies of Israel, Holocaust, and the Palestinians and how they resonate in her life: "'What does it remind you of?' I ask my mother, and read her the *Newsday* article about the Palestinian men in Rufus: rounded up by the Israeli police, they're told to lie face down in a nearby field. 'I know what it reminds me of,' she answers and says nothing more."

For Klepfisz, given the images etched in the collective consciousness of the Jewish people, how can this *not* remind Jews of the Holocaust? "What is it that we have been asking everyone to remember? Is it not the fields of Ponary and those nameless fields on the outskirts of dozens of *shtetlekh* that we're all pledged to remember? Am I to feel better that the Palestinians from Rufus were not shot by the Israelis but merely beaten? As long as hundreds of Palestinians are not being lined up and shot, but are killed by Israelis only one a day, are we Jews free from worrying about morality, justice? Has Nazism become the sole norm by which Jews judge evil, so that anything that is not its exact duplicate is considered by us morally acceptable? Is that what the Holocaust has done to Jewish moral sensibility?"[11]

Klepfisz extended these thoughts as she addressed a group of survivors on the forty-fifth anniversary of the Warsaw ghetto uprising in April 1988. Speaking of the idea of mourning, she asked what it is that the survivors mourn. In the case of Anne Frank, for example, do the survivors grieve that she was deprived of being a great writer, or that she was deprived of the ability to nurture what was inside of her, to explore the world around her, to enjoy the "normal process of growing up free to experiment, to experience the pleasures of success, the difficulties of failure." For Klepfisz, Jews should mourn that Anne Frank was denied an "ordinary, anonymous life." That lost experience of the ordinary serves as a reminder and also ultimately a link to the present: "I have come to believe that ordinariness is the most precious thing we struggle for, what the Jews of the Warsaw ghetto fought for. Not noble or abstract theories, but the right to go on living with a sense of purpose and a sense of self-worth—an ordinary life. It is this loss we mourn today."

Klepfisz then issues her challenge specifically in relation to the Palestinian people: to apply the "fierce outrage" of the ghetto fighters at the destruction of the ordinary lives of their people to those who live on the other side of Jewish power. Jews are called upon to feel outrage whenever we see signs of the disruption of Palestinian common life: "The hysteria of a mother grieving for the teenager who has been shot; a family stunned in front of a vandalized or demolished home; a family separated, displaced; arbitrary and unjust laws that demand the closing or opening of shops and schools; humiliation of a people whose culture is alien and deemed inferior; a people left homeless, without citizenship; a people living under military rule."[12]

In her moving address on the meaning of Holocaust memory as the sacredness of ordinary life, by including and naming Palestinian life within the context of Jewish memory, Klepfisz implies what the Jewish community has yet to realize: no matter what the resolution of the conflict, even were the agreements to fulfill the demands of justice and equality, the destruction of Palestinian life by Jews is now a part of Jewish history that must also be remembered.

Though Klepfisz does not state the corollary, it seems obvious that the image of the Warsaw ghetto uprising, symbolizing the dignity and violation of ordinary Jewish life, is complemented by the Palestinian uprising, which functions in a similar way for Palestinians. This suggests that not only the violation of Palestinian life but also the defense of that life must be remembered in Jewish history. In this context those Jews who seek to defend Palestinians are to be remembered at the same liturgical moment, perhaps in the same liturgy, as the heroic Warsaw ghetto fighters. Klepfisz further intimates that loss of the ordinary common life of any people is worthy of remembering and that the destruction of that life by Jews threatens to violate the memory of the destruction of ordinary Jewish life. The fight to remember Jewish suffering is tied to the fight to mitigate or even reverse Palestinian suffering.

In her poem "East Jerusalem, 1987," Klepfisz captures the images of a suffering history and the inclusive nature of this history. After a meeting of Jewish and Palestinian women in East Jerusalem, they part for the evening, with the Jews returning to West Jerusalem, in a sense returning to their safety, to their ordinary lives, to their history. But the haunting voices of the Palestinians, with their safety, ordinary lives, and history violated, remains:

> All of us part. You move off in a separate
> direction. The rest of us return
> to the other Jerusalem. It is night.
> I still hear your voice. It is in the air
> now   with everything else   except sharper
> clearer.   I think of your relatives
> your uncles and aunts   I see the familiar
> battered suitcases   cartons with strings
> stuffed pillowcases
> children sitting on people's shoulders
> children running to keep up
>
> Always   there is migration
> on this restless planet   everywhere
> there is displacement   somewhere
> someone is always telling   someone else
> to move on   to go elsewhere.
>
> Night. Jerusalem. *Yerushalayim.*
> Jerusalem. If I forget thee
> Oh Jerusalem Jerusalem Hebron
> Ramallah Nablus Qattana if I
> forget thee oh Jerusalem
> Oh Hebron may I forget
> my own past my pain
> the depth of my sorrows.[13]

What Klepfisz sees in the Palestinian forced migration is the loss of Jewish innocence and, with that, the loss of Jewish ability to stand firmly, as the Warsaw ghetto fighters did, on the side of dignity, justice, normality. Hence the conclusion of her poem " '67 Remembered," where the Israeli victory, once celebrated, is now a lesson in power:

Things fester.   We compromise.
We wake up   take new positions
to suit new visions   failed dreams.
We change.   Power does not so much corrupt
as blur the edges
so we no longer feel   the raw fear
that pounds in the hearts
of those trapped   and helpless.
In '67 in Chicago   we thought we'd be safe
locking the windows   till Speck was caught.
We did not know   there was a danger
in us as well   that we must remain vigilant
and open   not to power
but to peace.[14]

In Klepfisz's poetry, the boundaries cited are ones of violation and inclusion. The messianic dream of the return to Jerusalem, the command to remember, and the sin of forgetting are now expanded. When remembering Jerusalem, she cannot forget the Palestinian women and the cities from which they come, including Jerusalem. They are now part of a shared landscape, one defined by dislocation and death.

Klepfisz is called to remember this landscape that forms a new boundary to be protected and nurtured. In these Palestinian women, she remembers her own displacement and sees the blurring of the edges in the Jewish return. Attachment to power is natural, especially after immense suffering, but safety through power is an illusion.

The blurring of the edges seeks to maintain the illusion but contains, at the same time, the subversive message that there is a "danger in us as well." Power as a way of security also seeks to shield Jews from the knowledge of the danger that Klepfisz witnesses in the faces of the Palestinian women. They speak of the danger of Jewish power, and Klepfisz understands this danger in light of the dislocation in her own life and among her people. The identification is immediate and irrevocable.

So, too, is the hope that springs from this encounter in Jerusalem. It is as if the uncovering of the danger within releases another power. The sadness of violating this boundary mobilizes mourning into a solidarity that is profound and active.

Wiesel's additional covenant is past, a memory whose future is limited in its political and spiritual potential. For the most part, its gaze is fixed to the past, while the present is a protected lament, innocence and power linked in an uncritical embrace. Klepfisz embraces the past by honestly facing the present, seeking the relationship of past and present so as to move into a future. In understanding that the danger within is actively expressing itself in the contemporary world, mourning is mobilized to create a future of no migration, where no one is telling anyone else to move on, where everyone can be safe.

The situation of Jews and Palestinians is similar, and the history of the Palestinians recalls the history of the Jews. The future holds out the same possibility—a new covenant, as it were, sealed in the ordinary that for both peoples would be extraordinary.

Tikkun of Ordinary Decency

There are many examples of Jews who, in mourning the past, seek inclusion in the present. One thinks of the Holocaust survivor who, in protest of the Israeli bombing of Beirut, went on a hunger strike outside Yad Vashem, the Holocaust memorial in Jerusalem, and offered this statement: "When I was a child of ten and was liberated from the concentration camps, I thought that we shall never suffer again. I did not dream that we would cause suffering to others. Today we are doing just that. The Germans in Buchenwald starved us to death. Today in Jerusalem, I starve myself, and this hunger of mine is no less horrific. When I hear 'filthy Arabs' I remember 'filthy Jews.' I see Beirut and I remember Warsaw." And there is Sara Roy, the adult child of Holocaust survivors who, as an expert on the Gaza Strip, has reported consistently before and after the agreements on the disintegration of political, social, and economic life in Gaza. Traveling to Gaza over the last decade, often disguised as a Palestinian, Roy is relentless in her observations of the price of occupation. Her witness is similar to that of Klepfisz's: affirming the ordinary life of people by protesting its denial, even, and especially when, it is denied through power wielded by her own people.[15]

What is extraordinary about these Jews is the boundaries they have crossed: the boundary of enemy, defined as a dangerous other, and the boundary of memory, which has been used as a shield to limit and filter contemporary life. To cross these boundaries involves more than courage. These survivors and their children are propelled by an intimate history and an intuitive sense that violation in the present increases the violation of the past. They also recognize that the past can only be approached in the present.

By acting with memory, using memory to resist rather than simply to mourn, they open the path of healing, if not for their parents and not even for their own generation, then perhaps for the next generation. It seems that they are preparing with their own lives a deeper framework for an eventual political decision for justice and peace. Surely they remind the politicians of the ordinary lives with which they have been entrusted and for which they are responsible.

Yet at the same time this crossing of boundaries has profound theological implications. Wiesel's additional covenant, which involves the memory of God's presence and the memory of a world infused with meaning, is in this context a memory mobilized to protest and restore. Perhaps the crossing of boundaries is itself a covenant being formed in the present, a tentative yet energetic hope that God's presence and a world infused with meaning are not simply past but can be felt and established in contemporary life. In their own way these Jews follow the Commanding Voice of Auschwitz, of which Emil Fackenheim wrote so forcefully years earlier. As with religious thinkers reflecting on the Holocaust, they have little to say in positive affirmation of God.

In Klepfisz, in the fasting protester of the Lebanese war, in Sara Roy, there is no mention of God. Their testimony, on the theoretical and theological level at least, is more distant from God-language than Wiesel himself. Holocaust thinkers are in a sharp, profound, and angry dialogue with God; with many of the next generation that dialogue has ceased, been repressed, or become inarticulate. Yet one wonders if active solidarity with Palestinians is an unspoken reassertion of this dialogue, a pretheological action that represents an intuitive desire to create a framework from which speech about God may become possible again.

Is this solidarity an example of a counter-testimony to Auschwitz, a counter-testimony that the Jewish world did not expect and perhaps cannot accept? Perhaps this testimony could initiate a restoration of the image of God so desecrated in the Holocaust.

Emil Fackenheim is of importance here, for along with Wiesel, he helped lay the groundwork for Jewish reflection on the Holocaust. In his early work Fackenheim pointed to the difficulties of belief in God and the need for Jewish identification and solidarity. As for Wiesel, Israel represents the focal point for that solidarity, even as the rupture with God and the world continues.

Fackenheim understands that the pressing questions about God and the world invoked by the Holocaust are unanswerable in the present. Mobilization of the Jewish people, however, cannot await these answers, as their complexity and depth can be addressed only over time in a community structure that survives the aftermath of the Holocaust. The additional covenant may provide a holding action while, over time, inquiry takes place. For Fackenheim, the threat to the community continues in the present, a threat that renders the questions mute. Only survival, especially in Israel, can provide the physical and psychological structure to continue on.[16]

Fackenheim's later work is important, for he explores the possibility of healing the rupture that came into being with the Holocaust. The Commanding Voice of Auschwitz, which for Fackenheim replaces the voice of the God, once heard at Sinai but silent in the death camps, is the call to Jewish survival. Indeed, Fackenheim posits a commandment that issues from this voice, the 614th commandment, which forbids handing Adolf Hitler a posthumous victory by refusing to do whatever is necessary to survive as Jews, including and especially in Israel. This call remains but is now complemented with the Jewish need for healing, a need Fackenheim articulates with the Hebrew word *tikkun,* meaning repair, restoration, mending.

Tikkun olam, the mending of the world, is necessary because of the unprecedented and inexhaustible horror of the Holocaust; *tikkun* is possible because of the unprecedented and inexhaustible wonder of resistance to the Holocaust among a minority of Jews and Christians. On the Jewish side, this resistance was diverse, from religious Jews who continued to hold fast to tradition and, therefore, to their dignity in the face of the ultimate attempt to destroy both, and those who, like the Warsaw ghetto fighters, fought the Nazis despite the odds against them. On the Christian side, there were principled protesters, like the German philosopher Kurt Huber and the Catholic priest Bernard Lichtenberg. In holding up the "idea of man" and the "Christian word," they forfeited their lives.

And yet for Fackenheim the greater witness came from those Christians who, without a great and noble cause, showed what in other circumstances would be considered ordinary decency: "In the Holocaust world, a Gentile's decency, if shown toward Jews, made him into something worse than a criminal—an outlaw, vermin—just as were the Jews themselves; and as he risked or gave his life, there was nothing in the world to sustain him, except ordinary decency itself." This Fackenheim names as a "*tikkun* of ordinary decency."[17]

Though Fackenheim understands that this *tikkun* does not mean that ordinary decency has inherited the earth, it nonetheless, like the Holocaust itself, has an ontological status. In fact, Jewish and Christian resistance to the violation of ordinary decency represents the healing of a rupture and becomes the ultimate ground of post-Holocaust thought and activity. For Fackenheim, then, these *tikkuns* ontologically root the moral necessity of the 614th commandment and the Commanding Voice of Auschwitz.

Humanist, Jewish, and Christian fidelity give birth to a future philosophy, Judaism, and Christianity. Though a future is possible because of fidelity in the past, post-Holocaust thought dwells between the extremes of despair and a certain faith. For Fackenheim, authentic *tikkun* is sought within the tension of despair and faith, affirming a "fragmentariness" that is both incomplete and laden with risk.[18]

It is important that Fackenheim's understanding of *tikkun* connects the ontological with the ordinary. In this sense the retention of ordinary decency is itself a dual crossing of boundaries. The rupture of the Holocaust, ontological in its significance, creates a boundary in which the ordinary flow of life is demeaned, denigrated, and made impossible. Because of this, ordinary decency is a crossing of the boundary within history and beyond; it is profoundly human and much more.

One might call the assertion of the ordinary a miracle, that is, a yes to life that is being systematically destroyed. At the same time that the crossing of the boundaries is for life in its ordinariness, it is carried out with a threat to one's safety and often without the support of or actively against the majority of the community. Therefore, the crossing of boundaries is a carrying of one's entire life toward others into a perilous unknown future that becomes, in an ultimate sense, a future for humankind. In a situation of utter horror, ordinary decency is found in the bonding of the ontological and the human.

The rupture, boundaries, and *tikkun* that Fackenheim articulates are within Judaism and Christianity and between Jew and Christian. They are expressed by both within their commitments to Israel. In fact, for Fackenheim, *tikkun* is Israel itself, the place of future life for Jews and the place of commitment to Jewish life by Christians. Yet even this *tikkun* is fragmentary, limited in terms of Israel's size, capacity, defense, and its ability to guarantee its Jewish citizens a Jewish culture or a strong Jewish identity. Fackenheim sees the enemies of Israel as implacable, attempting to renew exile for its Jewish inhabitants. Internally, the exile for the Jewish people continues with the denial of the obligation to further identifiable Jewish life in response to the Holocaust.

Fackenheim does not pursue this analysis in relation to the Palestinians and, like Wiesel, would surely object to such a proposal. One wonders if the exile that Fackenheim analyzes continues because a further rupture has occurred between Jews and Palestinians, a rupture, which, itself, is in need of *tikkun*. It could be that this *tikkun* is also both ontological and ordinary and that only the assertion of ordinary decency in this time of trial could mend the contemporary world, a mending that Fackenheim so much desires.

It could also be that those Jews who embrace Palestinians are simply carrying on the *tikkun* of Jews and Christians in the Holocaust and therefore preparing a possible future for both peoples. Will Palestinians write one day of the righteous Jews as Fackenheim writes of the righteous Gentiles? Could this ordinary and unprecedented *tikkun* be a search for a covenantal framework, which in asserting ordinary decency over against political practicalities and enduring in a tension of fragmentariness, is nonetheless affirming a grounding that has been undermined and even in some cases destroyed? Surely these boundary crossings, though still incomplete and risky, represent a search for a *tikkun* that has evaded the Jewish world.

Perhaps the healing of the rupture, between Jews and Christians and Jews and Palestinians, can only come into being within an expanded covenantal framework. Such a *tikkun* is grounded in ordinary decency and suggests the possibility of God. The additional covenant Wiesel proposed—a covenant of memory and mourning and, within that covenant, the additional commandment that Fackenheim proposed, to deny Hitler a posthumous victory through survival and continuance—represents the understanding that Jews must live forever within the realm of the Holocaust. In this view, Jewish life in Israel and elsewhere is simply an extension of that event; there is no life after or independent of Auschwitz. By contrast, the expanded covenantal framework suggested by those on the margins of Jewish life views Jewish life within, after, and at the end of the era of Auschwitz.

The rupture Wiesel and Fackenheim affirm is accepted in this covenantal framework and is transcended in the only way possible: through acts of ordinary decency. Because these acts are unprecedented and risky, they, too, have an ontological status. They can help create a future only when there is content and continuity to these acts, that is, a political framework that allows these acts a foundational and efficacious structure. Clearly the lack of such a political structure was the reason for the initial rupture itself and relegated the ordinary decency of some Christians to the category of witnesses, to be remembered in the context of helpless bystanders rather than people who prevented the Holocaust.

A similar lack has separated Jews and Palestinians and thus rendered ordinary decency after the Holocaust to a witness position. Perhaps the creation of such a structure is what Shimon Peres was alluding to when he spoke these words: "On our side there are many mothers and fathers and children who suffered tremendously and on the Palestinian side, too, there are many people who paid with their fortunes, their freedom, and I really feel the Lord has offered us a real opportunity to change the course of hopelessness and desperation and bloodshed into something more promising, more noble, more humane."[19]

Here the commentary of Edward Said is crucial, for he challenges the words of Peres, which point to the *tikkun* of ordinary decency, with the details of the agreements between Israel and the Palestinians that structurally deny such an achievement. Of the 1995 extension of the Oslo accords, Said writes that the Palestinians have achieved a "series of municipal responsibilities in Bantustans dominated from the outside by

Israel. What Israel has got is official Palestinian consent to continued occupation."

On the one hand, Palestinians will have municipal authority over the towns and some four hundred villages, but they will have "no real security responsibility, no right to resources or land outside the populated centers and no authority at all over Israeli settlers, police and army." The settlements will be untouched and a "system of roads will connect them to one another, making it possible for settlers, like whites in the old South Africa, to avoid or even see the people of the Bantustans, and making it impossible for Palestinians to rule over any contiguous territory." Said refers to this situation as a "mirage of peace," and in an unsettling allusion concludes that Arafat and the Palestinian Authority have become a "sort of Vichy government for Palestinians."[20]

Clearly, on a political level, the *tikkun* of ordinary decency—in Klepfisz's language, the restoration of the ordinary—is unresolved. Said warns that the structure of peace itself is flawed, a mirage, as it were, which, if permanent, would seal an unjust division between Jews and Palestinians. In this sense, the haunting words of Rabin and Peres, which articulate in the political arena the vision of Klepfisz's poetry and point to a *tikkun* in the lives of ordinary Jews and Palestinians, ring hollow. The dramatic expectation of fulfillment raises the stakes: on the one-hundredth anniversary of Israel will Jews see the *tikkun* of ordinary decency as embedded in a way of life, or will they survey an Israel that celebrates a victory shadowed by a segmented, almost ghettoized, and, if possible, bypassed Palestinian population?

The next generation of Jews raised within this framework might simply accept this division without thought. Or will they discover a rupture that remains 100 years after the Holocaust? The question then will be whether that generation has the substance and desire to repair the break and mend this division or the ability to recognize the rupture at the heart of Jewish life.

Those Jews on the margins, like those today, may utter a cry of anguish but one that has no audience to recognize the covenantal obligation or even the possibility of such an obligation. Jewish life—once anchored in the covenant; then, after the Holocaust, anchored in anguish over its brokenness; and, with the flourishing of the state of Israel, at least symbolically, on the brink of its repair—might lapse into a lethargy that forgets both the reality of brokenness and necessity of repair.

As important is the question of whether Jews on the margins, Jews who before and after the Holocaust have contributed so much to Jewish life, will continue as Jews. The children of Holocaust survivors, for example, cross boundaries in a pre- and post-theological way, carrying a past, now inarticulate, religious sensibility into the future. The chance of their

children carrying forth this commitment to Jewish life—especially with
a further brokenness—is questionable.

Will the same energy, which propelled post-Holocaust Jews to cross
boundaries as Jews, propel the next generation to cross over into
another boundary without any kind of Jewish identity? Surely the
prospect of "losing" these Jews is great. Therefore the posthumous victory that Fackenheim seeks to forestall in the engagement of Jewish solidarity might be accomplished in a Jewish solidarity that isolates the
other of contemporary Jewish history: that is, a solidarity that refuses
to take the next unprecedented step.

This next unprecedented step might place oneself outside Jewish life
as we know it today. The personal and communal embrace of the other
may be, for some at least, either a projection of future Jewish life or an
abandonment of it. Is the understanding that Palestinians are now an
intimate part of Jewish life in repair and fulfillment of the covenant or a
final break with one already shattered?

Restoring the ordinary in the *tikkun* of ordinary decency may fulfill
the Commanding Voice of Auschwitz, or, in some views, may represent
its logical extension. That commandment might read as follows: the victory over Hitler is complete when an empowered Jewish people recognize that only an interdependent empowerment, especially in Israel and
Palestine, will usher in a time of security and healing for Jews; the end of
the era of Auschwitz is possible and worth pursuing but that end can
only come when the restoration of the ordinary life of Jew and Palestinian is complete.

A Thick Wall of Scandal

Yitzhak Rabin's assassin, Yigal Amir, tried to forestall the movement
toward the end of the era of Auschwitz. As with Baruch Goldstein, the
sense that solidarity could be extended to Palestinians threatened the
Holocaust worldview they cultivated and felt at home in.

Even the first tentative steps toward a restoration of the ordinary were
seen as fundamental betrayals of the Commanding Voice of Auschwitz.
Political compromise violated the boundaries of Auschwitz, as both
Goldstein and Amir felt Palestinians to be the new Nazis. The era of
Auschwitz, in their view, had to continue lest Jews fall into a lethargy that
would allow the actual Auschwitz to be reconstructed. Continuing the
era of Auschwitz is following the will of God, whose renewed voice can
be heard in the Jewish settlements that spearhead the reclamation of the
greater land of Israel.

In commentary on the assassination of Rabin, the need to mute religious voices was set forth. Cynthia Ozick, a Jewish novelist and conservative commentator, sought to refute those who placed the issue of Jews and Palestinians in a utopian, transcendent framework, arguing that the issue of messianic perfectibility from the right and the left encouraged destruction and death. For Ozick, the situation suffers from a "common arrogance" relating to this search for perfectibility: "There are too many seers in the land, too many utopians. There are too many dreams of Eden, right and left, pious and profane. A murdered prime minister will not increase holiness. A Palestinian state will not insure paradise."

Surely Ozick is correct; the issue is not one of messianic perfectibility. Instead, the issue of Jews and Palestinians could be one of covenantal responsibility. The removal of politics from millenarian fantasy is quite different than seeing a religious grounding and basis from which ethical and political judgments arise. In the wake of the Rabin assassination, Michael Walzer, a Jewish ethicist and liberal commentator, also longs for a naked public square in Israel where the "politics of calculation and restraint," a politics "without God, without myth and fantasy, without eternal enemies, without sacred causes or holy ground," triumphs over a religious politics.[21]

The truth is that all competing parties within the Jewish narrative appeal to Jewish history and the covenant, however interpreted, for their understanding of the present and the path to the future. There is reason for such an appeal: Israel does represent a dramatic, difficult, and ambiguous unfolding of Jewish history. Rabin's meeting with Yassir Arafat was highly charged in the mind of Amir and no doubt in the minds of most Jews, for more was represented than politics in their first reluctant handshake.

The facing of the other—the new other of Jewish history—was recognized as a rendezvous with Jewish history. Such a facing of the other should be seen in the context of the Holocaust and the 1967 war as the possibility of ending an era of history as well. The handshake represented the possibility of ending a cycle of suffering and violence that Jews first endured then perpetrated. When Rabin spoke of ending that cycle, one felt an opening toward a responsibility grounded in history and hope.

This opening could be the culmination of a history of suffering and violence and the beginning of a reconciliation with the traumas of Jewish history: a possible healing of the Holocaust that has not occurred through Jewish empowerment in Israel and in some ways has grown deeper through the conquest of another people. Surely, the humiliation of the Palestinian people, which has reminded many Jews of the historic humiliation of the Jewish people, cannot heal the Jewish people. To do so would require working through the idea of the covenant itself. With Jews mobilized and militarized after the disaster of the Holocaust, where God and humanity were found wanting, the possibility of healing by ending the cycle of suffering and violence is itself jarring.

For if the covenant, once given, now broken, and found again in the Commanding Voice of Auschwitz, is demobilized and demilitarized, what will happen to Jewish identity, Jewish defense, Jewish assertion, and Jewish power? Could that covenant promised to and accepted by Jews, a covenant carried throughout a long and difficult history, now be renewed by sharing it in the promised land with another people?

The next step of Jewish history might begin with the realization that the cycle of displacement and death can only end with the sharing of a land and, therefore, a history which once featured and even now promises an aloneness and exclusivity. *The new challenge of the covenant is to find Jewish chosenness within and among those who share the land often called holy.*

Paradoxically, Ozick laid the groundwork for such an understanding years ago in an essay, "Notes toward Finding the Right Question." Though this essay addresses the issue of feminism, asserting that the inclusion of Jewish women in Judaism on an equal basis with men is a sociological rather than a theological question, it may apply to the inclusion of Palestinians in Jewish life as well. After arguing that contributions to Jewish life must be valued regardless of whether they come from males or females, Ozick sees the urgency of that inclusion not with regard to the upsurge of Jewish feminism but in light of the Holocaust: "The timing is significant because the present generation stands in a shockingly new relation to Jewish history. It is we who come after the cataclysm. We, and all the generations to follow, are, and will continue to be into eternity, witness generations to Jewish loss. What was lost in the European cataclysm was not only the Jewish past—the whole life of civilization—but also a major share of the Jewish future. We will never be in possession of the novels Anne Frank did not live to write. It was not only the intellect of a people in its prime that was excised, but the treasure of a people in its potential."[22]

Because of this loss, and the resultant mournful language, "having lost so much and so many," for Jews there are no longer any "unrelated issues." A "thick wall of scandal" separates Jews from the covenant, however, and according to Ozick this scandal is twofold. On the one hand, the scandal denies a decimated people the needed contributions of women; on the other hand, the very injustice denies women their rightful place in Jewish history, especially after the Holocaust. Ozick's discussion of injustice is important: "What is injustice? We need not define it.

Justice must be defined and redefined, but not injustice. How to right a wrong demands ripe deliberation, often ingenuity. But a wrong needs only to be seen, to be seen to be wrong. Injustice is instantly intuited, felt, recognized, reacted to."

Recognition of injustice gives rise to the feeling that there is "something missing." In Ozick's understanding, that is the reason that the written law, found in the Hebrew Bible, is complemented later by the oral law found in the Talmud. The written and oral law become an extended Torah and covenant that, in every instance, "strives to teach No to unrestraint, No to victimization, No to dehumanization." When the Torah is silent in relation to injustice, injustice calls the Torah into question: "Where is the missing Commandment that sits in judgment on the world?" With regard to women, the question is strong: "Where is the commandment that will say, from the beginning of history until now, *Thou shalt not lessen the humanity of women?*"[23]

When the Torah is silent on injustice, it is unable to judge. Instead it "consorts" with the world at large. It is as if the covenant is in search of the missing commandment that will return it to its proper role in the world and remove the wall of scandal separating the people from the covenant and the people from each other. The reaction of the Jewish people to these missing commandments throughout history has been to strengthen the covenant by discovering new commandments to confront injustice. As Ozick writes, to strengthen Torah is to "contradict injustice; to create justice, not through fragmentary accretions of *pilpul* but through the cleansing precept of justice itself."[24]

Ozick relates the unfolding of Jewish teaching and living—the unfolding of the covenant—to the search for missing commandments. When found and implemented, these commandments are recognized after the fact as having been born of the covenant itself. The next step in Jewish life is, in retrospect, obvious and granted validity as the reality that it addresses becomes an acceptable part of life.

Therefore, the commandment about women is within the Torah before it is spoken and recognized as it is added. The covenant unfolds as new questions are asked and answered; the covenant expands as the people and their history journey through time. The next question demanding action is in response to injustice that, if allowed to exist over time, perverts the covenant. A thick wall of scandal is erected that can only be overcome when the Torah ceases to consort with what created the scandal in the first place.

How many Jews hear the commandment, *"Thou shalt not lessen the humanity of Palestinians?"* Did Rabin's soldiers hear it when they had difficulty carrying out the "harsh and cruel" actions of expelling Palestinians from Lod and Ramle? Did Rabin himself hear the commandment when he wrote of this difficulty in his memoirs? Did the Israeli censors hear it when they refused to allow inclusion of that passage in Rabin's published memoirs? Perhaps Rabin heard it again when he invoked the image of a shared humanity at the signing of the first accord in September 1993: " We, like you, are people—people who want to build a home. To plant a tree. To love—to live side by side with you. In dignity. In empathy. As human beings. As free men."[25]

Ozick states that to right a wrong demands "ripe deliberation, often ingenuity." Perhaps the hearing of this commandment—illustrated by spoken word and affirmed in public in a haunting and beautiful way—simply leapt ahead of Rabin's ability to implement these words in concrete deliberation and ingenuity. Perhaps the commandment, once uttered, is so powerful that the prospects of implementation have to lag behind the recognition of the injustice itself.

For if recognition and implementation occur simultaneously, the fear is that all will be lost, that the enterprise of empowerment will be undermined, and that, instead of steadfast purpose, a sense of confusion and remorse might predominate. Was Rabin balancing the hope and fear of finding the missing commandment of his own personal life and the life of his people because it was so earthshaking and explosive?

In the context of the Torah and the covenant, then, Amir's assassination of Rabin debased both. Amir thought that by murdering Rabin he could banish the commandment against lessening the humanity of the Palestinians. He was frightened of the commandment's corollary: the recognition that the covenant can only unfold with the understanding that Jewish and Palestinian destiny is a shared one, and the only question is how that humanity and destiny will be shared. *By murdering Rabin, Amir was really attempting to murder the covenant itself.*

From this perspective, the condemnation of Amir by most commentators—including liberal commentators like Amos Oz and Michael Walzer who favor a "divorce" of Jews and Palestinians—should be seen as a holding operation to isolate the murderer and, in so doing, to displace and manage the missing commandment, which continues to surface. Amir and Walzer are, in a paradoxical way, to be seen together as guardians of the covenant that consorts with injustice, one speaking in overt religious language, the other seeking to banish that language completely.

It is ironic that the murderer of Rabin and the managers of his legacy are closer together than either would allow in their own mind or could physically stomach. They both hear the Commanding Voice of Auschwitz at least in its initial formulation. However, its unfolding message—that what has been suffered by Jews should not be visited upon another people—is either denied or explained away. As guardians of the covenant that consorts, they both, like Oz and Ozick, are part of the thick wall of scandal that surrounds the covenant.

Ozick does not analyze how missing commandments are found, who is likely to find them, or how, once found, they are to be implemented. If injustice is obvious, when does it become so? Are there stages of development when what was not obvious becomes obvious in the present? Does the community see the obvious, or do leaders understand before the people? Does the generation that recognizes injustice find the missing commandment? Or does that await the next generation? Do the leaders who participate in implementing the commandment do so with pure intentions and backgrounds, or do they come to understand injustice because they have helped to create or maintain it? Can the missing commandment, once located, be lost again for the moment or forever, or, once found, is there a momentum that, like the cycle of violence, takes on a life of its own?

What happens to those victimized while the search for the new commandment takes place? Do they simply wait out the process and celebrate as the victorious community comes to grips with its own complicity? Are the victims of injustice better off with the assassins or the managers of the covenant? Are the oppressed simply suffering students, learning their own potentialities when empowerment, in the long cycle of history, finally comes their way? Or is the struggle against injustice the path toward finding the missing commandment and, thus, as essential to the history of the oppressor as it is to the oppressed?

This latter reality points to the interdependence of victor and victim. The other holds the key through its oppression and the struggle against that oppression. The way forward for the powerful can only be found when the other is seen within the history of the powerful. The oppressed, then, serve as a permanent reminder of the victors' capacity for injustice and as judgment on whether the found commandment has been implemented. The commandment, *"Thou shalt not lessen the humanity of Palestinians,"* is a reminder to Jews and renders judgment on the Jewish past, present, and future.

Though the past cannot be changed, reconciliation with the past can occur as time unfolds. That is why Rabin, as well as Jewish politics and thought after his assassination, will be judged by the future that unfolds for Jews *and* Palestinians. The Palestinian response to Rabin's assassination is crucial for Jews to listen to and understand, as their profound ambivalence represents a deep challenge and beckons Jews to move beyond the celebration of right-wing settlers and the management style of some Jewish intellectuals, indeed, beyond the symbolism and limitations of the peace process as presently constituted.

From the perspective of the covenant, a permanent and forced separation of Jew and Palestinian is impossible. The thick wall of scandal cannot be penetrated by a thick wall of separation hiding Palestinians from Jews. The divorce that Oz advocates is an attempt to end the scandal of Jewish displacement and humiliation of Palestinians while retaining the wall, *as if the scandal can be removed by making those who remind Jews of the original offense disappear.* In terms of women, it would be like replying to the injustice against them by removing women from view; the commandment would be interpreted as ceasing to lessen the humanity of women within Jewish life by banishing them from it. Consorting would become the covenantal norm whose violation would invoke the penalty of exile.

With regard to the Palestinians, the commandment to cease lessening their humanity would be met by further banishment from their own origins and homeland into a segmented, almost ghettoized entity, as if the challenge of the offense could be contained and exiled with them. The consorting covenant becomes a banishing covenant and the missing commandment, once surfaced, become a commandment in exile residing in the Palestinian case on the outskirts of Jerusalem. This would be happening as Jews celebrate and solidify their return to Jerusalem.

Still there is a choice. With a covenant that says no to unrestraint, victimization, and dehumanization, celebration at the deepest level and over many generations is impossible when an exiled Jerusalemite population remains outside its gates. Jewish mourning at Yad Vashem takes on a new perspective if, within the context of the found and implemented commandment, Palestinians *and* Jews mourn the expulsion of Lod and Ramle.

So, too, Jewish prayers at the Western Wall will become more authentic when a substantial and free Muslim and Christian population live and pray in Jerusalem as well. Jewish mourning and prayers take on another level of authenticity because the thick wall of scandal is removed, or rather is dealt with by facing the other and the commandment that they embody. This seems to be the original function of hospitality and the stranger in the covenantal framework: welcoming those who might carry with them a message essential to the fulfilling of Jewish destiny.

Jews correctly demand a shared covenantal framework with Christians in the West, especially after the Holocaust. Jews refused a second banishment that Christians, in order to preserve their own sense of superiority, might have proposed after the Holocaust. Jews insisted on this common framework for security; Christians needed it to recognize the commandment that they missed completely, *"Thou shalt not lessen the humanity of Jews."*

Though differing in severity, length of time, and historical circumstance, the displacement of Palestinians functions for Jews in a similar way. Palestinians insist on a shared covenant with Jews for their security; Jews need it for the commandment that has been missed completely. The Palestinian demand is as authentic as the Jewish demand. It is as important to Jewish history as the Jewish demand is to Christian history. The Palestinian refusal of a second banishment is therefore understandable and, in a covenantal sense, essential.

The time of mourning for Rabin has come to an end, as has the time to continue the consorting, ambivalent, and managed covenant. For the consorting covenant is a form of murder repeated daily in acts of injustice that lessen the humanity of the other who, paradoxically, resides at the center of the victors' history.

One day there will be an Israeli prime minister who pays a condolence call on a Palestinian mother whose son was killed by a Jewish soldier during the occupation. That prime minister will carry a letter of apology that asks forgiveness, articulating that Palestinian martyrdom is a marker of Jewish history and a turning point in the life of the Jewish covenant.

For the covenant remains today in a struggle for life in the heart of every Jew, religious and nonreligious alike. It is murdered or given life as the other, the Palestinian, is banished or embraced by the Jewish community.

The covenant cannot be strengthened while the gates remain closed in a new and more sophisticated way. Instead, the covenant can revive and take on a startling dynamism when the missing commandment and the other cease to be strangers.

As distance becomes proximity and separation becomes embrace, particularity and commonality come into a new configuration. The other becomes a partner in a shared enterprise and so, over time, ceases to be other and becomes a wonder of diversity, an engine of development, a discoverer of a shared destiny.

Then mourning is overcome in a celebration that answers the charge of visionary politics and messianic perfectibility. For the road has been paved with a "tainted greatness" that combines suffering and hope and now rests secure in the ordinary life of an ancient and newly covenanted people.

CHAPTER FIVE

The Great Debate over Jewish Identity and Culture

If the *tikkun* of ordinary decency and the commandment not to denigrate Palestinian life are at the heart of the Jewish covenantal obligation at the turn of the millennium, they remain ideals too often violated in the realm of culture and politics.

Israel's Fragmentary *Tikkun*

Regrettably, the inclusion of Palestinians in theological writings lags behind even the political sphere, where practicalities force their inclusion, however grudging and paternalistic. If Palestinians are mentioned in Orthodox religious reflections, they are seen within the biblical struggle to empty the land of the native inhabitants and secure the land of Israel for Jews. Palestinians are present in their opposition to the fulfillment of God's promises and thus take on the symbolism of a people opposing God's will.

Jews and political authorities are counseled by Orthodox leadership that they are obligated to pursue the cleansing of this foreign element from the land. If political authorities attempt to institute policies that withdraw from lands deemed to be part of this promise, then it is the responsibility of Jews to oppose these policies, democratically in the first instance but, if that fails, then militarily as well.

The liberal Orthodox who oppose such militant understandings do so in the biblical framework as well, though one wonders about the significance of the opposition. While the right-wing Orthodox see the Palestinians in opposition to God's will and, therefore, in need of expulsion, the liberal Orthodox argue that though the land of Israel has been promised to the Jewish people, God also counsels Jews to accept and be just to the strangers in the land. Palestinians are left in a bind between these two positions, defined in the Orthodox covenantal framework as enemy or stranger in their own homeland.[1]

Seen in light of the Orthodox sensibility, the biblical allusions offered by Yitzhak Rabin in the White House ceremony in 1993 and even featured in some of the celebrations of Israel's fiftieth anniversary in 1998 seem progressive to the extreme. The conservative and liberal Orthodox use the Bible to define the mission of the Jews in the contemporary world without reference to history and politics as they occurred and are evolving. While looking from the present to the Bible, they are involved in a dialogue that seeks justification for their own sensibilities. In their religious reflection, the mission of the Jews is all-consuming and renders Palestinians invisible even in their extreme visibility. In the end, the discussion excludes the Palestinians as participants, as if their understandings are insignificant and as if decisions about their future are to be made without even a minimal consultation with them.

A military man and a politician, Rabin was aware of the Palestinians from the beginning, as he had to take them seriously as enemies. Over time, he was also able to undergo an evolution in his understanding. Whatever the war and political experiences of the Orthodox theologians, their positions represent an inability to confront history in an authentic way. Their retreat to the protection of the Bible is an abstraction that has political consequences, as the assassination of Rabin demonstrates, and theological consequences as well, as the bifurcation of the Jewish world deepens. The specific language and symbolic imagery of the Jewish covenant become more distant and suspect, culpable in displacement and atrocity, contributing to the growth of the Jewish exilic community.

If the Orthodox positions are abstract and culpable and, because of this, a negative influence on Jewish life, other theological positions that point to a future are equally suspect. Emil Fackenheim's *tikkun* of ordinary decency and Cynthia Ozick's desire to free the covenant from consorting with injustice are suspect because of their inability to embody the logical extension of their reflections.

Fackenheim's *tikkun* is analyzed within the experience of Jews in the Holocaust and the possibility of Jewish rapprochement with Christians in the West. As an extension of the *tikkun* witnessed to in the Holocaust, *tikkun* in the present is found in Israel. Thus support of Israel by Jews and Christians witnesses to the continuation of this *tikkun* as well as the possibility that the *tikkun* will grow from a fragmentary undertaking to one that might eventually become complete. For Fackenheim and Ozick, present support for Israel determines whether the Jewish struggle and Christian witness in the Holocaust were ontologically valid, indeed whether the hope for the repair of the world is real or simply illusory.

Twinning the Holocaust and Israel charges judgment about the state with the enormous burden of rescuing those who died in the Holocaust, as well as the Jewish and Christian traditions, from oblivion. Palestinians, who embody the critique of the Israeli state and its policies, pose this threat in the extreme. To become visible in the narratives of Jews and Christians is to complicate Fackenheim's understanding of *tikkun* tremendously: the suffering of Jews and the witness of Christians in the Holocaust are shadowed by the Jewish violation of Palestinians and the silence of Christians in the face of the Palestinian catastrophe. History becomes more complicated, and the ontological significance of Jewish and Christian resistance to degradation and brutalization is lessened when Jews and Christians are involved in both.

Interestingly enough, Fackenheim understands that the exile remains within Israel because the *tikkun* that Israel represents is fragmentary. The fragmentary quality of the *tikkun* functions to continue support of those Jews and Christians even as Israeli policies increase dissent within both communities. Fackenheim wrote of this *tikkun* during the controversial Lebanon war and at the time when the occupation of the West Bank and Gaza was under increasing scrutiny in the 1980s. By his leaving Palestinians virtually unmentioned, one wonders if Fackenheim was proposing a *tikkun* of ordinary decency that deflected political opposition to the war and the occupation and, at the same time, deliberately removed Palestinians from the possibility of inclusion in his ontological healing.

A movement toward Palestinians, then, completes the rupture caused by the Holocaust and extends it to the point of no return. For Fackenheim, the exile continues in Israel precisely because of those Jews, Christians, and Palestinians who critique Israeli policies, refuse to emigrate to Israel or to leave it for other countries, or abandon the state politically. As Fackenheim relates it: "*Galut* [Exilic] Judaism may have ended; but there is no end to *Galut* itself, inside as well as outside the state of Israel."[2]

That the exile may continue because of the history that has accompanied the state or that the *tikkun* remains fragmentary because of the exclusion of Palestinians is beyond the realm of Fackenheim's imagination. The fragmentary quality of the *tikkun* is laid at the door of non-Jewish critics who, in a disguised fashion, express their anti-Semitism in their criticism of Israel and Jews who criticize Israel as a way of courting favor with the Christian world and, thereby, betray their own people because of self-hate.

Ozick's limitations are also significant. While she espouses a politics that prevents a "slide from the worldly into the wishful," she at times finds it difficult to accept present-day realities. Support for a Palestinian state as a Jewish obligation is hardly a wishful or an eschatological statement. That a Palestinian state, like any state, will be imperfect is without question. Does that render support for such a state unworldly, or does the right of Palestinians to self-government exist regardless of its imperfections?

Also troubling are Ozick's national and linguistic sensibilities, which join the Hebrew language to Jews and Judaism and so see non-Jews who speak and write Hebrew as interlopers on foreign terrain. This subject was broached at a conference of Israeli and American writers in 1989 when Anton Shammas, a Palestinian Israeli who thinks and writes in Hebrew, referred to himself as American Jews' "biggest nightmare." This because the rebirth of the Hebrew language in Israel has made that language his own as well.

The linguistic link that Jews have shared and assume to be exclusively Jewish is no more. In Shammas's view one can think of this as an expansion of the language or a perversion of it. Ozick angrily denounced Shammas as having no right to claim Hebrew as his language. For Ozick, Hebrew is "our language," and non-Jews working in Hebrew would render the language "sterile." What Shammas interjects into the discussion, and what angers Ozick, is that a state with a minority population shares more than land and a common citizenship: a linguistic universe comes into being with the state that has a capacity to evolve and diversify, even change its audience and direction. A Jewish-Israeli writer, Haim Be'er, responded to Ozick's comment by asserting that the Jewish past was with Ozick, but the future is with Shammas. For Ozick, Shammas's linguistic skills are a violation of her universe; for Be'er, Shammas opens up a future beyond the past.[3]

This future could distance the European dimension of Jewish history, even eclipse it, in a Middle Eastern venture of untold significance. The historical and symbolic orientation of such an enterprise could leave European and American Jews in an identity crisis from which there is no escape. Be'er lives in the present with Shammas so that their immediate sensibility and identification, even within the context of struggle, is engaged and intense. At some point, their experiences and hopes for ordinary lives might converge, giving birth to a new configuration and a new history.

In such a scenario the Holocaust recedes, as does the idea of Israel as solely a response to that event. New realities are pressing as a history and a people struggle to move forward. Ozick, who lives in America and writes in English, is anxious that Shammas, indeed Palestinians, might replace Western Jews as the significant partners of Israeli Jews. For Ozick this would represent the final break in Jewish history. But would this be the final break or the next logical step in the evolution of a history that Ozick seeks to control?

It is as if both Fackenheim and Ozick are desperately attempting to hold back history, to maintain a separateness and an innocence long vanished. The Holocaust is known and defined, as are the expected responses of Jews and Christians. Dwelling in the Holocaust, the *tikkun* of ordinary decency is undisturbed and uncomplicated by its post-Holocaust violation in Israel. So, too, the Hebrew language remains the language of an ancient and dispossessed people unsullied by the history of Hebrew in its rebirth as a living language in Israel.

Perhaps Shammas's intimacy with Hebrew is a nightmare to Ozick simply because she considers it a foreign intrusion into Jewish symbolic space. But it is also possible that his knowledge of the language threatens to expose its use as a carrier of dispossession, expulsion, torture, and murder. By not applying the possibility of *tikkun* to Jews *and* Palestinians where it is really needed and by denying the Hebrew language to those who already possess it, Fackenheim and Ozick seek a sensibility that can no longer be maintained.

Clearly part of the problem relates to the public and empowered quality of Jewish life that these thinkers either deny or pass over. Though they affirm empowerment as a necessity, they do little in the way of grappling with the consequences of that empowerment.

If Jews are displacing Palestinians, then the violation of ordinary decency is part of that displacement. Hebrew as the language of a Jewish state will be involved in all that the state does. Rabin's order to expel Palestinians from Lod and Ramle and Begin's congratulatory message on the news of the massacre at Deir Yassin were in the Hebrew language, as were the interrogations and tortures of Palestinians during their uprising more than forty years later.

In the camps that held Palestinians, these prisoners often mocked their captors in Hebrew, advising them of the transformation of a language that carried an exilic people through suffering and now had participated in exiling another people. In turn, as Ari Shavit reports, Jewish soldiers guarding these prisoners often referred to themselves in Nazi jargon, as carrying out an *aktion* or as serving so many days in the reserve as to merit promotion to a senior *Gestapo* official.[4]

At one level this seems a massive confusion, Hebrew being used as a language of the occupier, Palestinians mocking their captors in Hebrew, and Israeli soldiers seeing themselves as Nazis. Thinkers like Fackenheim and Ozick seek to straighten out this confusion or, if possible, hide it from view.

Though resistance to this transformation is understandable and has engendered much discussion, the power of its articulation is its intuitive nature. The symbolic universe of the Jewish people is inverted because of the history that is being created. While Fackenheim and Ozick seek to deflect or explain away what is actually occurring, the transformation is articulated by those experiencing it.

The present is found here in that transformation, more complicated and more vulgar, to be sure, without innocence and redemption, and with others who have experienced the linguistic and symbolic universe of Jews as a carrier of their oppression.

Perhaps this transformation also represents the future, as Be'er indicated in his remarks to Ozick. A history has already developed among Jews in Israel, among Jews and Palestinians within Israel, and between Jews and Palestinians across the boundaries of Israel and Palestine. An ancient landscape has evolved into a contemporary one, with disparate elements of early and modern civilizations confronting one another, sometimes fusing into a new configuration.

That configuration is as yet unnamed, burdened as it is with suffering and oppression. Tradition seeks to confine the new to definitions already in place, just as history pressures for a new sensibility. Still, the struggle of birthing a new reality is accompanied by a death that many refuse to accept. For in this birth, Jews and Palestinians, Israel and Palestine, have been changed in great measure. Returning to the past is a mirage, and holding the evolving configuration to the Holocaust or historic Palestine is impossible.

Jewish thought and religion that attempt to hold and mold the present in the context of the past will succeed only when the present is genuinely premised on the past. The Orthodox, for example, see their piety in returning to the Western Wall in Jerusalem. They do so, however, in such a vastly different context that the messianic promise of the diaspora is transformed almost beyond recognition. In their view, of course, the ancient promise is simply re-embraced, the messianic now protected by sophisticated military prowess. The biblical injunction to take the land is enforced by the military, and because of this strength the end times are approaching.

But can a contemporary community actually embrace the conquest of Palestine as a fulfillment of the divine commandment without turning its back on developments within Judaism over two millennia, its own journey of thought and suffering within that time, and changes within the thought patterns and religiosity of other religions as well? Though the time is much shorter in relation to the Holocaust, the attempt to mold the entire history of the state of Israel forever in that context also covers over developments in Jewish life and the world during the last century.

In the condition of suffering, the liturgy of destruction is haunting, a devastating critique of unjust power and genocide. When mobilized for empowerment, when it seeks to hide the injustice perpetrated by the same people, then it becomes something else, a liturgy of empowerment and sometimes a liturgy of retribution.

What does it mean when Fackenheim writes about the chasm that opened in the Holocaust yet refuses to acknowledge the chasm opened by the birth of Israel? Or when Ozick, who thinks and writes in English, accuses a writer in Hebrew, who received this "sacred language" through the conquest of his own people, of invasion and perdition? One wonders if the threat that Shammas poses is the sterilization of the Jewish symbolic universe or intimate knowledge of the culpability of the Jewish people.

The memory of Auschwitz held forth by Fackenheim and Ozick as *the* defining element of Jewish life becomes an orthodoxy practiced at its own Wailing Wall. It is an unacknowledged displacement and empowered affluence that creates the context for the prayer and theology which can be seen by the conquered only as a violation of the *tikkun* of ordinary decency, a thick wall of scandal surrounding the covenant.

As Ari Shavit pointed out on Gaza Beach and in Qana, the Holocaust and the covenant ring hollow and are inverted when they are articulated in the face of the conquered. This disparate insistence of their articulation is found in the distance between the past and the present. The obligation that Shavit realizes in the cries of the tortured is the break that renders the continuity of the messianic and the Holocaust impossible to assume.

The Seventh Jewish Culture

Continuity, like memory, is problematic, for it distorts as often as it illuminates the journey of a people. The designation *Jew* invokes a continuity, and the tradition into which Jews are born and which they learn carries that continuity forth. Paradoxically, myth and history reinforce and contradict each other, for the assumption of a lineage in symbolic, religious, cultural, and linguistic terms is both true and false.

Jew has meant similar and different things in different epochs and in different geographic and cultural milieus. An isolated sense of what is known as "the Jewish tradition" denies the borrowings and the changes from other cultures and then is assumed to be intrinsically Jewish, even as it neglects the different cultural and political situations that help determine fluctuations in Jewish affirmation and identity. Tradition is often seen as uniform, but it can also be seen as a succession of winners and losers, where the latest winner redefines the tradition without announcing the victory.

The call for Jewish unity is heard within a framework that often has just emerged. The substance of the call, however, has depth only in its appeal to the most ancient of Jewish motifs. For example, calls for the Holocaust and Israel to become central to Jewish life were made in the dialectic of past and present. The attempt to annihilate the Jewish people and the subsequent birth of a modern state could be seen as a radically different situation for Jews. Yet, if responded to properly and with the right symbolic and religious language, they could cement the fragile continuity of the people. Such a continuity is asserted within the context of the Sinai covenant even as that covenant is found wanting; the additional covenant and the 614th commandment, in some ways radical departures from the tradition, are in fact expressed within the tradition and dependent on it.

Why seek a covenant and new commandment at all as a response to the situation if not to appeal to an unbroken lineage of symbol and culture? The very shattering of the tablets begs their reconstruction.

For those interested in establishing a continuity, the struggle is ongoing. Holocaust theology and Zionist ideology constitute an ongoing struggle to establish their understandings as the authentic heirs of the long line of Jewish tradition. Shammas is a "nightmare" because his knowledge of Hebrew and how it has been used is intimate to him, while likewise representative of a larger event that has introduced new elements into the tensions of a tradition already fragile and under assault.

Recognition that the Palestinians are victims of the twinning of the Holocaust and Israel confronts this sensibility with questions it is not prepared to and cannot answer within its own framework without acknowledging its decline. Instead of confronting the issue by critically addressing the complaints of the people who suffer from it, Jewish thinkers often attempt to silence or denigrate the complaints. Continuity takes precedence over the fractures that are suggested by the cries of the suffering.

If the future of Jewish life cannot be built around Sinai (as if the Holocaust had not occurred), and if it cannot be built around innocence and redemption (as if Israel had not displaced the Palestinians from their land), what then will help provide the foundation for Jewish life? The exilic Jewish community is dispersed and often inarticulate regarding the foundations of Jewish life. At the same time, Palestinians are seen as distant and other by a majority of Jews. It is almost impossible to envision a future without Sinai, the Holocaust, or Israel as center, and Jews in exile seem destined to be lost to Jewish history. When Jewish culture and life are seen only in a linear sequence, the bifurcation of Jewish life can only widen.

Commentators on the Jewish experience either seek to fashion a unity where less and less exists, or they speculate about the divisions of the Jewish world purely in terms of divergent political and sociocultural interests. As early as 1964, the French sociologist Georges Friedmann speculated that the formation of Israel and the "Israelization" of Jews within the state was already leading to the formation of a new people. In Friedmann's view, this formative event of statehood will override theologies and ideologies that seek to create a unity where individual and collective experiences diverge so radically. The unity of the Jewish people, Friedmann writes, is a "pragmatic concept that to some is part of a mystique deriving from a messianic vision and to others is a plank in a political platform for buttressing the state." Attempts at maintaining unity can be considered to some extent "rearguard" actions, holding back a future that is already evolving.[5]

Friedmann's study was published before the 1967 war and the surge of unified support for the state of Israel. Yet, his sociological work raised questions about asserting the concept of Jewish peoplehood, questions subsequently banished by Holocaust theologians. The rearguard that Friedmann spoke about was an Orthodox religiosity as yet unmobilized. After the war, Orthodox religiosity was mobilized and nationalized in a thoroughly modern way as was Holocaust theology, which appealed to sections of the Orthodox community and to Jews on the path of secularization. A unity was fashioned around concern for fellow Jews and an emotional connection to Jewish history and destiny, in short, a point of mutually acceptable identification without demands for a unity in lifestyle or geography.

By 1990 David Vital, an Israeli and historian of Zionism, warned that this identification was falling apart and that the split of the Jewish people into two separate peoples was a distinct possibility. The reasons that Vital cited were similar to Friedmann's: Jews in America and Jews in Israel are living two separate lives, and the demands of the Jewish state cannot be understood by Jews living within states where they are a minority. Vital writes that the longer the tension and instability between these two experiences lasts, the greater is the likelihood that two Jewish peoples will emerge: "One here, one there; one largely middle-class and Euro-American, scattered in ever smaller packets, highly differentiated, part-time in its Jewish involvements; the other largely proletarian and Euro-Mediterranean, relatively compact, bound together ever more strongly by language, culture, political and military institutions, and, of course, immediate circumstances."[6]

It is likely that this separation will continue to grow. The danger and triumph of the 1967 war that overcame this divergence and that seemed to invalidate Friedmann's analysis was temporary. Vital sees the only prospect of bridging this gap in a future misfortune, something on the order of a massive military defeat or an increase of anti-Semitism to a level akin to Europe in the 1930s. Both scenarios are unlikely and are for Vital "intolerable" solutions to the crisis.

Even in such a situation, the possibility of mobilizing the Jewish people is unlikely; it would mean a collapse of the Euro-American or Israeli community and therefore a final narrowing of the Jewish people. Survival would take place within a ghetto-like framework without appeal to the tradition itself, for the additional covenant of memory and solidarity would be shattered as the original covenant was in the Holocaust. It is a situation from which no reconstruction could occur.[7]

Vital presents the problem of this separation in the form of a dilemma. The dilemma is the "hidden flaw" of nationalism in Jewish life, where the expectation of a great national revival of Jewish life has been frustrated. Paradoxically, the flaw does not lie in an inability to recreate a national life after a diaspora existence of 2,000 years. Nor is it found in the opposition of Palestinians or others to the establishment of Israel. Rather the flaw is the unwillingness of so many Jews to physically join the enterprise of nation building. Aside from political and financial support, Jews in Europe and America have chosen to continue their lives outside of Israel. Vital does not mention the fact that many Israelis live permanently outside Israel, reversing the hoped for return and creating another diaspora community within the context of Jewish empowerment.

As do many Zionists, Vital ponders this "flaw" with confusion and sadness. A unique opportunity is being lost to solve the question of Jewish suffering and revival that has plagued the Jewish people for millennia. The prospects for division of the Jewish people in Europe/America and Israel are doubly problematic, for not only are Jews passing up a historic and perhaps unique opportunity for the solidification of nationhood, Jewish prospects for a future in modern Christian Western civilization are bleak.

European Jewish communities are too small to sustain "full societies of thinking and creative people of distinctive (and necessarily alien) culture." American Jewry is much larger and more vigorous, but without direction, lacking central, all-embracing Jewish institutions, inculcating a superficial veneer of Jewishness, and facing the forces of assimilation in loss of distinctive Jewish culture, language, and intermarriage. Vital finds the American diaspora ill-fated and concludes somberly: "Today, at the end of the unspeakable twentieth century, it is not too much to say that the survival of Jewry as a discrete people, its various branches bound to each other by common ties of culture, responsibility and loyalty, is entirely in doubt."[8]

Vital suggests that the task before Jews is to account for and explore the reasons behind the "waning of the Jewish nation." As with Yosef Yerushalmi, Vital sees the situation of the Jewish people in the context of bifurcation. Though Yerushalmi concentrates his analysis on the relation between myth and history, while Vital focuses cultural and demographic trends, both see the center, which should provide coherence and a sense of unity, as fragmenting. Only a new configuration can rescue this unity.

Still both are silent on the future as it slips toward an unknown destination. Ozick and Fackenheim seek to deny this fragmentation through an insistence that Yerushalmi and Vital are unable to assert. It is as if the decentering of Jewish life recognized by Yerushalmi and Vital is a struggle that Fackenheim and Ozick take on as an ontological battle. The struggle is historical, political, cultural, and theological. In different ways and with different emphasis, through analysis and an over-determined insistence, the consensus is that the battle is being lost.

The "rearguard action" that Friedmann surfaces is therefore not confined to the Orthodox, as is often charged. And the situation cannot be seen within the struggle between the religious and the secular, as is often pictured. Nor can it be confined to the competing opinions of conservative and liberal, as the debate about Israeli policies has often been defined. All are attempting to influence the present situation as their opportunity to define the future of the Jewish people, to define the center, as it were, as a place of unity.

To claim this unity within the tradition is to assert a continuity with the center that is more and more elusive. The center as an engine of unity is being claimed by competing interests even as it dissolves. This may account for the raised voices, the anger that accuses and makes Jews with different perspectives an "other." The argument increases in tone and fervor as there is less and less to argue about or as the possibility of resolving the issues fades.

Although it seems that the decentering of the tradition and the consequent loss of unity is the issue, the reality is more complex. An ancient tradition has a variety of centers, and unity is achieved when one of those centers reemerges in a different context or when a new center arrives unexpectedly. Either, of course, constitutes a reconfiguration of elements in the history and tradition of a people responding to new realities. Therefore the assertion of old and new, orthodox and innovation, is illusory.

Still, the defining unity remains elusive, for it is difficult to define unity or how it is demonstrated and maintained. Is unity asserted within the designation Jew? Does the synagogue service or do certain secular proclivities define unity? Is this a myth without history, a theological category that is not demonstrable sociologically? And how is unity defined within the context of the covenant or nationhood, or are both of these categories irrelevant?

Efraim Shmueli, a historian of Jewish culture, defines unity within the context of Jewish culture or, more accurately, within the context of Jewish cultures. The covenant and nationhood find their definitions within different Jewish cultures that evolve over time and provide a center during their ascendancy. This center in turn helps define the culture: unity is found to the degree that various Jewish communities see that culture as their own and thereby ascend to the center that the culture proposes.

In Jewish history, Shmueli finds seven Jewish cultures that have helped establish a unity and a center for the Jewish people: Biblical, Talmudic, Poetic-Philosophic, Mystical, Rabbinic, Emancipation, and National-Israeli. Though his listing establishes a rough chronology, Shmueli is careful to point out that each culture is not delimited by a specific time-period, though their birth and ascendancy can be roughly outlined. Rather, Shmueli sees these cultures as constantly invading each other's domain, as "vanguards, rearguards, or as rivals."[9]

At the same time, those who advance the importance of a particular Jewish culture feel their culture to be essential and to differ from other cultures in fundamental ways. As Shmueli writes: "The cultures diverged over the most decisive and momentous issues, over life-styles and articles of faith. Each culture perceived itself as a new revelation of God's truth, bestowing a new comprehension of divine providence and of human and societal conduct (an insight its members denied, of course, to the antecedent cultures)." The disagreements are indeed significant and Shmueli lists ten general areas which illustrate the nature of that divergence. Among others, they include the nature of human happiness, definition of sin, attitude toward death, the giving of the Torah at Sinai, idea of redemption, and the character and mission of the Jewish people.

Though the cultures differ in fundamental respects, the superordinating concepts are common—God, Torah, Israel—as are the archetypal collective experiences—exodus, covenant, exile and destruction, expectations of the messiah. What differs is the meaning attached to these concepts and experiences. These differences have political ramifications as they influence the organization of Jewish life.

In each Jewish culture there arise disputes over what these concepts and experiences mean and how they are to be organized into a coherent system "capable of exerting control in all spheres of life." According to Shmueli, each system of cultures creates its own language of images, concepts, and symbols, a language that clearly defines it over against the previous culture.

Contrary to expectations, the language of one culture is not necessarily understood by the next. Shmueli uses the example of the biblical culture, which would barely comprehend the meaning of the images and symbols used by the Talmudic or Mystical cultures. Shmueli's point is important: "The thinking of a people within a historical culture is circumscribed by the imagery it employs; only within the range of the imagery can terms be used meaningfully. In each new culture a certain set of experiences had a decisive impact upon the imagery and conduct which became unique to that particular culture. The central new experiences were articulated in an innovative terminology, new images, reinvigorated symbols."[10]

If each new culture sees itself as a revelation, it also attempts to organize Jewish life around this revelation. According to Shmueli, each new culture is accompanied by an "exuberant outburst of creativity and enthusiasm, a marveling at the miracle of innovation and an intense zeal." Perhaps this is because each culture sees itself as possessing the way of transforming an uncertain world into an understandable and significant order.

As culture is a set of shared symbols that attempts to express the meaning of individual and collective life, then a sense of purpose and zeal in the creation of a new culture is to be expected. Paradoxically, and perhaps out of necessity, each new Jewish culture sees the culture it is competing with as outdated, at the same time claiming a connection with the original culture. In this sense, a new cultures must "slay" the culture it seeks to surpass, even as it claims a continuity within the tradition. New cultures mask their innovation, and the struggle for cultural hegemony is often fought in the context of an orthodoxy that itself is a series of succeeding cultures. For Shmueli, the search for orthodoxy is couched in the language of return but actually represents an innovation: the idea of a continuous, linear tradition that posits an essence of Judaism or Jewish life is a fallacy. Shmueli is adamant on the subject of the essence of Judaism: "There is no principle of unity which would illuminate the true essence of Judaism as the ultimate synthesis, once and for all." In Jerusalem, Babylonia, Cordoba, and Krakow, Jews constructed and reflected on their experiences in different ways; the commonalities are in the most general characteristics that hide the particular expressions of Jewish culture, which vary widely.[11]

Still, the particularity of each Jewish culture is limited in that these various cultures share superordinating concepts and archetypal experiences. Shmueli also argues that they share three important tensions: between nationalism and universalism, between the Jewish individual and the collectivity, and between the elements constituting a culture—land, language, religion, state, contemporary life, and hopes for the future. Furthermore, the Jewish cultures that Shmueli identifies do not cease to exist when a new culture appears as the organizing principle of the community.

Aspects of the culture continue in the common life of the people, while superordinating concepts and archetypal experiences are open to various interpretations. Even as the center is redefined, a symbolic and material negotiation is at work. New cultural elites appear, often trained by the previous elites. New institutions that translate the insurgent meanings into an organized center often use the old elites and their institutions as a sign of legitimacy and as a bridge to the future.

In short, the new comes out of the old, and residues of the old mingle with the new. As more cultures come into being, the layering of Jewish life becomes more complex. Though Shmueli is correct about the succession of cultures posing the questions of unity and essence, he also understands that the old cultures do not disappear. Yet, the demarcation is clear: Jews in the Rabbinic period and in the National-Israeli period, for example, have less in common than Jewish historians and theologians usually assert.[12]

What, then, are Jews left with? Shmueli subverts the idea of a linear continuity and specific essence to Judaism and Jewish life, while at the same time affirming a continuity in symbolic landscape and struggles of affirmation to Jews across cultures. A dialectical understanding emerges that involves a choice in viewing Jewish history in the present. Shmueli acknowledges this as a choice between a sense of Jewish history as a series of discontinuities and ruptures or as creative continuity, stressing the need for contemporary Judaism to "enrich itself with the many insights and experiences legated by past generations."

This creative continuity is found within the newest Jewish culture, the National-Israeli culture, that Shmueli sees as the creative force for Jews in the present. For Shmueli, this culture is a "new, surprising, and creative breakthrough," announcing a renewal of Jewish life with "innovative assumptions and unique ontology." The establishment of the state represents a breach more complete and more vigorous than with any previous Jewish culture and that is why Shmueli sees a need for an adjustment and a harmonization, a creative interpretation and integration that will allow the various sectors of Jewish life to catch up with this massive change.[13]

Shmueli published his understandings about Jewish cultures and contemporary Jewish life in 1970, just three years after the 1967 war. He died in June 1988 as the Palestinian uprising reached its peak. Though his son, in a biographical note to the English translation of his father's work, notes that Shmueli favored a territorial compromise or partition of the land between Jews and Palestinians, the discussion of the National-Israeli culture takes place with little reference to Palestinians or to the surrounding Middle Eastern cultures.

Throughout his discourse on Jewish cultures, Shmueli is aware of the dialectical tension between continuity and discontinuity and the fact that Jewish culture is an amalgam of internal development and a sharing with other cultures. Because of this, Shmueli does not argue the uniqueness of Jewish life or its essence. Instead he analyzes the different configurations that Jewish cultures have attained; adaptation to different circumstances and cultural contexts are, for Shmueli, the creative dimension of Jewish history. If there is such a thing as uniqueness, it resides in the category of creative adaptation, maintaining, at one and the same time, the superordinating concepts and archetypal experiences, while being open to the possibility and creativity of other cultures.

Yet, despite this analysis and the tensions that he identifies as accompanying these cultures and that force an internal reckoning *vis-à-vis* the cultures around Jews, Shmueli analyzes the breach and continuity of the National-Israeli culture only with reference to Euro-American Jewry. The national and Israeli trajectory of Jewish life is a response to the failure of the Rabbinic and Emancipation cultures to provide the organizing principles for the Jewish people; the revolutionary leap of national determination comes from this failure and rests securely in its answer to it.[14]

There is no sense in Shmueli that, while the seventh Jewish culture may in fact be a response to the situation in Europe, its ontology might evolve beyond its phase of response. That is, Shmueli is unable to contemplate a National-Israeli culture expanding beyond a European cultural configuration and assuming a dialectical life of continuity and discontinuity with its immediate predecessors.

But if the National-Israeli culture is indeed the organizing force of contemporary Jewish life, and if this culture maintains the superordinating concepts, archetypal experiences, and fundamental tensions that accompany all Jewish cultures, why will this culture be immune to its immediate circumstances and geography? And if immediate circumstances and geography are seen as mobilizing forces for protection and internal development, should they not also be seen as places for creative encounter and expansion of this seventh Jewish culture?

A period of adjustment and harmonization with past Jewish cultures is important, but that can hardly take place creatively without adjustment and harmonization with the cultures that are part of the future. To stop with the past or only to see the present within the past is to opt for an understanding of Jewish history that Shmueli rightly criticizes. In fact adjustment and harmonization may only be the first step toward that truly radical departure which Shmueli characterizes the National-Israeli culture to be.

Shmueli's work was translated into English in 1990, the same year that David Vital published his analysis of the division of the Jewish people. In twenty years, the celebration of the birth of a new Jewish culture had turned to an analysis of the divisive effects of that culture. The period of adjustment and harmonization that Shmueli hoped for was derailed by the very assertion of the ontology of that culture, the processes of settling, determining, and expanding the boundaries of Israel. The inward sense of connection was emphasized as the external connection with the surrounding cultures was minimized. Or, more accurately stated, the internal European sensibility within Israel was cultivated as the surrounding cultures were declared alien and threatening.

Because of this strict division between internal and external in Israel, the National-Israeli culture assumes an unexpected continuity with previous Jewish cultures, perhaps the one continuity most feared. That is, the National-Israeli culture takes in its Middle Eastern isolation an almost ghetto-like reality, the fundamental difference being that this Jewish ghetto is an empowered one.

Clearly, the sense of the National-Israeli culture as a revolutionary break with previous Jewish cultures is exaggerated by Shmueli, even as he misidentifies the internal characteristics of that culture which might bring it to maturity. In fact, within the Jewish community in Israel is a significant minority, some even speculate a majority, of Jews whose culture is Jewish and North African or Arab. They are underrepresented in Shmueli's description of previous Jewish cultures as they remain virtually invisible in his description of National-Israeli culture. Though their history of interaction in North Africa and the Arab world is complex, these Jews provide a natural bridge to the geographic and cultural location of Israel.

Both Shmueli and Vital neglect this piece of the National-Israeli culture and for good reason: as the number of North African and Arab Jews increased in the early years of the state, the culture they brought with them was denigrated by the European establishment in Israel. The challenge was thought to be the elevation of their cultural status by inculcating in them Western values and sensibilities and thereby ensuring unity within the new Israeli culture. Paradoxically, this unity was based on a European model in a Middle Eastern world, in a sense opting for a linear continuity with previous European Jewish cultures over a creative adaptation and innovation of these distinct Jewish cultures in a new environment. The truly revolutionary break of creating a European/North African/Arab Jewish culture in contact with and within the context of an Arab and Muslim world was never seriously contemplated by the founders of Israel or Jewish intellectuals like Shmueli and Vital.

Ammiel Alcalay, himself a product of this Jewish North African/Arab culture, sees the National-Israeli culture as wanting on this crucial point. From his perspective, this new Jewish culture is not only built on a European model that disparages his own culture, but the force of the National-Israeli culture also fragments the world he grew up in and ultimately led to its destruction in its geographic locality.

The settling of North African and Arab Jews in Israel is for Alcalay a dispossession, an exile, which is furthered within Israel. As the National-Israeli culture developed in continuity with European Jewish culture, the diversity and strength of the North African and Arab Jewish cultures was denigrated and stripped from them. Thus a second dispossession and exile occurred within the cultural configuration that sought to organize contemporary Jewish life. The superordinating concepts and archetypal experiences were seen through the history of European Jewish culture rather than that of Eastern or Oriental Jewish culture, which Alcalay names Levantine culture.[15]

This analysis complicates the emergence of a seventh Jewish culture, and even the division between Euro-American and Israeli communities, as the central drama of contemporary Jewish life. European Jews in the diaspora are uprooted in the Holocaust. They are seen as foreign to Europe by those who dispossess them but in fact have been European for more than a thousand years. The isolation of Jews in Europe, culminating in the Holocaust, leads to Zionism, which seeks a home and state for dispossessed Jews. The idea is that those Jews native to Europe who are also seen as foreigners will one day become native to the land from which they were dispersed two millennia ago. Yet in their yearning to be native to a particular geographic place, they dispossess Palestinian Arabs from their native soil and disrupt the native lives of Jews in the Middle East.

As Alcalay understands it, from the earliest European Jewish settlers in Palestine, the world of the Arabs, Muslim and Jewish, is submerged in European imagery: "Haifa, Jaffa, the Arabs, and even the Arab Jews simply became a backdrop for superimposed images from another world: the Cossacks, Poles, and Russians of the Ukraine." The world of the native, of Muslim and Jewish Levantine culture, is either ignored or seen as hostile. Jews fleeing their native European geography in search of a secure native land view the natives of Levantine culture as foreign and threatening. National-Israeli culture ultimately projects its own isolation and foreignness on the other, rendering them homeless in their own native culture and geography.[16]

Alcalay suggests the remaking of Levantine culture as a way for Jews of North African and Arab descent to recover their own heritage and reorient themselves in present-day Israel. He also proposes a larger project by which the sense of isolation that European Jews experienced in Europe and now experience in Israel may be mitigated. Here Alcalay proposes that Holocaust reflections and Israeli literature become articulate on this aspect of the hitherto hidden ontology of National-Israeli culture. By mapping out the space of Levantine culture where Jews were and still are native to the geography and culture, the same place and culture where the National-Israeli culture makes its home, the sense of isolation may decrease.

The need continually to assert that European Jews are not strangers in the Middle East betrays an estrangement that displaces a culture in recreating its own. What Alcalay surfaces is that the displacement of Palestinian Arabs is only the most obvious displacement in the creation of Israel. The National-Israeli culture is a culture of disruption, by which displaced European Jews displaced Jews of North African and Arab lands and the Levantine culture that forms their lives. Though fragmented, Levantine culture exists alongside the European culture in Israel and has a mission beyond its own reclamation. By reiterating a space where Jews were at home, the possibility of such a world existing in the future is envisioned.[17]

In this sense, even the homeland visions of Judah Magnes, Martin Buber, and Hannah Arendt are seen as distinctly Western in emphasis and scope. The Jews of North African and Arab background were at home in the Middle East, and the coming of European Jews, even within the homeland vision, was a sign of uprootedness that might have been mitigated by those of Levantine culture. Fleeing Europe, Jews of the Levantine were as invisible to those who sought a homeland as they were to those who established the state.

This is another of Alcalay's insights; Zionism and National-Israeli culture represent an internal struggle over the definition of what it means to be Jewish and the culture that will emerge following the failure of Jewish emancipation and the attempted annihilation of the European Jews—*from a European perspective*. This internal dispute is of interest to Jews of Levantine culture only insofar as it seals their fate and makes them strangers in their geographic and cultural space. They remain, however, the bridge from the isolation of what they might term the European-Israeli culture that has developed in the state of Israel.

It is Alcalay's view that those belonging to Levantine culture can be an internal *and* external bridge, broadening the national debate and shifting the perspectives of Israel in relation to the Arab world. Those within Israel who are native to the Middle East can cross internal and external boundaries and, in so doing, change the psychological and cultural landscape of the seventh Jewish culture.

As the landscape changes, so do categories of interpretation: the ontology of the National-Israeli culture, frozen in its European limitations, is challenged to include Jews of the Levantine as part of its own central core. The dialectical tension of National-Israeli culture is thus expanded considerably, as is the possibility for its growth.

As a mature culture, the challenge is to integrate West *and* East, being the stranger *and* the native, participating in dividing Jews *and* aspiring to Jewish unity, seeking to undo the separation of Jews and Palestinians and thus address a large part of the Jewish population joined by culture, language, and history to the culture that Palestinians embody.

With Ammiel Alcalay, the challenge of creative continuity is broadened. Alcalay's challenge is to recover a past where Jews were native, "not a stranger but an absolute inhabitant of time and place." He proposes to create a new Levantine culture by recreating the symbolic and linguistic world of North African and Arab Jews within Israel. By recreating the memory of a lost world, the possibility of its reappearance within a new configuration is enhanced. If there is a European sensibility within the state, so too is there the sensibility of Alexandria and Baghdad.

A Fatal Embrace

Yet, to recreate this world, the connections between Levantine culture within Israel and the broader Levantine culture outside Israel must be reestablished. Euro-Israeli culture has strong ties to the West and sees itself as part of the Western world. That is why the National-Israeli culture is an extension of European Jewish history. To continue and nourish Levantine culture among Jews necessitates a similar tie to the world from which it originated, the world designated as enemy by the National-Israeli culture. It means reimagining and reestablishing the connections between the cities of Damascus, Jerusalem, Cairo, and Beirut before the division of the Middle East by the colonial powers and before the establishment of Israel.

This requires above all a crossing of state boundaries in the search for a native space and the broad contours of the Arab world, which could support the rebirth of Levantine culture among Jews. From this vantage point, Alcalay sees the 1967 war quite differently than Elie Wiesel: not as a response to the Holocaust but rather as a continuing assault on the Arab world and its culture. For Wiesel, the 1967 war held out the presence of God to those who had suffered terribly in the European Holocaust. For Alcalay, the war allowed a renewed contact with those of Levantine culture, opening the frontiers of Israel so that Jews and non-Jews of the same culture could become aware of each other's plight. Though the interaction was often of a military type, the need for Arabic in commerce and translation increased tremendously. Paradoxically, it is through military occupation that the significance and possibility of Levantine culture comes into view.[18]

As David Vital informs us of the division of the Jewish people, it is now clear that he is speaking of the division of European culture into a Euro-American and National-Israeli culture. With Alcalay, the National-Israeli culture is likewise fragmented into two cultures in Israel, the Euro-Israeli and the Levantine-Israeli. The former tends toward the West and experiences a tremendous anxiety if Europe or America is tentative or threatens to separate from it. Geographically located in the Middle

East, its heart lies somewhere else. The latter culture tends toward its native lands in the North African and Arab world yet lives in a recently created state that has defined itself over against their home and culture. Levantine culture is fragmented further by its pull toward and away from Israel: on the one hand, Israel is its only realistic place of life today and, on the other hand, Israel frustrates the longing for its own symbolic and material landscape.

With Alcalay's analysis, the fragmentation of Jewish life becomes more complex, and bifurcation as defined by Yerushalmi and Vital is hardly sufficient to describe the situation. Further, the diversity within the Euro-American, National-Israeli, and Levantine cultures makes the definition of a contemporary Jewish culture seem almost impossible. Can representatives of these various cultures, people like Wiesel, Ari Shavit, Cynthia Ozick, Emil Fackenheim, Shmueli, Vital, and Alcalay, be understood within a singular cultural configuration?

The difficulty in the present is only compounded with additional figures from the past. Where do Buber, Magnes, and Arendt fit in? Or for that matter, Irena Klepfisz and Anton Shammas? Even this listing is limited, as it leaves out the various and diverse Orthodox religious and settler movements, as well as the political actors like Yitzhak Rabin, Simon Peres, Ariel Sharon, and Benjamin Netanyahu. Where do Baruch Goldstein and Yigal Amir belong in this definitional structure? Since they are so much a part of the discourse and policy consideration and implementation, where do the Palestinians fit in? Are they the unannounced shadow of all these cultures, the other that is invisible *and* present, distant *and* intimate?

As it turns out, diversity is perhaps the foundational element of contemporary Jewish life, and the seventh Jewish culture is one of many Jewish cultures that flourish today. The organization, within which these diverse cultures find themselves living, is Euro-American and National-Israeli, but this tells us as much about the power of ideology and theology linked with institutions and the state as it does about the life of these cultures in their own spheres. Both the Euro-American and National-Israeli cultures flourish within the confines of the European, American, and Israeli states and do so because of intellectual and material links with those states.

Shmueli correctly points out that the definition of these cultures is dependent upon their articulation of the superordinating concepts and archetypal experiences, but it also has to do with the manner by which these definitions reflect and serve the state in which they exist. Those cultures, or aspects of them that do not serve the primary articulation of the dominant culture or the state, are relegated to a subordinate status. They may even be defined as outside the culture that organizes contemporary Jewish life. Are those parts of Jewish life not mobilized in support of the state, or even in opposition to it, to be excommunicated from the contemporary understanding of what it means to be Jewish?

It may be that looking to define Jewish culture in a linear or creative continuity, or even the breakdown of cultures according to geographic, linguistic, and religious categories, is itself an attempt to create a simplified conceptual pattern where diversity and complexity exist. Even the definitions of *Jew, Jewish,* or *Jewish people* may be constructs that hide as much diversity as they explain.

Introduction of modern historical and cultural analysis places a burden on these definitions that closer scrutiny may not allow. At the same time, the advent of the state as crucial to the definition of Jewish culture further complicates the situation. For can there be a national definition of the Jewish people within a state that represents a majority of Jews on matters of the utmost importance to the definitional concepts of Jewish culture? Or can it only mobilize certain sensibilities within Jewish culture for a limited amount of time, thereby introducing a destabilizing element into Jewish life as it seeks to unify an essentially decentralized, sometimes complementing, sometimes conflicting, series of cultural configurations?

Jewish culture and its relations with the state are complicated. Over the last 700 years, Jews have been instrumental in the construction of important states in the Mediterranean and Atlantic worlds. In many cases, Jews were crucial in developing and staffing institutions of administration and coercion that mobilized and strengthened political and economic elites in their struggle to fashion a new order. Jews were important in these areas in part because they maintained a separate culture and because of the international connections gained from a diaspora existence.

This importance was also balanced by a periodic need for protection from those who were displaced and defeated by those very same states. Thus the Jewish community often helped to build, suffered within, and sought protection from the state. For Benjamin Ginsberg, the relationship of Jews and the state over the last centuries has been paradoxical and dangerous: the state has represented to Jews both opportunity and safety, but it has also been the chief catalyst for anti-Semitism. That is why Ginsberg refers to this relationship as a fatal embrace, a need and a danger that continue to this day.[19]

Ginsberg sees a continuity of relationship between Jews and the state. While the history of this relationship is primarily found in Europe and its colonial outreach, it continues today in the United States. To most the relationship seems quite different, moving from a fragile dependency in Europe to an empowered independence in the United

States. But Ginsberg warns that as a minority in a non-Jewish culture, the situation of American Jews is quite similar to diaspora Jews in general; the flourishing of Jewish life in the United States parallels past periods in other countries where Jewish life flourished, only to suffer the ignominy of persecution and expulsion.

What Ginsberg introduces here is the possibility that America for Jews is similar to what it was for their counterparts in Europe. Europe serves as a warning for Jews in America, as the embrace of the state can be lucrative and fatal. His counsel, though not explicit, is to steer a middle ground between being seen as outside the state or completely tied to it. Despite the rhetoric of a sea change in the Jewish situation after the Holocaust, the Jewish situation seems to have remained the same: a minority culture in a world that can be alternately accepting and threatening.

Ginsberg's analysis of Israel is in relation to the situation of Jews in America, and here his caution is similar to Vital's. The more visible Jews are in support of Israel, the more vulnerable they become to attacks that cite a special relationship between the Jewish community and the American state. Vital sees public support of Israel as one of the areas in which a division is occurring between Jews in America and Israel, not because moral support itself is waning but because the interests of the Jewish community in America are internal rather than external.

Jewish support for Israel in America is tied to its own interests in status and influence within America rather than to the actual needs of Israel. As symbolism and concrete needs diverge, the communities drift apart. Ginsberg warns that the day will come when pressure within America will make it necessary for Jews to fight their own battle to survive in a changing environment. That might make it necessary to mitigate or even withdraw support for Israel.[20]

Yet Ginsberg neglects the other side of this equation, namely the Jewish embrace of the state of Israel. The fact that Jews are a majority within the state and that their symbolism provides the foundational aspects of that state is a revolutionary change in Jewish history. In Shmueli's understanding this fact is part of the ontology of National-Israeli culture. Yet parts of the old dependency exist, an example being Israel's dependence on the United States for military and economic aid. It has also been dependent on a narrative in the West cognizant of the special place of Jews in Western civilization and religion.

Christianity is crucial here, as Christian liberal and conservative support for Israel comes from a confessional acknowledgment of historic Christian anti-Semitism in Europe and the centrality of the Hebrew Scriptures in the founding of Christianity. Israel is beneficiary of an often fatal embrace in the West, for the shadow side of state and religious philosemitism in the present is the anti-Semitism of the past. If the embrace of the states that Jews have served and by which they have been persecuted is inherently unstable, so too is the embrace of the religion that Jews helped found and whose recent recognition of its own sins has led to strong support for the state of the Jews, Israel.

If this external embrace of Israel has been absolutely crucial to the founding and continuance of Israel *and* to the advance and identity of Jews in America, then both Euro-American and National-Israeli culture continue a tradition of dependence on the state. The difference is that Jews are now also dependent on their own state as an engine of identity and survival, or rather they are dependent on a dependent state. The embrace is twofold, on others and on themselves, a dependence and interdependence for which Jews and non-Jews carry an equal weight and responsibility.

This configuration is as complex as previous configurations in Jewish history, and, while the military power of Israel adds a dimension of security previously missing, the stakes are even higher than in most periods of Jewish history. The Euro-American and National-Israeli cultures that embrace the state represent the two largest concentrations of Jewish population in the post-Holocaust and Israel era. With the Holocaust and the birth of Israel, the diaspora populations of Europe, North Africa, and the Arab worlds have dwindled to insignificance.

Today more than two-thirds of the Jewish population lives in America and Israel. In essence, the safety-valve of the diaspora has disappeared as the concentration of Jewish population has increased. Therefore the Euro-American and National-Israeli cultures carry a burden of responsibility rarely known in the last 2,000 years of Jewish history. Amid the celebration of America and Israel lies a profound and unsettling anxiety, an anxiety that, along with the other, is another hidden ontological element of contemporary Jewish cultures.

Monumental Anxieties

If the other is both internal and external to the dominant contemporary Jewish cultures, so too is the anxiety revolving around the narratives and states that protect Jews. External pressure is most obvious, as the memory of persecution by Christians and the states that Jews have been dependent upon is embedded in the archetypal experiences of the Jewish people. The Holocaust event presents this anxiety in its most extreme form, and remembrance of the event has become a cornerstone of Jewish and Western life.

The very monuments erected throughout the Western world, especially the United States Holocaust Memorial Museum in Washington,
D.C., mirror this anxiety. The museum in Washington in the heart of the
capital of the most powerful country in the world is a testimony to Jewish suffering. In a culture where Jews have faced minimal discrimination
and where they have reached the pinnacle of success, the monument
chosen by Jews in this community is one of incredible suffering experienced in Europe.

As important as the choice of suffering to be the defining element of
Jewish life, is the narrative of that suffering found within the Holocaust
museum. The factual description of the history of anti-Semitism and the
brutalities of the Nazi period is followed by the release from suffering
and the hope that such an event will never happen again.

The end of the narrative is the freedom enshrined in America and the
promises of equality and citizenship contained in the Constitution and
the Bill of Rights. Touched upon but hardly emphasized is the refusal of
the United States to admit Jewish refugees during the Nazi period and
the refusal of the military to bomb the railroad tracks to death camps
such as Auschwitz.

So, too, the role of Christianity in laying the groundwork of anti-
Semitism and its failure during the Holocaust to oppose the policies of
the Nazi regime in any substantive way are missing. Since most of the
visitors to the museum are American and Christian, and since the purpose of the museum is to initiate non-Jews into the suffering of the Jews
rather than a critical evaluation of American and Christian culture,
downplaying these themes is understandable. The idea is for visitors to
affirm Jewish suffering and, therefore, the special situation of the Jewish
people, and to be able to affirm their country and religion.

Rather than critique or separation, the message of the Holocaust
memorial is one of broadening the non-Jews' parameters of cultural
inclusion. The reason for this inclusion is not Jewish contributions to
European and American civilization or even the special mission of the
Jewish people; rather it is the enormity of Jewish suffering in Europe. In
a peculiar transposition, by broadening the parameters of inclusion with
regard to Jews, America and American Christians demonstrate their distinctiveness and their mission.[21]

The Holocaust museum is an appeal to the non-Jewish surroundings
for protection and special privilege narrated by a suffering that is deeply
embedded in Western and Christian culture. America and American
Christian culture demonstrate their exceptionality by rejecting anti-
Semitism. Even Israel is relegated to a peripheral status with regard to the
Holocaust narrative and the redemptive aspects of American freedom
and Christian repentance. Standing on donated land in the center of the

capital of the United States, dependent on continued government funding for its financing, and visited by millions of Christians every year, it is difficult to subvert the identity of either the secular or religious sponsors of the museum.

Thus the Jewish narrative of suffering must logically present itself within the larger and more powerful narrative that has created a space for this Jewish exhibition. Such a place would not be donated and maintained if Jews and Jewish culture were seen as fundamentally undermining the basic consensus of Americans and Christianity. This embrace of the United States and Christianity in the Holocaust museum is the culmination of a long struggle by which the Euro-American Jewish culture has demonstrated its loyalty to both, and where even the dissenting Jewish voices have been muted, excommunicated, or, in critical analysis, transformed into voices that impel America and Christianity to their higher calling.

Yad Vashem in Jerusalem is likewise complex in its symbolism and message. Like the museum in Washington, its relation to the state is assumed, yet National-Israeli culture took time in embracing the Holocaust as central to its existence. While the reality of the Holocaust is deeply embedded in Israeli life, the early post-Holocaust years were spent trying to distance the new and vibrant society from what was often considered the shameful experience of mass death. A main reason for Zionism was to end this history of weakness and dependence and to emerge as a nation able to defend itself.

This was the focus of the Zionist revolution; the diaspora mentality and the suffering that came with it were things of the past. The Holocaust, as a reminder of this weakness, should best be forgotten. A new age in Jewish history had dawned and divided the history of the Jewish people into a "before" and "after." The "after" in National-Israeli culture defined Jews as reborn in another form, the *sabra* whose interior sensitivity was hidden by an exterior of strength and force. The people of the Book were now the people of Land and Power.

Still the contradictions remained. By the early 1960s, David Ben-Gurion decided that the memory of the Holocaust was important to link generations of Jews within Israel with Jews outside the state. The decision was multifaceted and revolutionary in Zionist understandings, for it proposed a renewed connection with diaspora Jews who refused to emigrate to Israel, thus recognizing, in a halting and ambivalent way, the ongoing validity of diaspora life.

The first step was taken toward recognizing the Holocaust as central to National-Israeli culture at the same time that it was being recognized by Euro-American Jewish culture. This recognition was more than a grudging admission that the diaspora would continue. Rather, it was a political recognition of the strength of the diaspora and the fact that Western Jewish support for Israel revolved around its sense that Israel was a response to the Holocaust and a possible refuge if European and American Jewry were ever again in need of rescue.

While Israel saw itself as the center of the Jewish world, European and American Jewry thought the same of themselves. For Ben-Gurion the bridge to the West was significant enough to allow both cultures to assert their centrality. In his mind at least, Israel would inevitably win the battle of Jewish cultures, for history would prove the diaspora to be ill-fated both because of continuing anti-Semitism and the dynamism of Israel. Both factors would ultimately lure the best and brightest Jews to Zion.[22]

Even more important, however, were the ties Ben-Gurion coveted with the non-Jewish West. In the Cold War alignment of powers, the decision was made to court Europe and America, since Israel modeled itself on a Western-style democracy and the Western narrative was favorable to Jews and Jewish interests. Since Israel had no natural resources vital to the economies or security of the West, protection of Israel's national security had to be based on other considerations. Additionally, Israel had to compete with the geopolitical and strategic value of Arab proximity to the Soviet Union and Arab oil.

The United States, which had asserted its primacy over Europe after the war, had to be persuaded that a Western outpost in the Middle East outweighed the loss of Arab resources and support or at least that it could maintain a balanced relationship with Israel and the Arab countries. Because Arab resources far outweighed those of Israel in terms of strategic importance, the debt owed to the Jewish people because of the Holocaust could tip the balance in Israel's favor. Strategic concerns were to be balanced by moral values. The Holocaust became the link between the Euro-American and National-Israeli cultures in the context of two states, America and Israel.

The centrality of the Holocaust was confirmed by Jewish reaction to the 1967 war, but the introduction of the Holocaust as central to Israeli life itself occurred with the trial of Adolph Eichmann in Jerusalem in 1961. The kidnapping of Eichmann in Argentina and his trial in Jerusalem were dramatic in the extreme: the trial of a major war criminal against the Jewish people by an empowered Jewish government was part of the accomplishment of Zionism. Though Eichmann could have been tried in Germany or in other European states for his crimes, the choice of Israel was significant. Yet while it demonstrated the maturation of Jewish self-determination and empowerment, it also became quite controversial among Jews around the world.

Many issues were involved, among them the crossing of national boundaries to apprehend and prosecute a Nazi war criminal, but the internal controversy surrounding Eichmann revolved around the nature of his crimes. Was his participation in genocide a crime against the Jewish people or against humanity, of which Jews are one part?

The technicalities are many, but the main issue was whether the particularity or the universality of the crime should be emphasized. Was the lesson of the Holocaust that never again should Jews be subject to mass death or that never again should humanity be subject to mass death? Was the assault against the history and body of the Jews, or were the crimes against Jewish people an essential assault against the history and body of humanity?[23]

The distinction may be a fine one, and perhaps the attempt to annihilate the Jews was an assault on the history and body of the Jewish people *and* humanity, so that particularity and universality are equally defining. But the decision by the court and by Jewish commentators that Eichmann's crimes were against the Jewish people had a decisive effect on Jewish culture and its involvement in the affairs of state, whether in Europe, America, or Israel. That the particularity of suffering during World War II was seen through the prism of the attempted destruction of the Jewish people focused the way Jews and non-Jews viewed contemporary Jewish life.

Because of this focus, political, military, economic, and cultural support for the state of Israel proceeded along lines different than for any other nation-state, and opposition to that state or its policies was also judged in a different light. Strategic concerns were seen within the context of a moral commitment. Those who opposed Israel as an ever-expanding settler state, including Palestinians displaced by its expansion, were viewed as denying or even seeking to destroy the moral imperative of Jewish survival.

From this moment on, Jewish Euro-American and National-Israeli culture were mobilized by virtue of the Holocaust. Yet, in so doing, elements of both cultures were submerged. In Israel, as the memory of the Holocaust grew in significance, the intermingling of strategic and moral sensibilities blurred the edges of both, even as it smoothed the rough edges of Israeli history. For where was the Palestinian Jewish community during the Holocaust? Did it prioritize the suffering of the Jews in Europe, mobilizing the entire society to do what it could do to save the vanishing millions? Or was the suffering of the Jews in Europe used to justify Zionist ideology?

The questions continue: Did the annihilation of the Jews in Europe take second seat to the building of the Jewish state, and were the plans for Jewish rescue skewed toward the young and committed who, in coming to Palestine, would be able to help build the state? Was there a form of ideological and material triage practiced by the Jews of Palestine in relation to the Jews of Europe? In short, were Jews in Palestine culpable in some of the ways that Europeans have been found culpable, through apathy, silence, and even at times, perhaps indirectly, complicity?

The involvement of Israel in defining the Holocaust as a crime against the Jewish people limited these questions, and the trial of Eichmann directed them outside the community. One wonders if the memory of the Holocaust could have assumed its immense proportions without somehow trying to discipline its shadow side, where the place of rescue functioned within its own needs and parameters rather than mobilized every resource to combat the evil of the Holocaust.

Perhaps the most obvious difficulty with Yad Vashem is internal to Israel and foundational to the birth of the state. There is no need to equate the Holocaust with the displacement of the Palestinians to realize the connection between the erection of the memorial and the end of Palestine. The memorial itself is within eyesight of Deir Yassin, and the foundation stone of Yad Vashem was laid even as the Jewish settlers renamed Deir Yassin, Givat Shaul Bet. Included among those settlers were survivors of the Holocaust. Moreover, Yad Vashem is situated next to the national cemetery where Israel's ideological founder, Theodore Herzl, lies, and thus was conceived as part of the infrastructure of the newborn state.

A new civil religion emerged as part of the foundation of the National-Israeli culture. Though in the beginning Yad Vashem played but a small part in the foundation of that culture, its meaning was clear: National-Israeli culture would never allow such an event to happen to Jews again. Yet the structure and the memory enshrined in the memorial make no mention of Deir Yassin or the Palestinian catastrophe.

Like most memorials to the dead, Yad Vashem stands commemorating a history of suffering without mentioning those who suffered in the settlement of the state that sponsors the memorial. In fact, a monument within Yad Vashem commemorates the heroism of the Jewish resistors against the Nazis and bonds them with the fighters in Israel's armed forces. Called the "Pillar of Heroism," and bearing the inscription in Hebrew that stands for martyrs, immigrants, and fighters, the monument seeks to unite past fighters of the ghetto with current Israeli soldiers. Built after the Yom Kippur War in 1973, it was dedicated by Yitzhak Arad, former partisan fighter and chief education officer of the Israeli army.[24]

Over the years a further element has entered into Yad Vashem as the memorial has become a site of pilgrimage and, to some extent, a tourist attraction. Pilgrimages and tourism have flourished as the Holocaust has become more prominent and, though this is a difficult term to apply to it, popular.

Today Yad Vashem is placed on personal and group itineraries with individual and packaged tours. The most prominent of the pilgrimages is the March of the Living, in which European and American youngsters travel to Auschwitz and then to Israel, enacting the journey from death to redemption that is the narrative of Holocaust theology.

This has led some Israeli thinkers to point out that in these pilgrimages the Holocaust *and* Israel are both mythicized and trivialized. The children of the affluent are flown to Poland and Israel to visit a past and avoid the complexities of the present for the purpose of identity formation as Jews. The Holocaust is linked to an Israel that exists in the imagination of the youngsters, and the difficult realities of the past and the present are lost, perhaps are irrelevant, to youth searching for identity. Organizers of these tours are determined to inculcate a mythic understanding of Jewish history as the only viable avenue to a positive sense of Jewish identity.

There is also the reverse pilgrimage, that of Israeli students being flown to Poland and then coming home with a renewed sense of the purpose of Israel. As youngsters growing up in Israel, there is an assumption of normal life, but the idea of the tour is to present Israeli youth with Auschwitz so as to remind them of the world they escaped. The point is to demonstrate that their normality is shadowed by the past—Holocaust—and the present—Palestinians and the Arab world. The danger from which they come is the danger to which they may return.

A reversal of Zionist understandings is involved here as the radical break from the diaspora and its suffering is transformed into a radical dependency on the Holocaust as the anchor of Jewish identity in Israel. Students are dressed in uniforms created especially for their pilgrimage to Auschwitz: a sweatshirt of bright purple with a Star of David and the word "Israel" in Roman letters on the back. Walking in formation and waving Israeli flags to demonstrate that there is life after the death camps, the students display themselves in the Polish cities they visit.

Israelis freeze Poland in the Holocaust as they freeze their own history of just emerging from the Holocaust. Jewish youth are thereby freed from a critical evaluation of contemporary Polish *and* Israeli life. The search for roots is in a past which no longer exists. Later, after the visit to Auschwitz, many of the students dance in the discos with Polish youngsters. Moods of despair and pride are released during the day; the pursuits of youth are taken up once again in the evening.

These journeys of American and Israeli youth are laden with symbols and emotion combining in a bizarre way a union of kitsch and death. The student groups are referred to as delegations; the booklet distributed to them states that Poland supports self-determination for the

Palestinians and Palestinian terrorist organizations, as if these two were one and the same thing. "The students were not told that the right of self-determination is a universal right of every nation," Tom Segev, an Israeli historian, writes. "Again and again the students were warned that the Holocaust meant that they must stay in Israel. They were not warned that the Holocaust requires them to strengthen democracy, fight racism, defend minorities and civil rights, and to refuse to obey illegal orders."

For Segev, the journey to Auschwitz "exudes isolationism, to the point of xenophobia, rather than openness and love of humanity." Emphasizing the particular suffering of the Jews within the context of an empowered state, the wrong lessons were being gleaned from the tragedy of the Nazi period. The lesson of the Holocaust, at least for Segev, is to embark on a deeply critical encounter with the past and the present, raising questions about suffering and its relation to state power, especially when it is wielded in an abusive manner by those who sponsor pilgrimages to Auschwitz.[25]

Jewish Culture and the State

The kitsch found at Auschwitz is a response to the use of the Holocaust by the Euro-American and National-Israeli cultures in league with the American and Israeli state. Trivialization is inherent in this situation: the Holocaust is used to mobilize the young who grow up in an environment distant from the event. The complexity and void of the present are avoided, at least until the emotion wears off and the students experience their everyday lives again. Ordinary life in both cultures is deemed insufficiently Jewish or incapable of inculcating the ontology of these cultures to its youth.

Only through a movement outside ordinary life can the culture be experienced. The living culture is judged to be moving toward superficiality and vulgarization, but can anything, at least in Segev's mind, be more superficial and vulgar than these tours to Auschwitz and Yad Vashem? Is there a fear that the dancing of young Israelis and Poles in the discos of Poland might lead to the same dancing of Israelis and Palestinians in Jerusalem? Even more, the fear is that facing contemporary Jewish history might encourage a recognition of the shadow sides of the Euro-American and National-Israeli cultures and thus lead to the emergence of a new ontology or even a new Jewish culture.

The fatal embrace Ginsberg analyzes is now extended, for the desired protection and advancement within the United States and the empowerment and expansion of the state of Israel necessitate a series of deals that strike at the foundation of Jewish identity and culture. The danger

Ginsberg surfaces, that the protection of the state—in this case the United States—might be undermined and transformed into a persecution by that same state, is also extended in a different way to the case of Israel. Because a Jewish state, like any other state, functions within parameters of self-interest and power aggrandizement, depending on the circumstances, it may or may not comport itself with the deeper resonance of Jewish history and culture.

In fact, just as Jewish culture is skewed to function and advance in a non-Jewish state, so, too, a Jewish state attempts to manipulate Jewish theology and culture to its own purposes. The distortions of history and the present seem to be inherent in such deals with the state, and, over time, it becomes difficult to distinguish where the culture and state are independent and where they join. Blurring the lines of culture and the state, it becomes more and more difficult to judge where affirmation is possible and where dissent is mandatory, even as the stakes of both are raised because of the connection with state power.

The Holocaust memorials in Washington and Jerusalem illustrate this point because of their location and function. Their existence and relevance have as much to do with power as they do with memory. The existence of the superordinating concepts and archetypal experiences within the configuration of state power undergirds both to the point where they might be unrecognizable to previous cultures and generations. At the same time, the state and those who articulate the deal between the culture and the state attempt to disguise the differences so that the continuity can be established beyond any doubt or critique.

Though Shmueli sees that every Jewish culture disguises differences with the past to assert its own legitimacy, the power configuration of the Euro-American and National-Israeli cultures accomplish this in a different and more substantive way through the agencies of state power. What is possible now is not only the embrace of concepts and experiences, which mean different things to different Jewish cultures, but the reversal and even the denigration of those meanings within the safety of a state that pretends to be innocent even in its culpability. That is, the challenge of the new configuration to the old, traditionally carried out in a struggle of ideas and interpretations, can now be carried out on the military battlefields of Lebanon and Palestine.

When ideas are in service to the state, the military often establishes the terrain for the discussion. The memory of suffering, including the Holocaust, becomes a way of mobilizing support for state policies that, if examined from a distance, would be judged reprehensible and contrary to the foundational elements of Jewish culture.

Once in place, the culture's connection to the state is also difficult to break. Just as the interplay between culture and state blurs over time, the status and advancement that come with this connection are difficult to renounce. This difficulty is compounded as dissent is characterized by the state as disloyalty or even treason. The penalties can be substantial, from demotion in class and influence to relegation to the status of the underclass or even expulsion. Furthermore, alliance with the state means that those within Jewish culture who benefit most from that alliance are reluctant to sacrifice their advantages for moral and ethical reasons. A split occurs within the culture between those who fight for the alliance and those who seek freedom from it.

A civil war between Jews can erupt, one side embracing the state, the other opposing it. In Israel the stakes are raised to such a level that an oppositional stance raises the possibility that the entire enterprise may come tumbling down, exposing the population to hardship or decimation. Though decisions about a Jewish alliance with the state are considerably less earth-shaking in their possible effects within America, the importance of such decisions as they affects Israel is difficult to overstate. The pressure for an alliance with the American state is therefore made less on its internal merits than on its significance to the Jewish community in Israel.

Decisions by Jewish leadership with regard to American involvement in the Vietnam war and even the civil war in Nicaragua are made within a cautionary scenario: how far and for how long can the Jewish community dissent to American foreign policy if that policy is crucial to support for Israel?

On the domestic scene, one wonders how much the decisions to question affirmative action policies and other civil rights causes reflect a reckoning with Jewish tradition and the concepts and experiences of Euro-American Jewish culture and how much they have to do simply with identification with the power that can elevate or demote Jewish status and position in the larger society.

Emerging from a series of emergency situations in Europe and Israel in the 1940s, this tie with state power is understandable. The alternative of being outside or on the underside of the state has been experienced in a devastating way. For many Jews, the building of state power in Israel and the bonding to state power in the United States were difficult, sometimes traumatic progressions. The "realism" called for was disorienting for many Jews, and the transformation of Jewish culture in America and Israel to accommodate this reorientation continues today in a problematic way.

Perhaps this is the reason that contemporary Jewish theology rarely deals with the complexities and culpability of power and dwells, instead, on the suffering and innocence of the Jewish people. Traveling to

Auschwitz and recalling the horror there may, in a strange twist, be easier to deal with than the torture of a Palestinian witnessed by Shavit at the Gaza Beach detention center.

The most difficult aspect of this alliance with the state is that, once it is made and the emergency has ended, a psychological and material dependency continues. The alliance with the state prolongs the emergency and even makes it mandatory. Once mobilized, the Euro-American and National-Israeli cultures exist and gain their energy from the emergency atmosphere. Therefore, emergencies keep arising, especially when the possibility of normalcy appears.

It is paradoxical that as Jews have become more and more settled in America and Israel, and, as the situation of the Jews around the world has become so distant from the Holocaust that tours are necessary to remind youth of that event, the state of emergency, at least in psychological terms, has increased. The ability to defend Jews in Israel and project its power as a dominant force in the Middle East is so different than the defenseless reality of European Jews during the Nazi period that comparison is almost impossible. Yet Holocaust theology continues to see the next holocaust around the corner, and Israeli victories are seen in the context of the miraculous rather than as manifest military prowess.

Perhaps this is the same reason why Jewish youth are brought to Auschwitz at a time when Jews are creating a continuing state of emergency for another people. The perpetual state of emergency may function to mobilize Jews to identify themselves as Jews out of fear that there are no other compelling reasons for such identification. At the same time, however, questions of the consequences of such a perpetual emergency situation are deflected. In this way, the emergency functions to mobilize and deny aspects of contemporary life that contradict the mobilization and its ideological veneer of innocence and redemption.

That is why the re-education of Jewish soldiers was necessary in Yitzhak Rabin's order to expel the Palestinians from Lod and Ramle, and why it is necessary in the Marches of the Living in America and Israel more than fifty years after the European catastrophe. The fear is that, with the emergency behind us and knowledge of the emergency that Jews are causing today to Palestinians before us, contemporary Jewish cultures cannot come to some understanding of both facts. How can Jews create a path where both are apprehended in their depth and significance?

CHAPTER SIX

Toward a New Sinai

The ambiguities of Jewish culture, allied with and compromised by state power, have clouded fundamental imperatives of Jewish identity today. Legitimated by a narrative of Jewish innocence and suffering, "Jewish-state culture" threatens to blind Jews to the suffering around them.

Since the Holocaust, and with responsibilities of state power assumed since then, many Jews feel that solidarity with others who are struggling for justice around the world entails a risk. Yet could these struggles become a central concern, the 615th commandment, as it were, of Jewish life?

Leaving behind the limitations and power of the emerging Jewish-state culture involves a wager many Jews are unwilling to make. For what if that wager, what if the 615th commandment—to be in solidarity with all struggling peoples, including and especially the Palestinian people—is lost? What if the interests of those suffering from injustice are contrary to the interests of the United States, Europe, and Israel?

Secure within the West, few responsible Jewish leaders will help sway Jews to side with peoples and nations who, if empowered, will surely have the same propensities toward injustice and abuse of power as are found in the history of the United States and Israel. Will the situation simply be reversed, so that Jews, once secure in the West, will now seek security in a newly empowered state configuration?

As Jews know only too well, the best is not always achieved, and solidarity with struggling peoples might be forgotten or misunderstood. Depending on the new configuration, Jewish particularity might be rejected or overemphasized. A desire for the disappearance of the Jews as a community might be enforced as a way toward a new universality or as a repeat of European anti-Semitism.

The dilemma here is almost impenetrable. Forecasting a future for the Jewish people is a game of mirrors. It involves constant revisiting of the past, doing everything in the present to keep the past from recurring, while anticipating the recurrence of the past as the *raison d'être* for Jewish life. Embracing the state is justified to keep the past from recurring, even as the possible recurrence of the past is ideologically and theologically essential for that embrace. Therefore a genuine future, emergent from the past that is also free to develop beyond it, is feared as the enemy of the Jewish people. Any person, group, or culture that proposes and embodies a real future is ostracized or banished.

The very focus of the Jewish-state culture is to stifle the future. Thus the exilic Jewish community, the Levantine Jewish culture, the past and present voices of dissent, are seen as ornamental and, at the same time, declared outside. Those Jews who dissent are externally hammered by the power of those who fear the future and are internally conflicted by the fear that a future may, in fact, contain the dangers warned against.

For how can that fear be absent after the history of Jewish suffering and with the almost compulsive memorialization of that suffering in monuments and discourse? When the rhetoric and emotion of both sides are stripped away, fear is the one element they have in common. It is difficult, if not impossible, to reconfigure Jewish culture, to move toward a future when proponents of and opposition to the status quo both fear the future.

The result of this dilemma is that Jewish life is adrift as the embrace of the state deepens. The negotiated surrender of those who carry the diaspora and homeland visions is discussed in terms that are, in the final analysis, peripheral to the larger issues that constitute the true emergency of contemporary Jewish life. It is not bifurcation, superficiality, or vulgarization, nor is it the division of the Euro-American and National-Israeli cultures that constitutes the emergency but, perhaps, the inevitable and irreversible bond between Jewish life and culture and the American and Israeli states. That bond places an anxiety at the very heart of Jewish life that makes creation of a future in the broken middle difficult, if not impossible, to imagine. This anxiety comprises fear for survival and fear for the culpability inherent in this return into history. Fear for survival dictates the path of "normalization"; fear of culpability calls forth the path of refusal and the search for a restoration of the ordinary within the complexities of the present.

Here we are left with the question of fidelity, for if the choice is for the normative, status, and affluence, an affluent security if you will, then there is essentially no choice. The culture in the making is the place for that "success." But as Efraim Shmueli reminds us, "every person lives between the opposing poles that characterize his culture," and surely that leaves a place for choice even when the community is moving in another direction. The choice of exile, always with the knowledge of belonging to a larger culture and history to which one is bound even in dissent, and the articulation of that choice for the sake of that culture and that history cannot eliminate the ambiguity of Jewish life on the threshold of the twenty-first century.[1]

Nor can it assure a continuity to that history or offer solace to those who have been and are being displaced by that history. Indeed, the opposing poles are within every Jew, and thus the choice is more painful and more necessary because a fundamental choice is possible. That the poles are common relieves one of a sense of isolation and ensures that the choice is never seen as esoteric or privileged or as an elevation above other Jews who make different choices. The choice of dissent cannot relieve a person or a group of the culpability of the culture and history, despite the fact that many decisions are made by the few who comprise the Jewish elite.

Fidelity is the task of understanding and, within the context of contemporary Jewish life, pursuing a path leading to a future beyond the fatal embrace of the state. That this fidelity can only be pursued within that embrace is part of the historical moment. Yet, knowing that others in the past as well as many in the present have chosen this path of fidelity means that the choice is personal *and* collective, a choice that comes from other Jewish cultures and, to some extent, continues to exist.

The continuity of dissent—which also purposes an alternative future—is alive through Jews who choose that path. When and if that path could ever become the norm is another question. The question itself involves one of strategy and cunning, two necessary ingredients to any political struggle, but the question can also overwhelm the path and, in the end, those in power and those in dissent may be different only in the rhetoric they employ. Being bound together then takes on a sense of inevitability with neither escape nor solace.

To be sure, fidelity is a bond that proposes a freedom to direct all efforts to the present. But to whom or what are we bound? And what does freedom mean? Do the bond and the freedom come within a particular Jewish culture? Are the superordinating concepts and archetypal experiences, foundational to being bound and free, to be interpreted solely within contemporary Jewish cultures? Is the question of fidelity, then, to be solely defined within the present?

Clearly a variety of Jewish cultures exist alongside one another. Are there possible paths of fidelity to be found within these cultures, or are they simply subsumed by the dominant Euro-American and National-Israeli cultures? Is being faithful within any of these cultural constructs simply a quiescent and ornamental assent to the emerging Jewish-state culture?

Analyzing the paths chosen within each culture, historically and in the present, may provide a possible anchor for the question of fidelity facing Jews today. Here a sense of depth to Jewish history arises, one beyond an assertion of linear continuity or constant change. The super-ordinating concepts and archetypal experiences, interpreted by each culture in the context of its time, are the points of reference for Jewish fidelity. They become more powerful as they are seen as orienting pos-sibilities, directional pointers that anchor the search for fidelity in the present. Shmueli surfaces the dialectics of Jewish life within each culture and person and posits an interaction with these concepts and experi-ences. The result of this interaction is unpredictable as layer upon layer of Jewish history is discovered, exposed, and renewed. This allows Jews to hear in Ari Shavit's lament the voice of Isaiah.

Whose voice was heard by the men who initially refused Rabin's orders to exile the Palestinians from Lod and Ramle? Will their voices be heard along with Ari Shavit's one day in the future? Are these voices, heard in their own time in their own language, also the voice of Isaiah? And could these voices, announced and unannounced, be the voice of conscience that comes from the covenant and from God?

The continuity of Jewish history might then be seen as the continu-al search for the missing commandments so that the covenant and the people of the covenant do no consort with injustice. The tendency is just the opposite, and the cultural, theological, and ideological pull toward a dominant cultural system, which defines Jewish belief and often gravitates toward power and injustice, lives in permanent fear of these missing commandments. For when they are found, the force for their implementation is anchored in another history, a subversive his-tory of the search for the missing commandments. This history tran-scends a specific cultural configuration even as it is found within each one of them. Creative continuity as analyzed by Shmueli is the search for adjustment and harmonization; it is thus reinterpreted as the search for the missing commandment in each Jewish culture. This search is the defining point of fidelity and the orientation for the paths that open to a future.

This subversive continuity is anchored in the past, provides a path in the present, and looks toward a future when the missing command-ments will be found and instituted. Yet while the missing command-ments await the future for their implementation, they are also found within the present in the pursuit itself. By finding the commandments, those on the path place them before the community as *the* fundamental choices to be made within in their context and their culture. By pursuing this path even when the community turns its back, the choice still remains before the community. It is a haunting reminder of the deeper contours of Jewish life, a subversive continuity that can be neglected and even silenced for years, only to reemerge.

Perhaps it is the search for the missing commandments that provides the superordinating concepts and archetypal experiences with their depth and possibility. Within history these concepts and experiences become fuel for a future of justice and peace rather than a justification for domination and exploitation. Perhaps this search for the missing commandments advises us that the Jewish return into history has violated the *tikkun* of ordinary decency, or rather, that to retain its own validity, that *tikkun* must be expanded to include those who have been displaced by Jewish empowerment.

Clearly, the missing commandments cannot be found in isolation or solely in an internal dialogue among Jews. Though internal dialogue is crucial, the search within the contemporary Jewish world for the missing commandments after Auschwitz and the birth of the state of Israel has yielded a prophetic critique without effective implementation. Those who seek this path have referred to the plight of the Palestinians with regard to Jewish morality and innocence and sometimes within the context of the covenant. The reference, however, has been internal and the Palestinians have remained other. The prophetic critique has been self-referential rather than inclusive: the particularity of Jewish history and Jewish destiny have been emphasized so that those who are suffering are peripheral actors, subordinate to the claims of Jews.

The internal discussion has been conducted between those in power and those who criticize the use of that power with the same main reference point, Jewish history and the Jewish future. The possibility of inclusion, even expansion, of the subject is a risk, almost declared off limits. The terrain is already mapped, and only those who assent to the terrain are allowed in the discussion.

Those who suggest that the terrain may shift, indeed, because of the history between Jews and Palestinians—*it has already shifted*—are outside of the debate and will be condemned by both groups. For, after this history of power and criticism, it is clear that the internal Jewish debate has suffered from limitations that have paralyzed the Jewish world and increased Jewish culpability in injustice over the years. Is this because the internal Jewish debate is conducted on ground that has disappeared? *It could be that the covenant itself, so often discussed in religious and secular terms, has fled the scene and with it the possibility of finding the missing commandments.*[2]

Dominant contemporary Jewish cultures therefore are celebrated, even as the terrain from which they come and from which they draw sustenance disappears. The emerging Jewish-state culture seeks a continuity with the Euro-American and National-Israeli cultures, indeed with all of Jewish history, as the foundational substance of Jewish life is lost. The bifurcation, vulgarization, and superficiality of Jewish life has less to do with the loss of Jewish ethnicity, language, religion, and knowledge than it does with the loss of the covenantal grounding that lends depth to Jewish life. This covenantal grounding is related to education, communal living, and religion, but it also involves the behavior of the people: at some point the use of power to secure Jewish life that also destroys another peoples' life becomes a scandal that can no longer be debated within the covenant. Therefore the debate ostensibly about the covenant occurs outside the covenant, as the covenantal framework for such a debate no longer exists. Seeking to define the covenant in a way that makes less and less sense, the covenant reemerges in a context where a new encounter and discussion can begin. The covenant rejects consorting with injustice and, at the same time, seeks to find a place of justice.

At some point, power and its critics form a bond of mutual need and reinforcement, compelling the covenant to consort with injustice, or, perhaps better stated, they reach a dead end of debate. They form a circle from which there is no way out save for a way so frightening that a need for each other is established. As the reference point shifts, the mutual need intensifies. Beyond the discussion is a looming void; at least for the participants, what lies ahead is only bifurcation, vulgarization, and superficiality.

Though frightening initially, the void is also the place of challenge and possibility. Indeed, what is seen to be the void is often simply unrecognizable within the parameters of acceptable discourse. On closer inspection, the void is paradoxically replete with life. Coming from a previously defined perspective, this life is confusing and unordered. There is a history here as well; awaiting definition is the deepest point of contemporary life unrecognized by the very actors who have created that history.

The fear and lack of recognition are understandable because at some juncture of history a new configuration is forming that moves beyond what has previously been known. The unknown is already being created and has a reality which will ultimately demand recognition. But since it is beyond the known, it is feared and pushed away. At one level, it is simply the struggle of one culture to maintain its hegemony over the competition of cultures yet to come, as if the continuity it represents is threatened. At another level, the fear is one of foreign influences that may introduce a radical discontinuity into Jewish life that threatens the entire structure of Jewish history. The Jewish return into history might then be the end of Jewish history.

Yet this is exactly the risk of empowerment and statehood, that is, the creation of historical events that radically change the context of Jewish life. The structures and cultures that contained and maintained Jewish life for almost 2,000 years have been altered by contemporary events and by responses to them. While the Holocaust concentrated Jewish energies toward survival and rebuilding, the state of Israel has ultimately dispersed these energies in its expansion and dislocation of the Palestinian people.

The Holocaust refocused Jewish attention to the covenant even in the questioning of it; empowerment has displaced the covenant itself because the history of the Jewish people has expanded its own territory and culpability. Acted upon, Jews understood the obligation of history, but, as actors in history, Jews misunderstood the consequences of that action. In both the Holocaust and Israel, a new history emerged with alarming speed. Though it is difficult to lay blame for the lack of vision that resulted in the almost consecutive formative events in Jewish history—the Holocaust, the emergence of Israel, and the displacement of the Palestinian people—the consequences remain.

The Time Is Now

By the time the whirlwind of recent Jewish history settles, when a distance from these formative events in Jewish life is gained, it may be too late. The question of fidelity in the Jewish-state culture will be so limited, so saturated with culpability, and so distant from the voice of Isaiah, that the consequences of fidelity will almost be nil.

If this happens, the act of fidelity will appear to other Jews as a spectacular and courageous act or one of madness, but one that hardly could become normative. The very exceptionality of fidelity will be a sign that the hour is past when the ordinary can be restored or even imagined. The question of fidelity that remains vibrant today will be unnoticed tomorrow. In Jewish-state culture, the voices of dissent will be relegated to a periphery less visible than the Palestinians are today. Worse still, Jews who choose this path will be defined as other. They may be seen as the Palestinians of their time.

Yet this is to get ahead of the story, for fidelity can be practiced neither retroactively nor prospectively. The path of fidelity lies always in the present. If the path of fidelity is the search for the missing commandments, which is really the search for the covenant as it manifests itself in the contemporary world, then the search is possible in every era and within every Jewish culture. This search, with its dialectical complexities, inevitable compromises, limitations, and inherent culpability, can in every era lead to the vision of justice and the embrace of the covenant that stands as the origin of the Jewish people and its mission to the world.

For without this embrace, or at least the longing for this embrace, there would be little reason to articulate a special and defining character to the Jewish people. Why form Jewish cultures and agonize over the per-plexing questions of particularity and universality? Why cite ancient Scriptures when discussing political agreements? Why proffer additional commandments? Why create and articulate liturgies of destruction that could be conveniently forgotten? Why cross boundaries to the suffering other when the only response is to be accused of betrayal? Why seek to restore the ordinary and include in the messianic vision of Jerusalem, Hebron, and Ramallah, if not for a longing to find and embrace a covenant so tried in the history of the Jewish people? Why remember Deir Yassin?

That the search takes one outside of the Jewish community to the Palestinians—leads one to the tradition of dissent and Levantine cul-ture, to a confrontation with Jewish state power and the broken middle of Jerusalem, and ultimately to the frightening void where, paradoxical-ly, a new vision, even a new culture awaits—is the legacy of a history both imposed upon and created by Jews. Will this new place of creation be Jewish in the way that we understand the term? Will it see itself in continuity with previous Jewish cultures or battle the Jewish-state cul-ture for the right to define the next stage of Jewish life?

One wonders if there will be the strength and language to articulate a vision to the Jewish people that they will embrace as a healing and a rec-onciliation with the Jewish past and present. Or the embrace of the covenant might be silent and hidden, awaiting a new language and opportunity, seeking fidelity by continuing the search for the missing commandments without a strategy of confrontation.

Perhaps this embrace will be like an unattended martyrdom, lost to the movers of history yet a witness to the possibilities that remain even as they become more distant. Another possibility is that this search will be lost to the Jewish community forever and that the embrace of the covenant will become the seed for the emergence of a new people.

One wonders if this people, coming from diverse histories and seek-ing the path beyond oppression and suffering, will be formed around a new Sinai. The Commanding Voice of Auschwitz *and* Deir Yassin could be calling Jews to a new holy place to re-encounter that most ancient voice, the one voice that called diverse tribes to become a people.

Perhaps we have reached the end of Jewish history as it has been known, recorded, symbolized, and articulated, and the fight to continue it is lost, just as the attempt to claim the covenant as one's own is forever doomed. While being attentive to the past, fidelity searches for the place from which the voice might speak anew, where the commandments that define the present can be found, and where the covenant might be embraced with a freedom and inclusion that startles the religious and the secular alike.

No one knows the history that will emerge from such an embrace or whether it will be recognized tomorrow, if ever. In this sense, Israel and the United States, indeed all states and configurations of power, are to be monitored, confronted, and relativized as the deeper path is pursued. Then the words and visions of Judah Magnes and Ari Shavit, Edward Said and Irena Klepfisz, Anton Shammas and Ammiel Alcalay, will assume a different configuration, a constellation that is familiar and, at the same time, unknown. The limitations of each in their words and vision will remain as they also transcend their place and time. When the struggles of each era come to an end, the judgment of history will be rendered and the call of fidelity will assume a new arena, the next arena where another missing commandment awaits being found. Perhaps another Sinai will appear and, no doubt, in the least expected places.

To be open to this new Sinai is to hear the voices that have accompanied Jewish history and the voices within other histories that speak of the path of fidelity. To hear these voices in the era of Jewish-state culture is to relativize the states of all cultures, including the Jewish state, and to relativize the identity found within all of these cultures, including Jewish identity. For while rooting a person in history and a contemporary context, identity can become a place of paralysis where commitments to a certain community can also distort perspectives.

The torturous arguments in support of Israel made by Jewish progressives over the last decades exemplify this problem. Those Jewish voices that worked toward the end of colonialism, who spoke for the civil rights of African Americans, and who pioneered rights for women and labor—who in the broadest sense championed human rights and an equitable international order—were often silent on Israel when it violated those understandings and rights. Loyalties were divided, and since the principles that underlie these loyalties are tied to Jewish history, the identity of many Jews was split at its core.

In many ways, Holocaust theologians like Elie Wiesel and Emil Fackenheim provided a religious explanation and justification for the priority of Israel over these other principles. It was a way of reducing the cognitive dissonance that Jewish empowerment in Israel introduced into Jewish identity and, at the same time, moved other areas of Jewish commitment into the neoconservative orbit. The priority of Israel necessitated a re-evaluation of other commitments to show the non-Jewish powers supporting Israel that the Jewish community could be counted on. It also created a logical sequence within the Jewish psyche so that the support of Israel would be a reflexive action.

In short, because of loyalty to Jewish identity as Jewish, many of the principles underlying that identity were jettisoned. The difficulty that Holocaust theology had was to justify this shift while convincing the Jewish community that a shift had not really occurred or rather that the world was shifting its sensibilities in an anti-Jewish and anti-Israel bias. That Jews found themselves outside many of the movements they were instrumental in founding encouraged a sense that Jewish particularity was disrespected. The isolation that resulted simply fueled this sensibility that the priority of Israel, while problematic in its founding and in many of its policies, was the only option for Jews. Like Shmueli's seventh Jewish culture, Holocaust theologians convinced Jews that they had chosen the priority of Israel in continuity with their history and identity.

As the world of Holocaust theology becomes less and less persuasive, the way back to these principles is problematic. It is problematic because Jews have lost the language and, to some extent, the right to speak authentically of these principles as central to Jewish life. It is also problematic because in these years of isolation and culpability, Jews have lost their bearings in the movements that have continued, even escalated, their commitment to these principles.

The idea that Jews can regain their bearings and re-enter these communities of struggle from the perspective of an empowerment that displaces another people is an illusion. One reason is that the commitment to empowerment in Israel, at least at this moment, necessitates the embrace of states and their policies that these communities are struggling against. Another reason is that the policies important to Jewish empowerment in Israel cannot be dismissed easily as foreign to the tradition when the entire Jewish establishment claims them as the litmus test for Jewish affiliation.

The only way out is to claim that one is part of the movement of these struggling communities *and* loyal to the Jewish heritage as well. For a Jew to be identified with progressive politics and culture today is to be schizophrenic; it is easier to retreat into a Jewish enclave where both sides of Jewish identity can be articulated with a minimum of dissonance, safe from outside critique.

It is this "safety," with its ambivalence and culpability, that anchors an identity resistant to the future. Here the isolation of the Jewish world and its consequent embrace of the state can only increase. The embrace of the state is the opposite of the embrace of the covenant, for it operates as a holding action against the future, at the same time deflecting the questions of political and social reality that suggest missing commandments.

The schizophrenic situation of Jewish identity is denied, and those who suggest otherwise are themselves deemed schizophrenic.

For who could suggest that Jewish identity itself might be the problem? Could a rational person, committed to the Jewish people, suggest that absolute identification with the mainstream of Jewish life is at the heart of the present predicament? And is not the proper attitude toward the experience at Sinai to believe that there is only one Sinai carried forth by the heirs of those originally present? What can a new Sinai mean, except an experience that takes place outside a Jewish framework, where Jews and non-Jews come together under a new religion and a new God?

Though the future remains to be defined, the prognosis is clear. *As the Jewish-state culture comes to dominate Jewish life, the richness and diversity of Jewish life will continue to decline in its depth, while the covenant resides elsewhere, waiting to be rediscovered.* The path of fidelity will lead many Jews outside and around the community into places that are defined by the mainstream as ill-advised and dangerous.

The struggle that could have been bequeathed to Jews and non-Jews without condition, as a trust for Jews and all of humanity, will continue to dissipate and be betrayed. The Holocaust will recede in consciousness, as will the place of Israel in Jewish history.

What will be remembered is a squandered opportunity; the legacy of Jewish martyrdom and struggle will cease to inform Jews and non-Jews alike about the possibility of God and the challenge of human solidarity. The Jewish path of fidelity, therefore, is precisely to preserve this heritage even as it enters without condition into the present. If it is true that the articulation of the Jewish place in the world is more and more difficult, only by embodying this place—*only by embracing the covenant*—can this witness continue.

In the end, perhaps, Jews have made the same mistake that other cultures and religions have made: to identify God and destiny with a particular set of symbols and experiences that emerged in that history but belong to the broader arc of humanity. In doing so, particularity has lent depth to Jewish experience and, at the same time, narrowed the possibilities of thought and action.

As does any religion and culture, Jewish life has a circular dimension that is both expansive and limiting. Fear of being lost in a broader universality, coupled with a significant empowerment, moves that dialectic of expansiveness and limitations to another level, a level of culpability and emptiness.

Being defeated by and barely surviving the onslaught of a religion that claimed universality and dominated the West for a thousand years has hardly made it easier for Jews to acknowledge the limitations of the circle defining Jewish life. In this sense, Jews are quite right in deflecting Christian critique of Jewish empowerment. For who could blame Jews, especially after the Holocaust, for emulating Christians in their use of power while retaining the claim to innocence?

The isolation of Jews and the internal contradictions inherent in contemporary Jewish life allows Jews to emulate Christian behavior and ideology while denying a similarity between the two communities. At the same time, many Jews conveniently overlook the millions of Christians who are effectively challenging the dominant Christianity by which they were conquered or from which they have benefited. Paradoxically, Jews, as significant and historic critics of Christianity, have emulated that behavior as many Christians have accepted the critique and distanced themselves from that history.

Could it be that those Jews in exile, along with those Jewish cultures that are submerged today, are accompanied by other communities and cultures in exile, including many Christians in the West and those of Third World countries? A new Sinai may be in the making among the most curious and paradoxical of religions and peoples, including historic enemies (such as Jews and Christians) and contemporary enemies (such as Jews and Palestinians).[3]

What would Jewish culture be like if this new Sinai occurred? Would the Jewish people cease to exist? Would Judaism be transformed into a new religion? Would the Holocaust be forgotten? Would Israel cease to exist? Would Jews be exposed to virulent strains of anti-Semitism and threatened with annihilation?

The reverse could be true as well: the Jewish people will exist and flourish in an era of justice and peace, as will a transformed Jewish community in Israel/Palestine. Judaism will continue and will be strengthened in its dialogue with other religions also struggling to come to grips with their own beauty and limitations.

Perhaps a new Jewish culture will come into being that brings to an end Jewish-state culture, which emerged in the difficult years following the Holocaust. Perhaps two archetypal experiences will be added to the foundations of Jewish culture: the experience of dislocating a people *and* the experience of reconciling with a people Jews harmed. Perhaps these archetypal experiences will open the superordinating concepts of God, Torah, and Israel to new interpretations and challenge the Jewish community to a new search for the covenant and its meaning.

Perhaps this will also lead to a vision of reconciliation and inclusion within the Jewish world, thus beginning an internal healing and rebuilding. Then the broken middle of Jerusalem can take on a new coloration, as remembrance of the abuses of power and the difficult path of fidelity take their place within the many layers of historic Jerusalem.

One day Jews and Palestinians will gather at Yad Vashem and Deir Yassin to honor the dead and later, perhaps midway between the memorials, they will celebrate the path that brings life and a new beginning out of the tragic past.

Revolutionary Forgiveness

Today the hope of Isaiah seems distant, almost unrealizable. The memories of the dissenter Martin Buber or even those of David Ben-Gurion, much closer in time and relevance, seem distant as well. Yitzhak Rabin and Simon Peres are likewise distant figures, part of the founding generation whose ideals and sins are forgotten.

The state of Israel has come to a place where even the rhetoric of justice is seen as a sign of weakness, and the possibility of a shared future of justice and peace for Jews and Palestinians is spoken about in memory.

At the same time, a new complication has arisen with the failure of Palestinian leadership to mobilize Palestinian society and institute a democratic and open society. Some Palestinians have equated the Israeli occupation with their own leaders, portraying those Palestinians who have returned from exile as the new occupiers. Corruption and commercial monopolies, political authoritarianism, and police brutality are charged by many.

Though the situation is unequal in power and possibility, clearly the dream of Palestinian empowerment is tempered by its reality. The arguments that have issued from this disappointment are tenacious, sometimes deadly, and, to Jewish ears at least, familiar. Edward Said's criticisms of Palestinian leadership are argumentative in an intellectual way and beyond. There is an anger that shouts betrayal not only in a political sense of choosing the wrong direction but also in the more fundamental sense of betraying an entire people.

It is as if the struggle of Palestinians to create a new society faithful to their suffering has been lost. This is why Said's commentary is so passionate and his call to prepare the next phase of the struggle so clear. For Said, at least, the oppressive qualities of Israel remain in the new settlements that close the ring of settlements around Jerusalem and in the continuing cleansing of Palestinians from East Jerusalem by confiscating Palestinian identity cards, depriving Palestinians of the right to live there.

One wonders if this mutual disappointment, this passionate anger over the betrayal of both histories, will bring dissenting Jews and Palestinians into a new relationship characterized by sorrow and the hope of life within and beyond empowerment. Both Jews and Palestinians come to nation-state building late and under circumstances of distress and catastrophe. In different ways, both are beginning to understand that empowerment, while necessary, is limited and helpful only when the basic elements of life are respected and supported.

Occupation of a land and a people's history, diminution of their prospects for culture and justice, can come in many forms, foreign and internal. There can even be a collaboration between the two forces so that empowerment may become another way of suppressing what was struggled for. Those who realize the need and limitations of empower-ment are thus in a new situation when the oppressor has changed cloth-ing or the new configuration of power limits the possibility of a future worth bequeathing to the next generation. When this situation presents itself, those who recognize the limitations of the present situation must prepare and embody a new vision. Surely the present power arrange-ments mitigate against the deepest values of Jewish and Palestinian cul-tures and traditions. The result is an exilic condition of many Jews and increasing number of Palestinians. Thus the meeting ground of those who worked for peace and justice during the years of the Palestinian uprising, a ground built around mutual recognition and support of a two-state solution, has shifted.

Large areas of Palestinian territory supposed to be ceded to the Pales-tinians within the context of the two-state solution have passed to Israeli sovereignty and are beyond the call of withdrawal. The fact is that a viable Palestinian state—a state in reality rather than rhetoric—is diffi-cult to imagine. One might say that those who meet under the banner of "two states" harken back to a period of possibility that has already passed. The experience of those working for justice is that a new vision must emerge.

The meeting ground today is one of exile but one also with the pos-sibility of becoming a new diaspora. In their mutual flight, strangers may come to recognize each other in a new way. For more than fifty years the recognition has been immediate and unrelenting, as Jews and Palestinians have defined themselves over against the enemy other. This is crucial for authorities of both communities and essential to legitimate state and communal violence. It is also important for the silencing of dissenters within both communities, as critical discourse is defined as traitorous.

The boundaries established by each community function to keep the other from discovering the oppressive aspects of one's culture and power structure because they are shielded by representing the enemy as being outside. Crossing the boundary of Israel and Palestine allows the possibility of seeing the other reflected in one's own community and thus recognizing the other as more than stranger or, in an obvious way, reflecting back to their shared history and geography, as a possible intimate whose paths have crossed in enmity.

The point of recognition in the present is not found by reverting to the past, as if the reality of being other in history can be surmounted by dreaming a romantic past, but by recognizing the injustice of the past and present as throwing exiles together in contemporary life where a future project can be discovered. Returning to the past is another way of freezing history, as if Jews and Palestinians are just emerging from the era of colonialism and the struggle for independence.

The encounter now, with all its difficulty and suspicion and if taken on its own terms, is a way of moving forward within a common predicament. This will spur discussion on many topics, including the past, though the past will fade in priority as the present crisis is clarified. When the past is emphasized even a dialogue in exile simply replicates old arguments and proposes truces while the future remains to be born. That is why the exile, even after some decades, continues to produce Jews and Palestinians who, though to some extent share a similar plight and hope, remain strangers to one another.

When exiles begin to recognize one another, then a condition of flight gives way to the possibility of solidarity. The present situation opens toward a future in which exiles form a diaspora community. Whereas exile denotes flight and wandering, diaspora is dispersion within the context of community; it is a movement away from empire and oppression and toward the creation of a new matrix of values and institutions.

In diaspora, the past is brought with those who form the new diaspora but only as possibilities, remnants, small contributions to be combined, confronted, transmuted with other pasts. The present defines the community more strongly than the past, as mutuality of experience is the guide for shifting through values and actions. Interaction in the present brings recognition of those parts of the past that must be jettisoned and those parts that have been abused and perverted yet might be preserved or reconfigured.

One thinks here of the sense of Jewish redemption in Israel and the desire among some Palestinians to reclaim all of Palestine. Though differing in duration and context, both claims are now disasters for those on the other side of the claims. If both are held as the highest value and are disasters, then the very concepts themselves must be re-evaluated. Furthermore, recognition that disaster for the other is likewise disaster for those who make the claim is a humbling moment. It prompts a re-evaluation that is itself a way of confession and reconciliation, especially when it is done in the face of and with the other.

Yet to move from exile to diaspora, the possibility of forgiveness must be faced. Forgiveness as a mutual accounting of the past and the present frees the person and the community to the possibility of a new future. When authentic, forgiveness is preceded by a confession that is searching and reflective rather than simply damning and univocal. Could this be the way forward for Jews and Palestinians?

Like the present, the past is complex in its various configurations, and its potentialities for violence and deceit are the same as confront the hoped-for future. Tendencies toward fidelity and betrayal are common patterns, even if adorned with specific symbols for particular epochs and peoples, and the very dichotomy itself may be part of the inability to move forward. Authentic forgiveness is mutual in that the cycle of fidelity and betrayal, is identified, and then seen in a larger context of a journey that is diverse in its content and intent.

In this journey the good and bad can be identified. But unless a more complex and ambivalent picture emerges, unless the dichotomy of victor and victim gives way, then the past is woven into the present as the defining point of the future. At that point the victor and victim have too often changed places, for is it possible to condemn forever yet maintain a self-critical stance? Can a future be created without the ability to forgive and be forgiven and even to move beyond the need for forgiveness to see a depth of life from which we emerge and to which we journey? Surely this is true for Jews and Palestinians.

Carter Heyward, a Christian theologian, has emphasized the need for forgiveness as a way of embarking on a path toward justice and reconciliation. Heyward terms this "revolutionary forgiveness," a process of forgiveness in which the righting of the wrong that has been done is given priority. The righting of wrong is itself a process of self-discovery and change and becomes, with the act of forgiveness, a way of viewing the world as it is transformed in confession and justice.

In this journey, healing takes place within and between those who were once strangers and enemies. The vision of a just future is essential to enable forgiveness to realize its authenticity and reach its revolutionary potential. For without the movement toward justice forgiveness is simply a piety without substance and leaves the world as it is. Freeing the future, of course, means a forgiveness that interacts critically with the past and seeks to minimize what originally gave offense in the first place.[4]

In her philosophical writings, Hannah Arendt has also written about forgiveness as a way of entering public life with an orientation toward the future. Her caution about forgiveness is important. For Arendt, some crimes in the public realm are so heinous that they exist outside the framework of the human. They, therefore, cannot be forgiven.

One thinks of the Holocaust in this regard, and here the challenge is simply to forge a path beyond the terrible nature of that atrocity. The tragedy of the Holocaust is exacerbated by the generation after the tragedy not because it refuses to forgive but because, by holding up that tragedy, self-critical reflection is diminished. The community chose a path that to some extent replicates what violated the community in the past. Instead of embarking on a new venture, the Jewish community seeks survival and security in the most obvious ways: territorial and national sovereignty.

The consequences for the Palestinian people are obvious, and the cycle of pain and suffering continues. One may argue that the pain of the Holocaust is extended to the Palestinians while the healing that Jews pursued through empowerment has been illusory. It may be that the cycle of dislocation and death continued by Jews after the Holocaust has increased the trauma of the Jewish people. Creating a future that antici-pates the replication of the past is more than a refusal of forgiveness for an unforgivable event. Rather it extends the unforgivable act to another people not responsible for the original injury.

The trap is obvious and one that Arendt knew only to well: life cannot be defined by the unforgivable or lived indefinitely within its shadow. The task is to move on with those who will journey with you, but first the desire to move internally must be manifest. Carrying the Holocaust as a sign of distinction is a recipe for isolation and mistrust. Trust cannot be earned within the context of an event beyond even the ability to punish, nor can healing be achieved.[5]

Forgiveness is less a definitive act than a posture of critical reflection and openness to a future beyond the past. Arendt stresses that the act of forgiveness itself is a realization of the complexity and limitations of life, as well as a release from grief. Forgiveness has future consequences for identity, culture, and politics that cannot be known in advance. Insofar as forgiveness is possible within the movement of a new solidarity, the shared history of the adversaries remains so, but in a new configuration.

In the West, the example of Jews and Christians after the Holocaust exemplifies this process. Once bitter adversaries, a new relationship of trust and mutuality has emerged. The transformed relationship is multi-faceted and may involve, among other things, a solidarity against new "enemies." Clearly part of the Jewish-Christian relationship in the pre-sent is an agreement to share the spoils of Western capitalism; in some quarters Jews can be elevated into full participation in the white and Western domination over other races and cultures. Forgiveness here is a deal to resolve one injustice and unite to perpetrate further injustices with a clear conscience. The other disappears to create a different other more convenient and more important in the present. Still the new relationship may develop a critical matrix from which Jews and Christians can recognize a constantly evolving estrangement.

The task, then, is to be vigilant in recognizing that resolution of one enmity may lead to still another projection of otherness. Could such a forgiveness, a revolutionary forgiveness whose path is justice, give birth to an Israel/Palestine where values formed in the Jewish and Palestinian exile help create a political structure that gives voice to those values?

It is more than coincidence that has Yad Vashem within eyesight of Deir Yassin. Rather, a shared history and geography have brought this memorial and this village into proximity. Deir Yassin remains unmarked by a memorial; only with justice can such a memorial to the Palestinian catastrophe be erected.

Yet, at the moment of its building, both the Holocaust and the Palestinian catastrophe will begin to recede in memory. Or perhaps the journey toward a shared Jerusalem and land will begin at both memorials, with Jews and Palestinians commemorating both tragedies. New possibilities will emerge in this journey as well as dangers, for a shared land will also be open to violation and injustice. Setting free from grief demands a vigilance in the present so what created grief will not be repeated under any banner or ideology.

Envisioning the Centenary of Israel's Birth

On the threshold of the twenty-first century, revolutionary forgiveness involving Jews and Palestinians seems distant. The exilic community grows daily, but, as yet, the recognition of solidarity is still tainted with "stranger" and "enemy." State power and authority increase, separating those who dissent and struggle and silencing them through charges of betrayal, torture, and even murder.

What will the future be? What will the land of Israel/Palestine look like at the centenary of the birth of Israel and the beginning of the Palestinian catastrophe? Despite the difficulties at hand, the ground is being prepared. As Israel and Palestine are trumpeted with symbols and banners, the embrace and release of both deepens. For can Israel and Palestine be embraced as they are, or can they only be realized together by letting go of both as they have appeared in history and myth?

This is the argument of Tikva Honing-Parnass and Azmi Bishara in relation to dissenters who argue only for the right of two peoples to live separately in the land without reference to the possibility of external and internal injustice. As a Jew and a Palestinian, they argue that the reality includes and is more complex than the definition and demarcation of Jew and Palestinian or even the clash of two national movements, for they share a history and geography. The struggle, then, is for a democratic state where all can enjoy the benefits of liberty and justice without reference to ethnic or religious background.

For Bishara, the Palestinians within Israel and those in the West Bank and Gaza should form a single political unit within a binational state. This will exist alongside a Jewish political unit comprising Jews within Israel and those in the West Bank and Gaza. A Jewish-Arab polity will come into existence with two separate legislative chambers as well as a common parliament. For Honing-Parnass, this vision needs to be complemented by a strategy of joint struggle between progressive forces among Palestinians, Jews, and Arabs in surrounding countries. Otherwise the structures of binationalism may continue an economic and political oppression in the name of fulfilling the ideas of peoplehood. The symbol of fulfillment, a Jewish and Palestinian state or even a binational state with two flags, may seek to disguise economic and political inequalities between and among both peoples.[6]

Both Bishara and Honing-Parnass envision a struggle toward recognition of shared history and geography with a critical sense of the possibility of all political configurations devolving into injustice. The challenge is to see the situation as it is and then proceed along a path that involves critical analysis and hope for a future beyond the injustice of the present. Both Bishara and Honing-Parnass adopt a homeland sensibility within a Jewish-Palestinian communal framework.

For Honing-Parnass especially, that communal framework is found within a radical political framework that seeks the end of colonialism, imperialism, and racism. As a secular Jew, she raises the question of living within a culture and state without privilege and identity defined by the past, religion, nationality, or ethnicity. Instead, identity is developed within the struggle for a new social order, and solidarity in the present takes precedence over a solidarity that existed in the past.

Will this solidarity produce an identity that continues the Jewish and Palestinian trajectory we find today? At Israel's centenary will the bastion of Jewish identity be assimilated to the Middle East, where Israel is located? Will those Jews from Middle Eastern and North African backgrounds also assimilate to the larger Arab culture and, in the struggle that Honing-Parnass anticipates, lose their Jewish identity as well? By de-Zionizing the Jewish state and Jews within that state, will the second largest concentration of Jews in the world disappear?

Another obvious question is whether Palestinians will retain their identity, or rather, how their identity will change in this process. Though Arab, the Palestinian culture is also distinctive in its experience and expression. At the centenary of Deir Yassin, will the healing of the Palestinian catastrophe envisioned by Bishara mean the end of Palestinian identity as we know it today? Will Palestinian identity assimilate to the larger Arab world or perhaps even with the evolving Jewish identity, whatever that might be?

At the same time that Honing-Parnass and Bishara represent the resurgence of the binational idea, Daniel Boyarin, an Orthodox Jewish scholar, represents the re-emergence of an advocate of diaspora consciousness. Boyarin proposes a Judaic understanding that is equally committed to social justice and collective Jewish existence and, therefore, supports an Israel that "reimports diasporic consciousness, a consciousness of a Jewish collective as one sharing space with others, devoid of exclusivist and dominating power. . . ." Boyarin's understanding would lead to an Israel where individual and collective rights become an essential part of its structure, "no longer coded as a Jewish State but as a binational, secular, and multicultural one." What Boyarin calls for is the end of the "emergency and temporary rescue operation" resulting from the Holocaust and the end of the "substitution" of a European cultural and political formation for a traditional Jewish formation that emphasizes sharing political power.

This traditional Jewish understanding emphasizes the practice of solidarity and a hoped-for messianic future. For Boyarin, traditional Judaism and the subsequent Jewishness in culture and politics have the possibility of disrupting the categories of identity and introducing a dialectical tension that advises Jews of the need for survival, hospitality, and justice. This dialectical tension tempers and enriches aspects of Jewish life that revolve around but are not defined by national, genealogical, or religious sensibilities. Boyarin ends his discussion boldly: "Either Israel must entirely divest itself of the language of race and become truly a state which is equally for all of its citizens and collectives, or the Jews must divest themselves of their claim to space."[7]

Boyarin's proposal to place diaspora consciousness and practice above national ideology and self-determination echoes the words and practice of Judah Magnes in an Orthodox framework. But what is most interesting is that Boyarin's analysis is in the context of having lived within Israel and in the discussion of postmodern textual, cultural, and religious sensibilities. Boyarin's orthodoxy harkens back and ahead, and his position on Jewishness and the state of Israel is prospective.

This is true of Bishara and Honing-Parnass as well. Though they carry on certain themes of past dissenters, they speak and act from a concrete experience of the reality of Jewish and Palestinian life within the history of the state. Their analysis is tried by a personal and collective history that now projects a future beyond the past. It is more than a coincidence that the future of the state, of Jewishness, of religiosity, and even the future of Palestinian life are being thought through by Jews and

Palestinians who speak in secular and religious, cultural and political, geographic and historical language.

What we see here are boundaries *and* the crossing of boundaries, internal solidarity *and* solidarity with the other, who now is recognized as a partner and possible intimate. While the past is recognized, the future is primary and emerges from the present. The present has brought Jews and Palestinians into a relationship that has changed everything: separation is no longer possible or even desirable. Rather, the future of Jewish and Palestinian life may bring a positive depth to both peoples and cultures in the rough edges of their meeting and the critical sensibilities needed to forge a future together.

The disruption of the categories of Jewish and Palestinian identities forces a rethinking of both identities, what they are and what they might be. Boyarin's understanding of what diaspora cultural identity teaches us is important: "That cultures are not preserved by being protected from 'mixing' but probably can only continue to exist as a product of such mixing." Cultures and identities are constantly being remade. If this is true for Jews, it is also true for Palestinian identity and culture within and outside of Palestine. But it is also certain that Jewish and Palestinian identities and cultures have been remade and will continue to be remade together. The question before us is in what image these identities and cultures will form, how they will interact, and what commonalities they will share.[8]

Communal loyalties as well as ethnic and religious solidarity can be positive or negative values depending on the political status of the group making these claims. What is resistance in one situation can be the matrix for domination in another. Hillel Zeitlin, arriving for deportation in the Warsaw ghetto with prayer shawl and tefilin, means something different than those who wear the same dress at the Western Wall today. The first is a testimony to the history of a people and a sign that domination can be subverted by values and sensibilities that predate oppression and may one day resurface after the Nazis are defeated. The second is a testimony to a sense of entitlement and domination in religious garb, since the place where the worshipers are standing has been stripped of its Palestinian inhabitants. The vistas of the Western Wall are open because the Moroccan Quarter was demolished after Israel's victory in the 1967 war.

Religious garb, and by extension religiosity in general, is contextual in its meaning and content. Therefore the problem is not Jewish communal solidarity or even Jewish attachment to the land. Rather it is the political framework in which Jewishness is practiced and theorized. This leads Boyarin to acknowledge the need for Jews to preserve their status as critics and seekers after justice rather than purveyors of power and domination. Only then can Jewish identity be a gift to Jews and to others. For Boyarin, this is the task of contemporary Jewish practice and theology.[9]

Group solidarity may reinforce the very type of oppression Boyarin seeks to undermine. That is, the pull of Jewish resistance may reinforce Jewish power by providing a series of seemingly important intra-Jewish disputes that deflect more serious questions of political oppression. Honing-Parnass sees the need to break with Jewish solidarity as it is expressed in the political arena and even among leftist Jewish groups. She asks what is to be gained if the civil war within the Jewish world escalates while leaving the overall structure of oppression in place.

Here Honing-Parnass differs at least in emphasis with Boyarin. While Boyarin thinks that the interaction of Jews and Palestinians and the evolution of a unified political structure that divorces citizenship and ethnicity is important, he stops short of analyzing the formation of a new community. Honing-Parnass sees a new solidarity coming into being that takes those who suffer under oppression—Jews, Palestinians, Arabs—and fashions a different politics and culture.

Still Boyarin moves significantly beyond the progressive Jewish position of two-state solution because he sees an equal sharing of power and geography with Palestinians and even the release of a specific Jewish empowerment. Though differing in aspects of political structure and communal sensibilities, Honing-Parnass and Boyarin break with the Jewish consensus and move into uncharted territory.

The ideas of Bishara, Honing-Parnass, and Boyarin may move Jews and Palestinians closer to the time when revolutionary forgiveness becomes possible. The complementary aspects of their visions as well as their differences may provide a path beyond the present impasse. Clearly the interaction of Palestinians and Jews as distinct entities in Bishara's vision is important as is the solidarity among those from both groups that cross lines in Honing-Parnass's analysis.

The religious sensibility represented by Boyarin is crucial as well, because the stakes in Israel/Palestine are more than economic and political. Though overtly religious, Boyarin's vision also contains a moral and ethical framework that has the possibility of ecumenical outreach and political substance. Palestinian Christians and Muslims can identify with aspects of Boyarin's religiosity as they add elements of their own traditions that grapple with these issues. The confrontation with Israel is common as is the struggle to refuse co-optation within the power structures of state and authority. Moreover, the combination of politics, economics, and religion may provide the public as well as the personal capacity to envision ordinary life together after this bloody history.

Toward an Inclusive Palestinian Culture

Revolutionary forgiveness is a movement toward healing, a release from grief. In short, revolutionary forgiveness provides a dynamic of interpretation and politics that may become more prominent in the future.

This dynamic is external and internal, moving with the currents in the Middle East as it critiques aspects of each other's vision that become dominant or lose their critical edge. It combines the political, communal, and personal so as to restore the ordinary life of Jews and Palestinians in their various dimensions including the possibility of healing. The religious dimension is crucial in its widest sensibility: the connection to a past with an opening to an unknown future. By relating to the deepest aspects of contemporary life and hoping for a world different than the one inherited, a new beginning is possible.

A new beginning represents a movement away from the eighth Jewish culture—the Jewish-state culture—toward the creation of a Jewish-Palestinian culture. Of course, such a culture is itself complex and the label problematic as Jews cross the boundaries of both communities. Palestinian Arab identity is likewise complicated, because the diaspora reality over many decades has found many born outside of Palestine and formed within different cultures. Perhaps in its final formulation, a renewed and transformed Palestinian culture will emerge, combining elements from Western, North African, and Arab Jews with those of Palestinian Arabs born inside and outside of Palestine and Israel.

In a renewed and transformed Palestinian culture, the categories of other will be challenged by the complex nature of identity formation. Notions of ancient and modern, native and stranger, so important to divisiveness and oppression, will, in the transition from conflict to integration, be re-evaluated. Over time, the distinction between Israel and Palestine, Jews and Arabs, will be less important or even disappear. Particularity will be defined differently as the overall structure of the culture changes.

The terms *Palestine* and *Palestinian* resonate in both communities, historically and in the present. At least for Jews in Eastern Europe in the 1930s and 1940s, Palestine assumed an increasingly important place in their world as Europe came under the domination of the Nazis. For Jews living in Palestine, Palestine was home. Jews of the North African and Arab worlds also identified Palestine as part of Levantine culture, a site of religious sensibility and pilgrimage. For Palestinian Arabs who remain in the land, Palestine is a home that has been dismembered in living memory; for those in the Palestinian diaspora, Palestine remains a haunting dream, much as it has been recollected in Jewish memory.

Palestine evokes many memories and hopes on both sides of the conflict. Could the recreation, reintegration, and transformation of Palestine and Palestinian culture be the way out of division, trauma, isolation, involuntary exile, and fear? Here the values of empowerment are tempered by the challenge of an interdependent struggle to place power at the service of justice and peace. Sharing the land and its resources, erecting a political structure that bridges traditions, histories, and aspirations—creating a polity that embraces revolutionary forgiveness—is the way out of a cycle of violence and suffering that seems intractable.

This could also be the beginning of a new start for Jews and Palestinian Arabs in the diaspora, the healing of old wounds, so they may begin their journey again in safety and peace. Jews and Palestinian Arabs in the diaspora will be released to live with their neighbors fully in the present and also maintain a healthy and harmonious connection with the land of Israel/Palestine. Diaspora politics will be localized, even as travel and involvement in the Middle East increases. A critical political relationship will develop in the countries within which the diaspora communities reside: no longer will alliances with various states be determined by their support or lack thereof of either side in the Israeli-Palestinian conflict. Tremendous burdens of responsibility for politics outside of their control—of separation and displacement, of grief and mourning—will be lifted.

Moreover, an inclusive Palestinian culture will allow Jews to feel at home inside and outside of the land, just as it will welcome Palestinian Arabs in involuntary exile. Both communities will be demilitarized and demobilized so that culture and religiosity can resume a pattern of normality and growth. Orthodoxy as a political weapon in Judaism and Islam might diminish, and the Christians of Palestine can be rescued from their declining numbers and prospects. Interdependence breeds trust and mutual decision making. It also encourages humility in the religious sphere, which can in turn encourage the same in the political arena.

Though the development of this kind of Palestinian culture will have many critics, the reality of a shared land and politics make it nearly inevitable. It is already in evidence, stunted to be sure, in the word borrowings, use of symbolic language, and enjoyment of food and music. As Ammiel Alcalay points out, the reservoir on the Jewish side already exists in the remains of Jewish Levantine culture.

In probing the North African and Arab cultures of Jews and Palestinian Arabs, Alcalay seeks to "map out a space in which the Jew *was* native, not a stranger. . . ." The urgency of such a task is historical *and* contemporary, one that needs to be done in order to revive the roots of an alienated population and to envision a future beyond the Western model of life and the conflict that has almost destroyed Palestine. If it is true that the natives of the region, Jews of North African and Arab background and Palestinian Arabs, have become or are seen as strangers in their own space, then the difficulty of being at home involves those who dislocated these peoples in the first place, that is, Western Jewish settlers who were themselves displaced from Europe. The complication is that those who helped estrange the native populations are themselves now native or at least in the process of becoming so. With the passage of time and the incursion of the West, another population has settled and been born in this same space. The challenge now is for this population to become natives and not strangers.[10]

Clearly the bridge to a future where all are native is two-way: the future will be a combination of Levantine and Western, bringing the Jewish, Christian, and Muslim cultures into a mutually enriching dialogue with modernity. The reversal of emphasis must now include what has brought much destruction, lest another destruction take place to make all strangers to their original cultures. For what would be the difference if the Levantine culture was mobilized to drive the foreign settlers away? Would that culture be any more worthy than the one it violently replaced?

This thought leads Shiko Behar, a Jewish Israeli of North African background, to comment: "All we can say today to our brothers, sisters and comrades—whether Palestinian Muslims and Christians or *Ashkenazi* Jews—is that we, critical *Mitzrahim*, will continue to attempt to construct such progressive, inclusionary, collective political identities." Inclusionary politics has the possibility of transforming culture without further uprooting. It is also carrying the past into a future configuration that is progressive rather than regressive.[11]

The movement toward a new Palestinian culture is thus found within the realities of the present situation and seeks to avoid the abstraction of pure identity formations. This Palestinian culture must recognize the diversity within it and come together with the knowledge that someday a new identity will emerge from that culture. What that identity will consist of is unknown, as the mixture of elements and how they will be configured cannot be determined in advance. "Native" is an evolving concept and reality; where it begins and its intermediate destinations are rarely known.

So, too, the notion of Jewish diaspora is evolving. Where does the diaspora begin? Is there an end to diaspora or simply a different experience of it? Surely the distinction of exile and return so prominent in Jewish literature and increasingly connected with the Israel is difficult to maintain. Being both inside and outside the land have been experienced multiple times in Jewish history, so much so that each is carried in the other. Jewish religiosity and culture are diaspora and homeland, homeland and diaspora until the separation of the two is impossible.

Feeling at home is possible in the diaspora, as is the feeling of the diaspora in the homeland. There is the possibility of being in exile in both places, an experience increasing in our time. Jewish-state culture, though postulating a return and security to continue Jewish life, is in fact testing the very viability of Jewish life. The end of the diaspora proclaimed by numerous Jewish intellectuals and religious leaders in the context of Israeli power has created an exile that threatens disassociation from the community itself.

Already, in the wake of the invasion of Lebanon, this reversal of diaspora/exile as applied to Israel was in evidence. As William Freedman wrote in 1983: "The moral image the nation has begun to project—as an occupying power determined to cement its occupation; as an increasingly iron-fisted occupying power; as a fierce avenger diving to the moral level of its attackers; as an increasingly divided nation of bitterly opposed and frequently aroused factions; as an increasingly anti-democratic populace headed by an increasingly autocratic and theocratic government—is unattractive, even repugnant, to some." Because of this Freedman suggests that Israel is part of a new diaspora, a term he defines not in the literal sense of geographical dispersion, but as "exile from a spiritual home or sense of home." Paraphrasing an early Zionist, A. D. Gordon, Freedman concludes that "domicile in Israel without tenacious adherence to Jewish social values is nothing else than a transference of diaspora to the state of Israel."[12]

Freedman's analysis echoes Daniel Boyarin's sensibility a decade later as he argues that Jewish values are themselves dependent on their context—whether or not they are used in alliance with state power or on behalf of those who are suffering under that power—and, at least to some extent, dependent on facing and learning from other cultures and political systems located in the same environment. In the West, for example, Boyarin sees a "dialectic of correction" between Jewish and Christian values and tendencies "as an antithesis to the other, correcting in the 'Christian' system its tendencies toward a coercive universalism and in the 'Jewish' system its tendencies toward contemptuous neglect for human solidarity. . . ." In Boyarin's view this dialectic of correction might lead beyond both to a more humane social order, though today they have combined in an "unholy alliance" combining the worst features of each system.[13]

One wonders if this dialectic of correction could issue forth, perhaps even become a central reality, as Jews and Palestinians form into a diaspora within a renewed Palestinian culture. Confrontation and solidarity between those from the East and those from the West could produce a dialogue about political, religious, and cultural-institutional and ethical life that is illuminating for both. The presumption of difference and specialness, for example, in Judaism, Christianity, and Islam, could be tested. Similarly the patterns of thought seen to reside differently in East and West could also be tested.

After the testing, that which is different and special could be retained and offered to each other, while that which is found to be held in common can be seen as a joint inheritance. Elements of culture, politics, and religion that, when empowered, tend to oppress can be identified and at least minimized. What then needs to be faced is the possibility that this solidarity might bring about an unholy alliance to dominate others. The hope is that this Palestinian culture will maintain as its watchword a solidarity that refuses to create new exiles and that those who have experienced exile from external or internal structures can become catalysts for a true homecoming.

Homecoming comes through a long and complicated journey. Through political, cultural, and religious contacts, with the wrestling of difference, values, and power in the context of a shared history and future, a new collective will form with innovative mechanisms for identity formation. In terms of Jewish identity, Richard Shusterman, professor of philosophy at Temple University, identifies as an intriguing possibility, "a life of continued Jewish self-expression and self-realization through cycles of *yeridah* and *aliyah*, departure and return to Israel." It is a movement away from a fetish for unity to a circular narrative of Jewish identity. The former seeks a unity that can only be imposed through myth and power; the latter recognizes a "fragile narrative unity embracing a confusing multiplicity and division of subnarratives that are (like the overarching narrative itself) open, at any moment, to divergent interpretation and future constructions."[14]

Shusterman fails to mention, however, the other obvious ingredient to this circular narrative, the Jews from North African and Arab backgrounds and Palestinian Arabs. With their inclusion, departure and return are not limited to the Jewish community in Israel and the West; they become the alternating rhythms of departure and return in relation to a shared culture in contact with the Western and the Arab world. Divergent interpretations and future reconstructions, in Shusterman's mind expanding because of Jewish comings and goings between Israel and America, are seen within the context of an emerging Palestinian culture to be quite limited. The important reconstruction of Jewish life will take place in a more diverse local and international milieu. The circular narrative of the future will involve the dialectic of correction and a cycle of departure and return that transforms the notion of exile and diaspora and even the question of solidarity.

Finding the Lost Agenda

Without belief in a new beginning for Jewish life, and without surfacing a dynamic out of which new life can grow—the restoration of the ordinary in circumstances of justice and peace in a new political and cultural configuration—we are consigned to a future that simply replicates the past. Though exact replication of the past is impossible, the refusal to see a nascent breakthrough results in the constant effort to maintain a system of division and injustice. The choice is between maintenance of the status quo and creation of a new configuration to redress present inequities.

This effort at creation, however, will be attempted only if the courage is found to admit that the projection of the status quo into the future is a disaster for both peoples and simply a postponement—at great cost to be sure—of the inevitable shift in judgment and structure of life. As Hannah Arendt wrote, "Courage is indispensable because in politics not life but the world is at stake." We might amend this by stating that both life and the world are at stake because both are intertwined and, within that, the traditions and cultures that make up life and the world.[15]

Thus new beginnings of traditions and cultures renew life and the world. Courage, therefore, is the crossing of boundaries in this spirit of renewal and life. The relief from grief, from the tragedy of destruction as well as from the tragedy of being an oppressor, of personal and communal loss in these tragedies, is the fruit of courage.

Surely the courage needed here to envision a centenary of justice and peace and the practice of the *tikkun* of ordinary decency must be implemented across ethnic and religious lines and enshrined in the system of governance of the new polity that emerges. Recognition of the brokenness of Jewish and Palestinian history, of the brokenness of Jerusalem itself, can help enshrine the values that both people have exhibited in their history and have submerged in their struggle for power and survival—hospitality, religiosity, and connection with the land.

The combination of courage and brokenness, of hope and suffering, may temper the will to dominate or the coming together against new "strangers" or "enemies." If the courage found to build toward the centenary emerges from brokenness and seeks to build a society in which brokenness is remembered as a violation of the ordinary rather than a call to arms, if the brokenness is a call to restore the ordinary rather than overcome it through new displacements, then suffering will be balanced by the prospects of healing. Jerusalem will then, as will the land of Israel/Palestine, herald a renewed vision of the possibilities of life for Jews and Palestinians around the world as well as people everywhere, and Isaiah's vision will become visible again.

Theories of forgiveness, evolving political structures, and diaspora religious consciousness—the creation of a reinvigorated Palestinian culture—are crucial to the future. The danger is that they may remain theories, abstractions as the possibility of implementing the vision erodes. Recognition of the brokenness of Jerusalem, the meeting place that emphasizes the ordinary rather than the symbolic aspects of the ancient city, cannot occur if few Palestinian Arabs are living in the city or if their presence is simply tolerated as a remnant. If Palestinian Arabs are treated as strangers in the land they once called their own, then clearly the possibility of a new polity or even the challenging and healing interaction of two communities in dialogue atrophies.

Time is crucial, for there comes a point of no return when the community can no longer create a mature political structure and a dialogue that leads to a future. In this case, the Palestinian diaspora will carry on in the surrounding Arab countries and in the West, but inside Israel/Palestine the will and the voice of the people will be stilled.

At the centenary, what will the face of Jewish life look like? What Jewish ethical and moral visions will survive? What will Judaism hold dear and propagate? Will the map of Israel and Palestine engender hope or an apathetic resignation? Will that map take its boundaries and sensibilities from Menachem Begin and Benjamin Netanyahu, Yitzhak Rabin and Shimon Peres, or from Martin Buber, Judah Magnes, Hannah Arendt, Henry Schwarzschild, Ari Shavit, Tikvah Honing-Parnass, Azmi Bishara, Edward Said, and Daniel Boyarin?

Though at times the future looks dim, the hope of the centenary remains. That there are Jews who have and continue to place ethics and morality at the center of Jewish life is cause for hope. That more and more Jews include Palestinians as part of that vision, as partners in restoring the ordinary that cannot be and should not be restored for Jews without Palestinians, is a sign that ethics has survived the state and may even be the seed for the movement beyond the state as it now exists.

Though historians write as if they can analyze the elements that bring about turning points in history, they write when history has already turned. Acts of resistance and solidarity are therefore celebrated after the event and often by those who attempted to hold the line at a previous point in history. To predict that power or dissent will triumph is dangerous: from the perspective of the present it seems that power will remain as it is. From the perspective of the powerful, of course, the future always seems to be theirs.

Dissenters, by definition out of power, are often projected as those who cannot continue or will be marginal to the future. Nonetheless, actions on behalf of a future different than the present carry within them unpredictable outcomes. "Human action, projected into a web of relationships where many and opposing ends are pursued, almost never fulfills its original intention," Hannah Arendt writes. "No act can ever be recognized by its author with the same happy certainty with which a piece of work of any kind can be recognized by its maker. Whoever begins to act must know that he has started something whose end he can never foretell, if only because his own deed has already changed everything and made it even more unpredictable."[16]

Epilogue

At the close of Daniel Boyarin's scholarly study of Paul, he appends a chapter titled "Answering the Mail: Toward a Radical Jewishness." To many readers, the reference to Paul, contemporary Jewishness, and the mail in the same breath seems odd. For could this ancient Jewish "convert" have anything to say to Jews today, and did Boyarin find a message in this long dead figure?

Boyarin's scholarly study had become a personal challenge: Paul's letters, which outlined his call to the Jews of his time, remain a challenge today. Paul's challenge is the following: "How can I construct a particular identity which is extremely precious to me without falling into ethnocentrism or racism of one kind or another?" As Paul had a vision of universal solidarity rooted in Hebrew monotheism and Greek longing for universals, Boyarin sees the articulation of Jewish particularity within an overall universal human solidarity. In dialogue with the Jewish tradition, Boyarin nonetheless concedes his response to be highly personal, engaged, and not always satisfactory.[1]

Answering the mail, that is responding to criticisms and challenges, is part of the territory when discussing contemporary Jewish life. And it seems that almost every discussion refers back to or projects itself ahead to the Holocaust and Israel. For Boyarin this means that his study of Paul ends with a theory of diaspora consciousness that can affect the life of Jews and Palestinians in the Middle East. His response to Paul suggests the possibility of affirming a particular identity while affirming the same in others. Even more, it seems that particular identity is challenged, deepened, and expanded by contact with other identities.

Identity can be formed over against an other, but it can also be strengthened in solidarity with a different identity that also becomes part of your own. Identity is particular *and* shared, always evolving in contact with other identities and embracing aspects of those encounters, so that what once was seen as alien becomes part of what feels like home. Over time, the original and borrowed elements of culture and tradition, even faith, are difficult to separate and name.

For Boyarin, at least, this challenge is unavoidable and to be embraced. From the time of Paul till today letters have been addressed to the Jewish people, often by Jews themselves. The replies help define what Jewish practice is and might be.

Surely the challenge to Jewish practice in our time moves far beyond the letters of Paul. The map of Israel, as it is on the threshold of the twenty-first century, is worse than the possibilities that existed earlier, and the facts on the ground signal their enshrinement as definitive and irreversible. The letters to Paul represent a challenge in the language of struggle and hope; the letters from Israel today, in the form of a final map of Israel and the Palestinians represent almost the end of possibility, a symbolic and practical death.

Jewish thinkers and activists who answer the mail are attuned to our time, with its conflicting currents of despair and hope. On my journeys to Jerusalem, for example, I am often asked whether all is lost or whether there is still hope. In conversations with Jewish activists in Israel and America, the question is asked about our own failure to confront Israeli power. Did we fail in some obvious way, a way we should have noticed and corrected?

Still I am struck by the ability of the mail to humble one's own analysis for not going far enough, especially mail from Palestinians who appreciate Jewish solidarity. In a recent essay I wrote the following with reference to the founding of Israel after the Holocaust: "That at this same moment a segment of world Jewry, with the acquiescence and later almost total support of Jewish leadership in Europe and America, would embark on the enterprise of state building and the dislocation of another people is unfortunate, though perhaps understandable within the context of the Holocaust."[2]

Though I continued by stating that the post-1967 and Oslo expansion of Israel was "unforgivable," Nuhad Jamal, a Palestinian who read my essay, responded by focusing on my use of the word *unfortunate*. "From the Palestinian point of view, 'unfortunate' is hardly the adjective I would have chosen to describe the utter destruction of a people and the death of a nation!" Jamal wrote. "As a Palestinian who has taught my young children about Nazi horrors, it is not 'understandable' to me that a non-European people were made to pay the price for European crimes against humanity!"[3]

Reading this letter, I knew my Palestinian correspondent was correct. "Unfortunate" is clearly not adequately descriptive of the tragedy that befell her people or even adequate to describe her own journey into exile in America. Though I marveled once again at the sensitivity that the issue of Israel/Palestine evokes—at the same time noting her being "moved by the clear recognition of Palestinian pain expressed" in my narrative—Jamal is clearly right. Reading a shortened version of the essay at a conference in Washington, D.C., before receiving her letter, I stumbled over the word *unfortunate* and quickly moved to the subsequent *unforgivable.*

When I vocalized the sentence it was clear that the idea behind the word, the strategy behind the sentence, sounded strained, unresponsive, inadequate. Perhaps I was attempting to remain within an acknowledged framework of Jewish discourse. At that moment, however, I realized the territory I entered was itself unforgiving, trying to express the understandability of an action in history while condemning it at the same time.

I could not do this on the issue of South African apartheid. I do not express an understanding attitude toward the imperialism of Christianity. It is impossible for me to explain the genocide against the indigenous people in Australia or the United States with this terminology. And I have never been able to make this kind of statement to the hundreds, perhaps thousands, of Palestinian exiles I have met personally over the years.

I think of the many meetings in which the journey of a Palestinian is outlined in vivid detail. Expulsion from Haifa in 1948 and from Jerusalem in 1967. Fleeing from Lebanon in 1982. Over dinner in Cyprus, the discussion is of this migration. Often the words are without bitterness, but the address is clear: this migration resembles our own and is caused by our "return." In person, recognizing the ordinary life that has been disrupted over and over again, words fail. Letters are inadequate.

What then do I say? Do I replace *unfortunate* with *inexcusable,* making the entire enterprise of state-building a travesty, as unforgivable as I label the later expansion of Israel's boundaries? The implications of this shift are monumental, for even the dissenting figures—Judah Magnes and Martin Buber for example—are culpable.

Those sources for the renewal of contemporary Jewish life are thereby compromised, for they were also involved in this tragedy. Indeed anyone who argued then, and by extension anyone who argues today, for a Jewish "return" to the land is part of the Palestinian catastrophe. If this desire was not understandable, especially in the emergency years after the Holocaust, then all are part of the exile my Palestinian interlocutor has suffered.

The road ahead, then, is clouded by a complicity that has unfolded in stages. This is what Benjamin Beit-Hallahmi, an Israeli historian of the Zionist movement, labels the original sins of Zionism and the state of Israel. For Beit-Hallahmi, the thought and theory of Zionism at the turn of the century was more than understandable: it was a response to the situation of Jews in Europe. As Beit-Hallahmi writes, Zionism at the "level of an abstract idea of Jewish sovereignty and territorial concentration cannot be faulted." We cannot fault its "morality."

The problem with Zionism is its implementation: "The trouble with Zionism starts when it lands, so to speak, in Palestine. What has to be justified is the injustice to the Palestinians caused by Zionism, the dispossession and victimization of a whole people." This wrong creates the need for justification, a justification that takes many forms and is intricate in its maneuvering. In the end, however, these justifications sound like excuses, "so many fig leaves designed to cover a shameful nakedness."[4]

"Zionism today is more and more in the position of not being commendable or acceptable as a general principle," writes Beit-Hallahmi. "Not justifiable, but maybe at best excusable or forgivable." The task is to judge the past—for without judgment, what kind of morality can there be?—but more importantly to confront the present. The original sin cannot be changed or erased, and the justification of that sin, or the silence about it, leads to its continuation and expansion in the present. The wrong must be understood and stopped lest the cycle continue.[5]

The letter from Jamal along with Beit-Hallahmi's analysis places my perspective in jeopardy: *unfortunate* is hardly the word to use, and the situation was a disaster before the 1967 war. The Zionist theory of the need for a place for Jews outside of Europe should be understood rather than faulted; the implementation of that plan must be understood *and* faulted from the very beginning, before 1948 and after.

Where does this leave Jews like myself? Misunderstandings, some deliberate, some out of ignorance, some out of pressure by others, flourish. In 1988, for example, just after returning from Jerusalem, where I visited Palestinian children in the hospital who were paralyzed or brain dead from the "rubber" bullets shot by Israeli soldiers, a man from a Jewish organization insisted that he publicly respond to one of my lectures. His insistence belied a profound anxiety: he told me that in my writing I had counseled suicide for the Jewish people because we had become oppressors. What I wrote was something quite different, namely, that the movement from being oppressed to becoming oppressors was like committing "moral suicide."

My words were a challenge to my own people to awaken to what we were doing, to think again of our own history and what we were becoming. I emphasize "we" because I have always placed myself among my own people sharing in our contemporary culpability. I showed the accuser the passage, and we spoke at length. It was clear to me that, though he wanted, indeed insisted, to challenge me publicly on my writing, he had never read anything I had written. My "letter" to the Jewish community was easily condemned without being read, and in our subsequent conversation it was clear to me that the man was not very far from my understanding at all. Subsequent to our discussion, this official criticized my stance on Israel publicly and remained silent on those issues we agreed upon.

How long have we remained silent out of a sense of duty, loyalty, fear? How many letters from Palestinians have we, as a community, refused to read? If letters are read by Jewish progressives, they are read only if they carry certain dates, 1993 for some, 1988 for others. This dating applies to Jews who write letters as well. Are we willing to read this letter, written in the spring of 1949, by a member of a Jewish kibbutz preparing to celebrate Passover? "Why are we celebrating our holiday in an Arab village? . . . Once there was an Arab village here. The clouds of Sasa floated high over other people one year ago. The fields we tend today were tended by others—one year ago. The men worked their plots and tended their flocks while women busied themselves at baking their bread. The cries and tears of children of others were heard in Sasa one year ago." Reflecting on the culpability of his kibbutz, the writer continues: "And when we came the desolation of their lives cried to us through the ruins they left behind. . . . What gives us the right to reap the fruit of trees we have not planted, to take shelter in houses we have not built. . . . On what moral grounds shall we stand when we take ourselves to court?"[6]

As a Jew, this writer juxtaposed the holiday that celebrates the liberation of the Israelites with the "liberation" that had just taken place. He was benefiting from a new expulsion and could see in his own tradition and experience a cautionary word. Liberation built on the oppression of others could not be seen as liberation at all. What he was left with was a celebration that conjured accusing images. These images remain years after the physical reality of expulsion and occupation, undermining the moral standing of his own kibbutz, Israel, and the Jewish world at large.

Like Martin Buber's letter to David Ben-Gurion, this letter remains unanswered. Or perhaps Beit-Hallahmi's book is a response to both. The fact that Buber's letter to Ben-Gurion is itself inadequate raises the stakes of the moral argument. The "black stain" on the Jewish people that Buber raises in relation to Deir Yassin is extended to the Zionist enterprise supported by such highly "moral" figures as Buber and Magnes. The arguments for a settlement within the context of a Zionist victory in 1948 refer to an internal Jewish argument about the moral future of Jewish settlement in the land of Palestine, now Israel. Buber and Magnes sought to limit the advance rather than reverse it. Already in 1948, courage in the moral realm is combating the excesses of a process that ultimately displaced people like Edward Said and, later, others like Jamal Nuad.

Thus the courage of Buber and Magnes is similar to the courage of contemporary Jewish progressives: limit the advance of Israel. The point of difference is important, however. The Jewish advance is now so significant that there is little left of Palestine. Because of this, moral urgency has atrophied to the point where power relations are the significant point of discussion. "On what moral grounds shall we stand when we take ourselves to court?" has been replaced in the mainstream of Jewish life at least with the fig leaf of justification or silence. Beit-Hallahmi is an exception. Jamal's letter raises too many questions about the enterprise of state-building itself.

While there is no way back, there is a way forward. Defeat comes in many stages, as do reversals; when defeat is reversed, another unexpected path opens. A future comes into view where only despair reigned years before. Reflecting on the present crisis, Naseer Aruri, a Palestinian political scientist who lives in America, writes that Palestinian hope has collapsed, with Palestine being "replaced by Bantustans and a Judaized Jerusalem." Worse still, Palestinian leadership has become a "police state without a state . . . the oppressed has become oppressor, the revolutionary collaborator and the resister Quisling."

Still, the Palestinians have not been defeated, only "our leadership has," Aruri writes. "But we are not doomed. There is sufficient fluidity in the regional and international (dis)order. There is a new vibrant generation and emerging civil society, a new critical demeanor and a tendency to be more honest with oneself and others. There is a universal condemnation of autocracy and new respect for democracy and human rights. . . ." Aruri echoes the sentiments of his father who, when the 1967 war began, spoke the following: "I lived under Turkish, British and Jordanian rule. I might spend the rest of my life under Israeli occupation. But a new generation will emerge."[7]

The wisdom of father and son is one born of suffering and a patience with history that is tried with the passing generations. Nonetheless, there is a sense, shared with Hannah Arendt, that new beginnings are possible, indeed inevitable, and that commitments when written and acted upon have unpredictable consequences. The timeline is long, too long, but nonetheless one that awaits the end of empires, occupations, pretenses to innocence, and even the internal autocracies that emerge within catastrophes.

For Jews this litany is all too familiar, but today the accusation is directed against us. I hear in this litany hope, a hope addressed to all of us, Jews and Palestinians, and those from other peoples and nations, that in the end the triumph of a critical solidarity is possible and new identities and cultures will emerge within and after the struggle.

Still, the mail is likely to worsen in the near future. My own journeys to Jerusalem over the years have made this impression on me
quite vividly. In 1973 as a college student staying in the Armenian
Quarter of the Old City, I witnessed a vibrant city defined by Arab
rhythms and diverse in religious and cultural practices. On the threshold of the twenty-first century, Jerusalem had clearly changed to an
almost monolithic Jewish city with smatterings of Palestinians, mostly
in the tourist trade, and with the Muslim and Christian holy sites
increasingly separated from a vibrant cultural and political life.

What should be an evolving religious sensibility rooted in faith, culture, and politics is quickly becoming a tourist mecca with shrines to an
ancient reality unconnected with contemporary life. Orthodox Jews
increasingly determine the pattern of life in Jerusalem, and Christian pil-
grims from the West celebrate their festivals as if there are no indigenous
Christians in the land and as if the Palestinians are backdrops to their
lifelong dream of coming to the Holy Land.

As the vans of Jews come in the morning to bring their children to
school and as I walk in the city and hear the ancient Hebrew prayers of
return and thanksgiving, I cannot help but feel a contradiction so great
as to be almost insurmountable. The deep resonance of Jewish history
within me forces a question that is so obvious and yet is considered by
many Jews to be traitorous: can Jewish festivals, prayers, religious pro-
nouncements, ring forth from a Jerusalem that has been conquered and
almost emptied of its inhabitants?

I wonder: Do these Jews see the Palestinians they are displacing? Do
they wonder where the Palestinian mothers are living today, or where
their children will go to school? Wanting to be so close to their religious
center, do these Jews think that Christians and Muslims might also be
attached to their religious center and city?

The blindness at the heart of the faithful, of course, is shared across
religious lines throughout history. And the secular leaders of Israel, like
secular leaders of other places and times, use religiosity to accomplish
their own goals. Still in Jerusalem, I wonder how Jewish religious and
secular life has come to this terminus.

For the mail has brought this home to me as have my meetings with
the refugees created by Jewish power. The Jewish poet Adrienne Rich has
written that truth "comes by accident and from strangers," and so it often
does. But who would have thought that this truth would be carried by
those who are seen as "enemies," and who would have imagined in the
century of the Holocaust that I would encounter this truth, carried by
another people, in the city Jews prayed for over two millennia of exile?
Who would have imagined that the answer to these prayers would create

a dual exile of Jews and Palestinians that one day will transform Jewish religiosity and practice?

Such is the contemporary journey of the Jewish people that I, with other Jews, have inherited and witness to. Jews have indeed returned to Jerusalem in triumph and in a boldness that defies expectation. In doing so we have wounded the Jewish spirit, made more distant the millennial hope, and have less and less resonance with the words of the prophets who spoke about the city we now call our own.

That the prophetic spirit lives on outside the gates of Jewish life is a reality difficult to articulate to the Jewish people, let alone to myself. Nonetheless, the spirit lives on, awaiting new voices, enfolded in an emerging solidarity. The creation of a Jewish-Palestinian culture in Jerusalem and throughout the land is worthy of our commitment even as the prophecies of Isaiah, ancient and renewed, seem distant.

Refusing Partial Practice

The distance of the dream of Israel/Palestine is itself a challenge: *to go forth, to risk everything, to begin again, to continue searching for the missing commandments, to embrace the covenant wherever it is to be found.* By doing this, the dream is made real, even if delayed or destined to be unfulfilled in our lifetime. Though the suffering continues and the healing is made more difficult, the journey itself testifies to a future beyond divisiveness and oppression.

Embracing the covenant does not in and of itself change the world, the Holy Land, or even ourselves, as if all is resolved and renewed. Like creation and humanity, we are tied to and limited by history. We are *en route*, unfinished, in process.

The covenant is not a rescue operation in which those who have been lost are now found; rather, it makes a focal point of our lives become more and more articulate. We are able to move into a deeper realm, where commitment and freedom are closely bound and the question of God is raised in a different way.

For after Auschwitz and Israel, after the mass slaughter of Jews in Europe and the displacement of Palestinians in Israel/Palestine, how are we to approach this most important question of God? The approach can only come through a renewed effort of trust, a renewed solidarity with humanity across borders and boundaries, a renewed commitment against the partial practice that is understandable and limiting.

Empowerment without solidarity, victory without the desire to lift up the victimized, leads to a practice of politics and faith that is stunted. The end of Jewish history as we have known it and inherited it is less a comment on Judaism itself or even the Jewish community at the threshold of the twenty-first century. It is instead an opportunity that issues into a command once articulated by the eleventh-century Tibetan yogi, Milapera: "It is the tradition of fortunate seekers never to be content with partial practice."[8]

The challenge of all traditions and disciplines is practice and overcoming the partial practice in every generation. Thus the limitations in each tradition and discipline are abundant and generational. Only by reifying it as both revealed and eternal—as if Judaism, or for that matter Christianity or Islam, are ontologically connected—can the covenant be seen as given and static. Overcoming partial practice involves taking the tradition and discipline seriously as a guide always in need of transformation and expansion.

Never being content with partial practice demands a movement within and outside inherited patterns, as it demands internal and external movement of the person. Rituals, learning, synagogue attendance, and prayer are only meaningful insofar as they direct us to the next place and next question, to the other who is suffering, in need, struggling. That other is also ourselves or our people, then, now, or in the future.

At one point in history, with the limitations that attend all practice, Holocaust theologians sought to overcome partial practice by investing empowerment with a religious dimension. Israel, to their minds at least, was less a political statement than a theological engagement with the questions that confronted them after Auschwitz.

The judgment of history, the news that the mail has brought us, is that this practice was partial because an entire people was ignored or denigrated. As these Jewish thinkers embraced the covenant within the context of their own experience and horizons, the covenant itself began to flee. A fuller practice is necessary, an inclusive practice that understands the connection between Yad Vashem and Deir Yassin.

Where will this fuller practice lead us? Will it lead us to a covenant that will always demand a further commitment? Will we be judged limited by the next generation? Will they have to overcome the partial practice of our generation? Does this need to move beyond the present invalidate our practice, as our practice seems to invalidate that of the previous generation?

Though it would be easy to see the fidelity of the next generation as *the* correct practice—thus judging past practice as insufficient and sometimes even criminal—fidelity, indeed history itself, is more complex. Rather than judgment as the final arbiter, as if judgment from one generation or people is without bias and limitation, history represents the challenge as a response that is demanded, with its own partiality and need for correction.

The sad part of history is that the challenge history provides is often recognized too late or implemented in a partial way. Even in the struggle to overcome partial practice, suffering continues. Embracing the covenant in our time, as in other eras as well, does not end suffering in general or even the suffering that comes from one's own history and community. On the threshold of the twenty-first century, the practice of Judaism itself is a form of survival *and* oppression. Can we justify the appeal to the same covenant that causes suffering for a healing that seems almost utopian?

Only when we realize that the Jewish community itself, like other religious communities, will not make the decision to overcome partial practice, can we be free to embrace that part of our inheritance that propels us outward to engage the world. The realization that the community itself, the Jewish people as a people in history, will not embrace the covenant as a way toward ending suffering and beginning the process of healing evokes sadness. For does not the covenant speak of a people chosen among the nations, with a destiny guided by God, particular and universal in significance, one of liberation and hope? Does the end of Jewish history and life, the end of Judaism as we have known and inherited it, mean turning away from this covenant in its fullness and promise?

We return to Daniel Boyarin's diaspora consciousness as partial, inadequate for the future, at some points recovering aspects of the tradition that allow a fuller practice, at other points seeking to define practice within a Judaic framework that is frayed almost beyond recognition. Boyarin moves back into an Orthodoxy that even the Orthodox hardly recognize, thus challenging that community with its own tradition, and he moves forward, challenging those who feel free of the tradition, with a practice that has a depth modern secular Jews often lack. A way back to a Jewishness that is religious and open, prayerful and just, particular and inclusive, is sought.

The paradox is that those who recognize, take seriously, and celebrate Boyarin's Jewishness are themselves for the most part non-Jewish. On the one side are Palestinians, who appreciate a Jewishness that is religious, non-statist, repentant and inclusive; on the other side are post-Holocaust Christians, who understand Jewishness as a subversive and searching response to God's call and seek to emulate that within their own faith tradition.

Surely, Boyarin's attempt to overcome partial practice is Jewish in its origins and depth. Should we think less of it because its primary appreciation is found outside of contemporary Jewish life?

At the same time, Boyarin's study of Paul demonstrates that his own Jewishness is in dialogue with Christianity, and the modern Christian community is also his reference point. For can Boyarin reclaim a diaspora Jewishness without a renewed Christianity? Is Paul simply an ancient person that Boyarin is studying, or is Paul an entry point into the contemporary world where Jews and Christians are in a dialogue characterized by solidarity and mutual affirmation?

Boyarin's audience—one might say his community in reality rather than theory—is neither *the* Jewish community nor *the* Christian community but those Christians and Jews (Palestinians and others as well) who are trying within their own histories and across boundaries to overcome partial practice on the threshold of the twenty-first century. Mutual recognition of the struggle is itself important because in that recognition lies a positive identification and dependency. The identification is recognition of a common search and goal; dependency is a sense that isolation from one another inhibits the practice itself.

Today there is no way of overcoming partial practice alone or simply within one community. Fortunate seekers are bound together even, and most especially, when particularity is emphasized. Recognizing one another as on the same journey means that particularity itself betrays a commonality. Could it be that the next generation will see commonality as its particularity?

Here it seems that a new path is opening beyond Judaism or, if you will, beyond Judaism and Christianity in the West and beyond Israel and Palestine in the Middle East. The fear of the end of distinctiveness, of particularity, of assimilation is understandable. Yet, in each generation and surely at formative moments of human history, distinctiveness, particularity, and assimilation have shifted in their emphasis and categories. At these momentous times, categories are drawn, defended, and crossed as if the very universe is at stake.

Yet I am struck at how often the shifts in naming and tradition are themselves mistakenly understood as monumental betrayals on the one hand, and moments of salvation on the other. The entire movement of Christianity and Judaism away from one another is a mistake and holds both ancient and contemporary significance.

For were Jesus and Paul discoverers of a new covenant and founders of a new religion or Jews in their own time struggling with the partial practice of first-century Judaism? The mistake on the part of the Jewish establishment was understanding this search for authenticity to be against and outside Judaism, and the mistake of the Christian church was to see this search as beyond a failed religion. Both establishments returned to, instituted, or defended partial practice as a sign of the covenant revealed exclusively to each community.

The historical baggage we carry often forces upon us false choices, narrowing the resources we can call upon for our struggle to be faithful. At this point in history, the attempt to categorize our fidelity within the boundaries created thousands of years ago—themselves created after the crossing of boundaries—is fated to fail. Either we cross boundaries to understand ourselves and our struggle, burying those boundary crossings when we come to identity and liturgy as if they did not occur, or we refuse the invitation and narrow our field of vision and possibility. The latter represents a slow death, for the resources for fidelity within one community are too limited. The former awaits a naming so that the explosive quality of the search for the missing commandments in all our communities can come to fruition.

On the threshold of the twenty-first century, the search for the missing commandments can be found in the challenge of overcoming partial practice. The resources for that search, like the covenant itself, reside in many places and no one place. Since overcoming partial practice is a constant demand—for all practice is liable to declaring itself *the* practice, repeating the mistake it once crossed over to avoid—the covenant is always before us, ahead of us, awaiting an embrace. The covenant appears here and there, shedding layers of culture and history. The appearance of the covenant is recorded in ancient Egypt, for example, as a patriarchal God leading his people through the desert. It is recorded later in the brokerless kingdom Jesus and his disciples experienced in table fellowship and, still later, in the many personalities and movements around the world that struggled deeply, often suffering in their own history.

Yet these recordings of the struggle to be faithful, of the search for the missing commandments, of the overcoming of partial practice, are for us windows on the possibility of a new engagement with God and each other. *If the covenant does not consort with injustice, neither is it defined in advance nor banished forever. The covenant creates boundaries only in the narratives we create around it, in retrospect as it were. When the boundaries are erected, the covenant is no longer there.* That is why the synagogues and churches—and by extension mosques and Hindu temples— are repositories for God and the covenant as they were once explored, embraced, and named. The religious calendar exemplifies, sometimes beautifully and dramatically, other times superficially and in a boring fashion, this narrative of the God and covenant of the past. In this sense liturgies are attempts to remember and recount this embrace and naming, and they remind us of the possibility of such an experience in our own time.

Unfortunately and too often, we mistakenly conclude that this is the God and the covenant that we must find again, or if we do not find it here and in that language it is nowhere to be found. The God and the covenant of the past can force us to a new struggle or render us passive or cynical in the face of this dramatic and ordered narrative. The danger is that we can become "stuck" in the God and the covenant of the past.

So the question remains: Where is the place that partial practice is challenged, overcome and challenged again? Is there a presence that continually calls us beyond our limitations, asking an embrace that seems difficult, if not impossible? And what mediates that presence, surrounds it, and places it before us, even when access to the source itself is hidden or absent? What can prepare the way for the reappearance of the voice that has been silent or unheard, buried in history and grief, in the violence and cries of atrocity?

Here another definition of the covenant comes into view: *as the historical carrier of God and humanity through time that overcomes partial practice in the present.* It is as if there is a reality within our lives and community that can carry us deeper within and beyond what we have known. The search for the missing commandments *is* the future *in potentia.*

Therefore those who answer the calls of their time, whether overtly religious or not, are fulfilling the demands of the covenant. What the covenant awaits then is its articulation by those who have access to more overt religious categories. Still, these categories are themselves evolving and without exclusive communal claimants. Those who have helped articulate the claims of the covenant for a certain time period should regard this as a privilege rather than a right.

By our facing the new challenge with others, a renewal of a particular community may take place, but one seen, like its practice, as partial, a contribution to an overall embrace of the covenant rather than *the* embrace. In this sense all religious traditions are at their end, at least as we have known and inherited them. Within this context, Judaism is just one among other religions, contested, failing, contributing, ending and beginning again.

The Grounding of Our Fidelity

Those who look out over Jerusalem know this feeling of endings and beginnings. For here, at least symbolically and within the monotheistic religions, is an entire history of the covenant and those who have sought to embrace it.

Many of the struggles within this history have been brutal and concerned with monotheism itself, setting forth competing claims to fulfill the covenant. And who can forget the cries of those who carried this covenant with them in the twentieth century, in Auschwitz, where the voice of God was muted, absent?

The answer to the question of God in Auschwitz is itself unanswerable. Only the fact that the covenant has re-emerged can be spoken because there continue to be those persons, Jewish and non-Jewish, whose pursuit of the missing commandments is palpable. Their response, rather than their answer—for is there an answer to Auschwitz or beyond?—challenges all of us to overcome partial practice.

We should be unafraid that this overcoming places the continuation of Judaism as we have known and inherited it in jeopardy. For where can the new come from if not from endings, and how can we know what symbolic and identity structure will emerge in the crossing of boundaries and overcoming of partial practice? In any case, the use of the covenant to oppress others already jeopardizes the continuity of Jewish life. If the way forward involves risk, there is no alternative. There is no way back.

Is God with those Jews who cross boundaries in search of the missing commandments, who embody the *tikkun* of ordinary decency, who reach out to Palestinians and others who are dispossessed and in need? Does God accompany those who refuse partial practice? Is God found in the midst of that refusal, listening and speaking to and through those who rarely articulate their hopes and fears in religious language? Does God become, as it were, "unstuck" in the overcoming of partial practice, and is this done with others from every tradition and culture who are themselves moving beyond the limitations of their situation?

In the new exile, of Jews and non-Jews together, is there a gathering place where a common struggle is recognized and so thereby is a common God? Is this new beginning—unpredictable as it is—the calling forth on the threshold of the twenty-first century, akin to the calling forth experienced at Sinai over 3,000 years ago?

Perhaps such a comparison is too grandiose, too sure of itself and predictable, in need of humility. A possibility, one more plausible in the eyes of the world, is that the voices of those in exile will be lost to contemporary Judaism and to the world at large. Jews in exile, and exiles from other religions and cultures as well, will continue on for a time and then be lost to history.

The attempt to overcome partial practice will be seen as a form of betrayal or will be unnoticed, unrecognized in the emerging Jewish-state culture. In its powerful continuation, the end of Jewish history will be unidentified. Deir Yassin will lack its monument and its place in Jewish history, and Jewish history, like other histories, will leverage affluence and power against memory and culpability.

So it may be. Still the covenant beckons, freely chosen and embraced, as the ground of our fidelity, from which a future can be envisioned. Here is found a rootedness that allows trust and exploration, a commitment that demands justice with compassion, a fidelity that is engaged without finality and with hope, a witness to more truth and life.

Our grounding and fidelity—our very witness—establishes the possibility of a future beyond the known and expected; it establishes the possibility of God or, if not God, the possibility of trust as a vehicle for understanding. What else do we need to sustain a journey into the unknown? Are we so unlike those who went before us?

They too crossed the boundaries of faith and community. They risked safety and honor in and for a history they were called to fulfill.

"You should not think that these great secrets are fully and completely known to anyone among us," the great Jewish sage, Maimonides, wrote. "They are not. But sometimes truth flashes out to us so that we think that it is day, and then matter and habit in their various forms conceal it so that we find ourselves again in an obscure night, almost as we were at first. We are like someone in a very dark night over whom lightning flashes from time to time."[9]

On the threshold of the twenty-first century, Maimonides speaks to our situation. Do we have the courage to take hold of the truth that flashes out to us? Or will matter and habit take hold and divert our attention, our practice, and allow us to continue on as if we are innocent? Lightning flashes in the dark night are glimpses of another way, a different embrace, a world waiting to be born. Though great secrets are never fully known to anyone or perhaps even to a generation, the way forward is lit, if only for a moment. Shall we respond to this light, seek it out, share and multiply it, as if our fidelity depends on it?

The choice is ours. The time is now.

Notes

1. Visions of the Diaspora and Homeland

1. For the situation in Gaza, see Sara Roy, *The Gaza Strip: The Political Economy of De-development* (Washington, D.C.: Institute for Palestine Studies, 1995). For descriptions of the situations in Gaza and the West Bank, see Ghassan Abu-Sitta and Abdullah Mutawi, "Arafat's Oppression, Israel's Demands," *New York Times*, July 2, 1996; and David Hirst, "Shameless in Gaza," *Guardian Weekly*, April 27, 1997.

2. For his essays on the peace process, see Edward Said, *Peace and Its Discontents: Essays on Palestine in the Middle East Peace Process* (New York: Random House, 1996).

3. The main outlines of the Labor policy follow the Allon Plan drafted after the 1967 war. For the details and evolution of this plan, see Mark Tessler, *A History of the Israeli-Palestinian Conflict* (Bloomington: Indiana University Press, 1994), 466, 468, 500–502, 520, 606.

4. A paid editorial advertisement elaborates this traditional diaspora position. Issued by the Central Rabbinical Congress of the U.S. and Canada and entitled "A Clarification of Torah Doctrine," it appeared in the *New York Times*, July 14, 1996. For a fascinating narrative about this secular diaspora, see John Murray Cuddihy, *The Ordeal of Civility: Freud, Marx, Levi-Strauss and the Jewish Struggle with Modernity* (New York: Dell, 1974).

5. I have written extensively on this shift in Jewish understanding, especially in relation to the development of Jewish religiosity. See my book *Beyond Innocence and Redemption: Confronting the Holocaust and Israeli Power* (San Francisco: HarperCollins, 1990), 1–31. For a powerful essay that contains some of these warnings, see Irving Greenberg, "The Ethics of Jewish Power," in *Beyond Occupation: American Jewish, Christian and Palestinian Voices for Peace*, ed. Rosemary Radford Ruether and Marc H. Ellis (Boston: Beacon Press, 1990), 22–74.

6. For a history of the binational idea, see Susan Lee Hattis, *The Bi-National Idea in Palestine during Mandatory Times* (Haifa: Shikmona, 1970).

7. An example of this understanding can be found in the essays of Hannah Arendt. See her essay "To Save the Jewish Homeland: There Is

Still Time," in *Hannah Arendt: The Jew as Pariah*, ed. Ron H. Feldman (New York: Grove Press, 1978), 178–92.

8. Quoted in the *New York Times*, September 14, 1993.

9. One way of looking at the ambivalent legacy of Rabin and Peres is through the lens of "tainted greatness," a concept developed by Nancy Harrowitz in the introduction to a book she edited *Tainted Greatness: Anti-Semitism and Cultural Heroes* (Philadelphia: Temple University, 1994), 1–4. For my application of this theme to Rabin, see "Murdering Rabin and the Jewish Covenant," *Middle East Policy* 4 (March 1996): 72–75.

10. This story was reported in the *New York Times*, November 10, 1995.

11. The significance of Arafat's journey into Israel seemed lost on the news media. That Arafat was flown into Israel for a condolence call to the slain prime minister's wife is of historical significance. See my own understanding of this in "Murdering Rabin," 74–75.

12. My own understanding of coming to the end of the era of Auschwitz and the difficulties it poses for the Jewish community can be found in Marc H. Ellis, *Ending Auschwitz: The Future of Jewish and Christian Life* (Louisville, Ky.: Westminster/John Knox Press, 1994).

13. For two early discussions of the non-Jewish population in Israel, see Ian Lustick, *Arabs in the Jewish State* (Austin: University of Texas Press, 1980); and Fouzi El-Asmar, *To Be an Arab in Israel* (Beirut: Institute for Palestine Studies, 1978). For reports on the struggle between religious and secular Jews in Israel, see Joel Greenberg, "Jerusalem Road Is Secular-Religious Battleground," *New York Times*, July 15, 1996; and Serge Schmemann, "Orthodox Israelis Assault Jews Praying at Western Wall," *New York Times*, June 13, 1997.

14. The story of Arendt's involvement in Zionism and her subsequent silence can be found in Elizabeth Young-Bruehl *Hannah Arendt: For Love of the World* (New Haven, Conn.: Yale University Press, 1982).

15. Contemporary literature on Jerusalem is enormous. For discussions on the political issues facing Jerusalem, see the issue of *Palestine-Israel* 2/2 (1995) titled "Our Jerusalem"; and Sami Musallam, *The Struggle for Jerusalem: A Programme of Action for Peace* (Jerusalem: PASSIA, 1996).

16. Buber's essays, testimony, and public debates on the issues of Jews and Arabs in Palestine and Israel can be found in *A Land of Two Peoples: Martin Buber on Jews and Arabs*, ed. Paul Mendes-Flohr (Oxford: Oxford University Press, 1983). For his debate with David Ben-Gurion see ibid., 239–44. For his letter regarding the massacre at Deir Yassin, see Tom Segev, *1949: The First Israelis* (New York: Macmillan, 1986), 87–89.

2. On Memory and Justice

1. Yerushalmi is the Salo Baron Professor of Jewish History, Culture and Society at Columbia University. In 1977, while on sabbatical in Jerusalem, he delivered a lecture at the Institute of Jewish Studies at Hebrew University on Jewish historiography in the sixteenth century. Though the topic was specific to that time period, it encouraged him to develop a series of lectures on the subject of Jewish memory and its defining role in Jewish life. See Yosef Hayim Yerushalmi, *Zakhor: Jewish History and Jewish Memory* (Seattle: University of Washington Press, 1982).

2. Ibid., 9–10, referring to Exodus.

3. Ibid., 5, 11.

4. Ibid., 99–101. Yerushalmi writes that some reorientation is required: "The task can no longer be limited to finding continuities in Jewish life, not even 'dialectical' ones. Perhaps the time has come to look more closely at ruptures, breaches, breaks, to identify them more precisely, to see how Jews endured them, to understand that not everything of value that existed before a break was either salvaged or metamorphosed, but was lost, and often some of what fell by the wayside can become, through retrieval, meaningful to us"(101).

5. Ibid., 95.

6. David Roskies, *Against the Apocalypse: Responses to Catastrophe in Modern Jewish Culture* (Cambridge, Mass.: Harvard University Press, 1984), 197, 198.

7. Ibid., 35.

8. Ibid., 275, 305.

9. Ibid., 262. Roskies suggests that the Hebrew word *shoah*, meaning calamity, ruin, desolation, and the Yiddish *der driter khurbm*, meaning Third Destruction, have problems of their own when referring to the Holocaust. See his discussion on 261–62.

10. Ibid., 268.

11. Ibid., 263, 268, 301. François Mauriac, foreword to *Night*, by Elie Wiesel, trans. Stella Rodway (New York: Hill and Wang, 1958).

12. Roskies, *Against the Apocalypse*, 302.

13. Emil Fackenheim is important in this regard, adding a philosophical voice and structure to the narrative elements provided by Wiesel. See Emil Fackenheim, *To Mend the World: Foundations of Future Jewish Thought* (New York: Schocken, 1982). In 331 pages Palestinians are mentioned once, in a footnote.

14. For a classic example of Wiesel's liturgical rendering of the Holocaust narrative, see his public lecturing of Ronald Reagan on the latter's visit to the cemetery in Bitburg, Germany, in 1985. See Elie Wiesel, "Your

Place Is with the Victims," in *Bitburg and Beyond: Encounters in American, German and Jewish History,* ed. Ilya Levkov (New York: Shapolsky Publishers, 1987), 42–44.

15. The invitation was sent on June 24, 1995. The historical sections on Deir Yassin are taken from the following sources: Conor Cruise O'Brien, *The Siege: The Saga of Israel and Zionism* (New York: Simon and Schuster, 1986), 281–82; Benny Morris, *The Birth of the Palestinian Refugee Problem, 1947–1949* (Cambridge: Cambridge University Press, 1987), 113–15; Michael Palumbo, *The Palestinian Catastrophe: The 1948 Expulsion of a People from their Homeland* (London: Quartet Books, 1987), 47–49.

16. The question of narrative and the Palestinian place in that narrative was first raised by Edward Said in *The Question of Palestine* (New York: Random House, 1979).

17. Quoted in Palumbo, *Palestinian Catastrophe,* 55.

18. This letter is found in Tom Segev, *1949: The First Israelis* (New York: Macmillan, 1986), 88–89.

19. Ibid., 89–90.

20. Morris, *Refugee,* 115; Segev, *1949,* 70, 90.

21. For his speech at Auschwitz, see *New York Times,* January 28, 1995.

22. Wiesel's response to Daniel McGowan, director of "Deir Yassin Remembered," is dated June 7, 1995. I reflected on the inability of the Jewish people to heal after the Holocaust in a lecture at the United States Holocaust Memorial Museum on March 15, 1995. The lecture was published in *European Judaism* 29 (Autumn 1996): 19–50, with the title "Restoring the Ordinary: An Inquiry into the Jewish Covenant at the End of Auschwitz."

23. The quotes from Pa'il and De Reynier are from Palumbo, *Palestinian Catastrophe,* 52, 53, 54.

24. Paul Mendes-Flohr, ed., *A Land of Two Peoples: Martin Buber on Jews and Arabs* (Oxford: Oxford University Press, 1983). 263–68; Segev, *1949,* 89.

25. Martin Buber, "Genuine Conversations and the Possibilities of Peace," *Cross Currents* 5 (Fall 1955): 292–93. On the subject of a federation within the Middle East, see Buber's "We Need the Arabs, They Need Us," in *Two Peoples,* ed. Mendes-Flohr, 263–68.

26. For the debate with Ben-Gurion, see Mendes-Flohr, ed., *Two Peoples,* 244. For Buber's protest against expropriation of Arab lands, see ibid., 262.

27. See Buber's "A Letter to Gandhi," in ibid., 113–26. Buber wrote critically of Gandhi's call to converting the Nazis to respect Jewish life through nonviolence. For Wiesel's reflections on the 1967 war, see his article "At the Western Wall," *Hadassah Magazine* (July 1967): 4–7.

28. Elie Wiesel, *A Jew Today* (New York: Vintage, 1978), 127.

29. Arthur Hertzberg, "An Open Letter to Elie Wiesel," *New York Review of Books* 35(August 18, 1988): 14.

3. Jerusalem and the Broken Middle

1. Paul Mendes-Flohr, ed., *A Land of Two Peoples: Martin Buber on Jews and Arabs* (Oxford: Oxford University Press, 1983), 115–16, 117. For a discussion of the term "broken middle," see note 12, below.

2. For the sign expressing solidarity and a general commentary regarding the religious right, see Thomas Friedman, "What about You?" *New York Times*, November 8, 1995.

3. Quoted in David Shipler, *Arab and Jew: Wounded Spirits in a Promised Land* (New York: Times Books, 1986), 34. It is interesting that this passage was censored by Israeli authorities and thus did not appear in Rabin's autobiography.

4. Henry Schwarzschild, "On Withdrawing from Sh'ma," *Sh'ma*, September 6, 1982, 159. For *Yesh Gvul*, see Ruth Linn, *Conscience at War: The Israeli Soldier as a Moral Critic* (Albany: State University of New York Press, 1996), 124–26.

5. For Oz's commentary on the war in Lebanon, see his book *The Slopes of Lebanon* (New York: Harcourt Brace Jovanovich, 1987). Oz argues for a "divorce" between Israelis and Palestinians. See his later commentary in *Israel, Palestine and Peace: Essays* (New York: Harcourt Brace, 1994).

6. For a survey of the Jewish literature that emerged during the Palestinian uprising see Marc H. Ellis, *Beyond Innocence and Redemption: Confronting the Holocaust and Israeli Power* (San Francisco: Harper-Collins, 1990), 73–86.

7. For an interesting debate about the use of religious language after the assassination of Rabin, see Daniel Frank, "Hunting Season for the Torah," *Hartford Jewish Ledger*, November 24, 1995; and Reuven Gerber, "The Keepers of the Gunmen," ibid.

8. Arthur A. Goren, ed., *Dissenter in Zion: From the Writings of Judah L. Magnes* (Cambridge, Mass.: Harvard University Press, 1982), 213; Ari Shavat, "How Easily We Killed Them," *New York Times*, May 27, 1996.

9. Shavit, "How Easily."

10. Roskies, *Against the Apocalypse: Responses to Catastrophe in Modern Jewish Culture* (Cambridge: Harvard University Press, 1984), 35.

11. Ari Shavit, "On Gaza Beach," *New York Review of Books* 38 (July 18, 1991): 10–11. For a detailed description of torture in Israel, see Stanley Cohen, "Talking about Torture in Israel," *Tikkun* 6 (November/Decem-

ber 1991): 23–30, 90. Also see B'Tselem, *Torture during Interrogations*: *Testimony of Palestinian Detainees, Testimony of Interrogators* (Jerusalem: B'Tselem, 1994).

12. For an extended discussion of the broken middle, see Gillian Rose, *The Broken Middle: Out of Our Ancient Society* (Oxford: Blackwell, 1992). In terms of philosophy, Rose defines the middle as acting as a "third, the middle, their own effectivity at stake between the potentiality and actuality of the world and engaging at the point where the two come into a changed relation: not *ex post facto* justification, even less *a priori* rejuvenation, but reconfiguration, oppositional yet vital—something understood" (xi).

13. Azmi Bishara, "Bantustanisation or Bi-Nationalism?" *Race and Class* 37 (October–December 1995), 49. For Magnes' letter, see Goren, ed., *Dissenter in Zion*, 279.

4. The Covenant on the Threshold of the Twenty-First Century

1. Hannah Arendt, "To Save the Jewish Homeland: There Is Still Time" in *Hannah Arendt: The Jew as Pariah*, ed. Ron H. Feldman (New York: Grove Press, 1978) 178–92.

2. Tikva Honig-Parnass, "Rabin's Assassination: The Golem Rebelled against Its Maker," *New Politics* 4 (Winter 1996): 24. Also see Stan Cohen, "Shalom Chaver?" *News from Within* 11 (December 1995): 3–7.

3. Netanyahu's speech was quoted in the *New York Times*, July 11, 1996.

4. For the execution of the Egyptian prisoners of war and Eitan's comments on the massacre, see Serge Schmemann, "After a General Tells of Killing P.O.W.'s in 1956, Israelis Argue over Ethics of War," *New York Times*, August 21, 1995. For the Kahan report on the massacres of Sabra and Shatilla, see *The Beirut Massacre: The Complete Kahan Commission Report* (New York: Karz-Cohl, 1983).

5. The reactions were solicited and published in *Newsweek*, June 10, 1996, 42–43.

6. Quoted in the *New York Times*, November 8, 1995.

7. For a detailed discussion of this tradition, see Anson Laytner, *Arguing with God: A Jewish Tradition* (Northvale, N. J.: Jason Aronson, 1990).

8. Ibid., 214–27. See Elie Wiesel, *Night, Dawn, Day*, trans. Stella Rodway (Northvale, N. J.: Jason Aronson, 1996).

9. The term *additional covenant* and the analysis of Wiesel's thought are found in Michael Berenbaum, *Elie Wiesel: God, the Holocaust, and the Children of Israel* (West Orange, N.J.: Behrman House, 1994), 125–51.

10. Irena Klepfisz, *Dreams of an Insomniac: Jewish Feminist Essays, Speeches and Diatribes* (Portland, Oreg.: Eighth Mountain Press, 1990),

124–26. I am indebted to Hilda Silverman for introducing me to the work of Irena Klepfisz.

11. Ibid., 130–31.

12. Ibid., 134–35.

13. Irena Klepfisz, *A Few Words in the Mother Tongue: Poems Selected and New 1971–1990* (Portland, Oreg.: Eighth Mountain Press, 1990), 237–40.

14. Ibid., 232–34.

15. The unnamed Holocaust survivor is quoted in *Ha'aretz*, August 11, 1982. For an example of Sara Roy's analysis of Gaza, see "The Seed of Chaos, and of Night: The Gaza Strip after the Agreement," *Journal of Palestine Studies* 23 (Spring 1994): 85–98.

16. For the classic statement of his early position, see Emil Fackenheim, *God's Presence in History: Jewish Affirmations and Philosophical Reflections* (New York: New York University Press, 1970).

17. Emil Fackenheim, *To Mend the World: Foundations of Post-Holocaust Jewish Thought* (New York: Schocken, 1982), 307.

18. Ibid., 312.

19. Peres is quoted in the *New York Times*, September 25, 1995.

20. Edward Said, "The Mirage of Peace," *Nation*, October 16, 1995, 413–20.

21. Cynthia Ozick, "The Consensus That Plagues Israel," *New York Times*, December 2, 1995; Michael Walzer, "Reasons to Mourn," *New Yorker*, November 20, 1995.

22. Cynthia Ozick, "Notes toward Finding the Right Question," in *On Being a Jewish Feminist*, ed. Susannah Heschel (New York: Schocken, 1983), 120–51.

23. Ibid., 135, 144, 149–50.

24. Ibid., 151.

25. Quoted in the *New York Times*, September 14, 1993.

5. The Great Debate over Jewish Identity and Culture

1. For two studies of the sociological and theological understandings of the radical right in Israel, see Ian Lustick, *For the Land and the Lord: Jewish Fundamentalism in Israel* (New York: Council on Foreign Relations, 1988); and Ehud Sprinzak, *The Ascendance of Israel's Radical Right* (Oxford: Oxford University Press, 1991).

2. Emil Fackenheim, *To Mend the World: Foundations of Post-Holocaust Jewish Thought* (New York: Schocken, 1982), 312. Fackenheim mentions the Palestinians in a note on p. 304.

3. This exchange can be found in Rick Hornung, "Family Feud: Israeli and American Jewish Writers Mix It Up," *Village Voice*, February 7, 1989, 27.

4. Ari Shavit, "On Gaza Beach," *New York Review of Books* 38 (July 18, 1991), 25.

5. George Friedmann, *The End of the Jewish People?* (Garden City, N.Y.: Doubleday, 1967), 235. His discussion on whether there is such a entity as the Jewish people is fascinating. See ibid., 235–42.

6. David Vital, *The Future of the Jews: A People at the Crossroads?* (Cambridge, Mass.: Harvard University Press, 1990), 142.

7. Ibid., 141.

8. Ibid., 105, 108–109, 147. Vital continues: "In sum, the old unity of Jewry, however fragile, however problematic, essentially a function of the old sense and, yes, the old reality of nationhood, lies shattered today, almost beyond repair"(147–48).

9. Efraim Shmueli, *Seven Jewish Cultures: A Reinterpretation of Jewish History and Thought* (Cambridge: Cambridge University Press, 1990)

10. Ibid., 5, 13, 14, 15, 35.

11. Ibid., 14, 33.

12. Ibid., 113. As to the tensions of Jewish culture, Shmueli remarks that "every person lives between the opposing poles that characterize his culture" and that in the course of a lifetime the "tensions that govern one's world may undergo some change" (113). Thus his understanding of culture within the larger framework of the people allows for the person to experience that culture in its ambiguity. For the most part Shmueli does not address the importance of that individual experience to the larger framework or even to the formation of new Jewish cultures.

13. Ibid., 250.

14. See Gila Shmueli's biographical note in ibid., xiv.

15. This is a main thesis of Ammiel Alcalay's book *After Jews and Arabs: Remaking Levantine Culture* (Minneapolis: University of Minnesota Press, 1993).

16. Ibid., 53.

17. Ibid., 1.

18. Ibid., 1. For this different view of the 1967 war, see 57–59. For his understanding of Alexandria and Baghdad in Israel, see 256–61.

19. For the overall thesis of the book, see Benjamin Ginsberg, *The Fatal Embrace: Jews and the State* (Chicago: University of Chicago Press, 1993), 1–59.

20. See the final chapter in ibid., 224–44.

21. These tensions are embedded in the very founding of the museum. See Edward Linenthal, *Preserving Memory: The Struggle to Create America's Holocaust Museum* (New York: Viking, 1995).

22. For an understanding of the Eichmann trial in the eyes of Ben-Gurion, see Tom Segev, *The Seventh Million: The Israelis and the Holocaust* (New York: Hill and Wang, 1993), 327–44. According to Segev, Ben-Gurion had two goals in relation to the trial: "One was to remind the countries of the world that the Holocaust obligated them to support the only Jewish state on earth. The second was to impress the lessons of the Holocaust on the people of Israel, especially the younger generation"(327).

23. The emotional tenor of the discussion about the trial can be seen in the correspondence between Hannah Arendt and Gershom Scholem over her controversial reporting on the trial. Their exchange of letters is found in "Eichmann in Jerusalem," *Encounter* 22 (January 1964): 51–56.

24. James Young, *The Texture of Memory: Holocaust Memorials and Meaning* (New Haven, Conn.: Yale University Press, 1993), 250, 256.

25. Segev, *Seventh Million*, 488, 502.

6. Toward a New Sinai

1. Efraim Shmueli, *Seven Jewish Cultures: A Reinterpretation of Jewish History and Thought* (Cambridge: Cambridge University Press, 1990), 113.

2. For an example of the circular argument—dissent that competes for the same territory as those who dominate Jewish discourse—see the many articles over the years in the progressive Jewish journal *Tikkun*. For a gathering of these articles see Michael Lerner, ed., *Tikkun: An Anthology* (Oakland, Calif.: Tikkun Books, 1992), 291–396. For his latest book on the subject of Jewish renewal, idem, *Jewish Renewal: A Path in Healing and Transformation* (New York: Putnam, 1994). Also see Lerner's latest experiment in Jewish renewal, as reported by E. J. Kessler, "Rabbi Lerner's Latest: A Shul Named Tikkun," *Forward*, August 23, 1996.

3. I have addressed this question more fully in *Ending Auschwitz: The Future of Jewish and Christian Life* (Louisville, Ky.: Westminster/John Knox, 1994) and in *Unholy Alliance: Religion and Atrocity in Our Time* (Minneapolis: Fortress Press, 1997).

4. The term *revolutionary forgiveness* emerged out of the journeys of Carter Heyward and a group of her students—collectively known as the Amanecida Collective—to Nicaragua in 1983–1984. For the recounting of their story and reflections which led to the concept, see Carter Heyward and Anne Gilson, *Revolutionary Forgiveness: Feminist Reflections on Nicaragua* (Maryknoll, N.Y.: Orbis, 1987).

5. For a fascinating interpretation of Arendt's understanding of the limitations and possibilities of forgiveness, see Adi Ophir, "Between Eichmann and Kant: Thinking on Evil after Arendt," *History and Memory* 8 (Fall/Winter 1996): 89–136.

6. The following paragraphs, which explicate aspects of Honing-Parnass' and Bishara's thought can be found in Tikva Honing-Parnass, "Binationalism vs. the Secular Democratic State," *News from Within* 8 (March 1997): 26–29; and Azmi Bishara, "Bridging the Green Line: The PA, Israeli Arabs, and the Final Status," *Journal of Palestine Studies* 26 (Spring 1997): 67–80.

7. Daniel Boyarin, *A Radical Jew: Paul and the Politics of Identity* (Berkeley: University of California Press, 1994), 244, 259, 260. Also see Yochanan Lorwin, "Judaism and Zionism: An Interview with Daniel Boyarin," *News from Within* 7 (September 1996): 21–25.

8. Ibid., 243.

9. Ibid., 242. As Boyarin writes: "In order, then, to preserve the positive ethical, political value of Jewish genealogy as a mode of identity, Jews must preserve their subaltern status" (242).

10. Ammiel Alcalay, *After Jews and Arabs: Remaking Levantine Culture* (Minneapolis: University of Minnesota Press, 1993), 1.

11. Shiko Behar, "Is the *Mizrahi* Question Relevant to the Future of the Entire Middle East," *News from Within* 13 (January 1997): 75

12. William Freedman, "Israel: The New Diaspora," in *Diaspora: Exile and the Jewish Condition,* ed. Etan Levine (New York: Jason Aronson, 1983), 235, 246.

13. Boyarin, *Radical Jew,* 235.

14. Richard Shusterman, "Next Year in Jerusalem? Postmodern Jewish Identity and the Myth of Return," in *Jewish Identity,* ed. David Theo Goldberg and Michael Krausz (Philadelphia: Temple University Press, 1993), 304.

15. Hannah Arendt, *Between Past and Future: Eight Exercises in Political Thought* (New York: Penguin, 1968), 156.

16. Ibid., 84.

Epilogue

1. Daniel Boyarin, *A Radical Jew: Paul and the Politics of Identity* (Berkeley: University of California Press, 1994), 228–29.

2. Marc H. Ellis, "On the New Diaspora: A Jewish Meditation on the Future of Israel/Palestine," in *Remembering Deir Yassin: The Future of Israel and Palestine,* ed. Daniel McGowan and Marc H. Ellis (New York: Olive Branch Press, 1998) 10–24.

3. The letter was sent via e-mail on June 14, 1997.

4. Benjamin Beit-Hallahmi, *Original Sins: Reflections on the History of Zionism and Israel* (New York: Olive Branch Press, 1993), 166, 190.

5. Ibid., 190.

6. Quoted in ibid., 167.

7. Naseer H. Aruri, "Out-Fight, Out-Organize, Out-Talk," *Mideast Monitor* 12 (Spring/Summer 1997): 2, 3, 4.

8. Quoted in Patrick Hart, ed., *The Other Side of the Mountain: The End of the Journey,* The Journals of Thomas Merton, vol. 7 (San Francisco: HarperCollins, 1998), 247.

9. Maimonides, "Guide for the Perplexed," in *A Maimonides Reader,* ed. Isadore Twersky (New York: Behrman House, 1972), 238.

Index